Paul's Gospel in an Intercultural Context

STUDIEN ZUR INTERKULTURELLEN GESCHICHTE DES CHRISTENTUMS
ETUDES D'HISTOIRE INTERCULTURELLE DU CHRISTIANISME
STUDIES IN THE INTERCULTURAL HISTORY OF CHRISTIANITY

begründet von/fondé par/founded by
Hans Jochen Margull †, Hamburg

herausgegeben von/édité par/edited by

Band 69

Peter Lang
Frankfurt am Main · Bern · New York · Paris

William S. Campbell

PAUL'S GOSPEL IN AN INTERCULTURAL CONTEXT

Jew and Gentile in the Letter to the Romans

Peter Lang
Frankfurt am Main · Bern · New York · Paris

CIP-Titelaufnahme der Deutschen Bibliothek

Campbell, William S.:

Paul's gospel in an intercultural context : Jew and Gentile in the letter to the Romans / William S. Campbell. - Frankfurt am Main ; Bern ; New York ; Paris : Lang, 1991
(Studien zur interkulturellen Geschichte des Christentums ; Bd. 69)
ISBN 3-631-42981-9

NE: GT

ISSN 0170-9240
ISBN 3-631-42981-9

Printed in Germany 1 3 4 5 6 7

In loving memory of my only son Allen
who was killed in a car accident 1st November 1990
having enriched my life for 26 years

Acknowledgements

Permission to reprint the following essays, which originally appeared in the sources indicated, is gratefully acknowledged:

"Why did Paul write Romans?" (Expository Times 85, 1973-74, pp 264-69).

"Christ the End of the Law: Romans 10:4", (Studia Biblica 111: Findings of the VIth International Congress on Biblical Studies), JSOT, Sheffield 1980).

"Romans III as a Key to the Structure and Thought of the Letter", Novum Testamentum, 23, 1981, pp 22-40.

"The Freedom and Faithfulness of God in Relation to Israel", (Journal for the Study of the New Testament, 13, 1981, pp 27-45).

"Christianity and Judaism: Continuity and Discontinuity", (International Bulletin of Missionary Research, Vol 8 (2) 1984, pp 55-58).

I am also grateful to the editors of the Scottish Journal of Theology and of Irish Biblical Studies respectively for permission to publish here articles due to appear later in 1990, ie "Did Paul advocate Separation from the Synagogue?" and "Paul's Missionary Practice and Policy".

CONTENTS

Preface

This book has been a long time in germination. Over the years I have delivered many lectures only some of which have been offered for publication. Some two years ago the present volume began to materialise. The first five essays were published separately and met with sufficient interest from scholarly friends to merit their inclusion here. The other six essays have not previously been published but two of them will appear in British journals later this year. Rather than revise and rewrite them, all have been included in their original form with only minimal alterations. In a volume of this kind, there is inevitably some repetition but I trust that the fact that there is a certain historical sequence in the essays (and their bibliography) may have prevented this from being excessive. Chapter 12 is intended to serve both as a conclusion to "A Theme for Romans" and as a general conclusion to the whole volume.

The main objective in producing this volume is to include together essays which were first published in different journals at differing times, thereby making them more accessible. Another objective is to put on record earlier essays documenting the progress of my research, particularly those articles whose findings have been substantiated by more recent scholarship. When I completed my doctoral research, the literature on Romans was very different from that presently available, and it is some small gratification on my part that several of the major lines of my approach to Romans have found support in, or been in accord with, subsequent studies. Although in some of the essays occasionally I have had to go outside the Letter to the Romans, such excursions cohere in the single aim of helping to illuminate Paul's attitude to Jews and Gentiles in Romans.

I am deeply indebted to the many scholars whose names appear in the following pages. In particular, I owe a debt of gratitude to Professors Hugh Anderson, Robin Barbour, Charles Cranfield, Anthony Hanson, Ernst Käsemann and Otto Michel whose support, both scholarly and personal, has been invaluable at different stages in my theological pilgrimage. The frequent interaction in this volume with other scholars' writings demonstrates, I hope, how much I have gained from their dedicated work.

I also owe a great deal to fellow teachers in Religious Studies and Theology in the Selly Oak Colleges and in the University of Birmingham. In the city of Birmingham I have been privileged to work both with professional scholars and with interested friends in the great issues of tolerance, anti-racism and social equality. Friends in other related areas in the University of Birmingham and in the Selly Oak Colleges have taught me much more than they realise. I have become particularly aware in recent years of the increasing debt I owe to colleagues involved in Jewish-Christian dialogue in the Centre for the Study of Judaism and Jewish-Christian Relations at Selly Oak, and to others similarly engaged in the work of the ICCJ.

To friends in Westhill, particularly in my own department, a word of thanks. To Marilyn Nefsky and Marius Felderhof, colleagues and friends, who listened patiently to my endless questioning over Paul and his letters, special thanks. They were a constant source of encouragement on dark days when teaching and administration rendered all personal research impossible. To Gordon Benfield, Principal of Westhill College, and the Governors and Trustees, sincere thanks for travel grants which enabled my longstanding participation in the annual conferences of the American Society of Biblical Literature.

Most of all I thank Kay and my children, Allen, Alison, Coleen and Cathie - firstly for putting up with a husband and father who started doctoral research after his family was nearly complete; what a day it was when we celebrated the completion of my dissertation by having a bonfire to burn all the superfluous versions accumulated over several years. Secondly, from a family one learns what it is to be part of a small community - it diminishes the tendency to think of oneself as an independent individual and helps one to learn the positive virtues of community and interdependence. A special word of thanks to Kay whose work both full-time and part-time, financially enabled me to undertake research and travel to libraries for my doctoral studies.

W S Campbell
Selly Oak
January 1990

Introduction

The rediscovery of the significance of the social context for theology has combined with other factors in modern thought to emphasise the importance of cultural background. As the world 'grows smaller', so we have become more acutely aware of our own cultural experience, commitments and limitations. In Paul's mission and theology, the cultural factor was exceedingly important, and nowhere so much as in the letter to the Romans.

One response to cultural diversity in the modern period has been the attempt to integrate immigrant minorities into the dominant or host community. The process of assimilation, it was hoped, would diminish major cultural differences to the extent that part or all of the original diversity would disappear and a more homogeneous or monochrome society would result.

However, it is now realised that this experiment offers no lasting solution to cultural diversity. Real issues of personal identity are bound up with one's religious and cultural background. Today, therefore, the pluralism of our societies in Europe and America is coming to be increasingly acknowledged, accepted and even appreciated. It is thus of some relevance to consider how the apostle Paul sought to bring the Gospel to a society where an historic divide existed between Jew and Gentile.

Paul's letters focused on contemporary issues and were addressed to the needs of the communities he founded. Although he himself was of Pharisaic background, his call to be apostle to the Gentiles meant that he was deeply involved in the conflicts surrounding relations between Jews and Gentiles in his own day. In a very real sense, Paul was a product of both Judaism and Hellenism. As a Jew born in the Diaspora, whose father was a Roman citizen, and as one schooled in the law of his fathers in Jerusalem, he was truly a debtor to both Jew and Greek.

The fact that Paul believed that the Gospel gave him the freedom to be flexible in his keeping of Jewish food laws exaggerated the complexity of his position. He felt free to relax laws relating to eating with Gentiles and yet he naturally lived as a Jew when with his own people.

The situation was further complicated by a central tenet of Paul's theology. Apparently, after the incident with Peter at Antioch when the latter stopped eating the Lord's Supper with Gentile Christians, Paul worked henceforth in pioneer mission work, founding new communities consisting mainly of Gentiles, where Jewish Christians must necessarily follow a more or less Gentile life-style as far as Jewish purity laws were concerned. In his own theology Paul maintained that in Christ 'there is no distinction' between Jew and Gentile - the phrase is repeated twice in Romans and also occurs in conjunction with the parallel, 'God is no respector of persons'. In much modern interpretation, this phrase has been taken to mean that Paul would actually dissuade Jewish Christians from continuing to live a Jewish life-style or even to circumcise their children. But Paul's gospel is more complicated than this. He is very much aware of the difference between Jew and Gentile. God, he knows, accepts both equally in Christ. But Paul did *not* hold that Christians should lose their cultural identity as Jew or Gentile and become one new humanity which is neither. Instead he emphasises the overcoming of the hostility between Jew and Gentile, and yet allows for the recognition of the difference between them in daily life.

This is clearly seen in the use Paul makes of the term 'Israel.' In his theology there is only one Israel, the historic people of God, and although Gentiles can be accepted into the covenant through faith in Christ, yet Israel remains Israel and Gentile believers can never be termed 'the new Israel!' Having such a theology, it is no surprise therefore that the relationship between Jews and Gentiles is a theme that permeates every aspect of Paul's mission and literary activity.

So the paradox is that the apostle who stressed that all are *one* in Christ, who recognised that he was debtor to Jew and Greek, nevertheless was acutely aware of, and gave lasting significance to, the unique position of Israel's faith and history.

The practical outcome of this is that Paul also felt it right to give recognition to the abiding differences between Christians of differing cultural backgrounds. On the question of food laws, he stipulated that each one should be fully convinced in his own mind. No one was to make his standard of faith a norm for others, nor allow them to force him to conform to their conscience, cf Rom 12-15. Above all, Paul fought for the right of Gentile Christians to be fully accepted into the people of God as Gentiles, without having also to become Jewish proselytes. Moreover, he regarded as 'false brethren' those Jewish Christians who refused to acknowledge Gentile Christians as full members of the community of faith.

The latter demonstrates that for Paul, although ethnic and cultural differences are significant and need to be recognised, they are still subject to the judgement of God as manifested in the revelation of His righteousness in the Christ-event. This is for Paul the ultimate criterion of all life and behaviour. The significance of everything is transformed by this event. In keeping with this, Paul's theology, we would exphasise, is one of transformation of the old into the new - not of its complete destruction or displacement.

The tolerance of diversity which we have already noted in Paul's letter to the Romans is significant and relevant to the modern interpreter in several respects. As interpreters who must make choices in coming to one's own particular understanding of the text, we cannot but be aware of our cultural and ethnic backgrounds. Indeed we now are aware as never before, that the answers we elicit from the text may be strongly influenced by the questions we bring to it, and that these are themselves, to some extent, the product of our own background and commitments. We are, indisputably, products of our own history and reflect it in the way we interpret the text.

But what is now generally recognised is that there can be no escape from this universal tendency; no longer can anyone pretend that real objectivity before the text is possible. There is no culture-free exegesis; exegesis can never take place in a vacuum. Conversely *all* properly conducted exegesis *is* acceptable. When brought under the judgement of God in the Gospel, one culture is as good as another and one's own particular history need not be denied.

Thus one may in the following essays, become very much aware of historic interpretive tendencies such as the Lutheran approach to Paul, or to be more precise, of the traditional German Lutheran understanding of his theology. Both cultures and schools of interpretation have strengths as well as weaknesses. Only in the interaction of scholarly debate across cultural, historical and other possible divides, can some measure of objectivity and impartiality be realised. Perhaps the best we can expect is that we should be as fully aware of the influence of our culture and commitments as possible.

On the positive side, the acknowledgement and acceptance of cultural diversity is but another way of recognising the particularity and significance, as well as the relativity, of all historical experience. This means that it is perfectly valid to have a 'Third World Theology' or a 'Water Buffalo Theology' just as much as it is to have an Indian or an Anglican.

It also means giving due significance to history itself. In my view, New Testament interpretation has suffered in the last fifty years from what might be termed a 'flight from history'; hence the conflict of Cullmann with Bultmann's existentialism in his book *Christ and Time*. Neither existentialist interpretations nor a theological supra-history are adequate for a Christian theology of history. In some sense, at least, Christians are obliged to see history as the field of God's activity, however hidden to the 'natural eye'. The fall of Jerusalem or the Holocaust cannot be ignored, though the significance of both can easily be misunderstood. The fall of Jerusalem certainly influenced early Christian writers and there can be no relevant exegesis in the modern period which writes as if the Holocaust had not happened. Scholarly debate must still decide the extent of the influence which this event should have upon interpretation, but it dare not ignore it.

The interpretation of historical events is itself no easy task. Again, part of the problem is the perspective from which they are viewed. It requires a major feat of imagination to think one's way back to the Judaism of the years immediately following the Jewish-Roman War and to imagine what it was like for Jews suddenly bereft of their temple and its rituals. This is difficult enough as a Jew but even more so for a Gentile. Again how can we, as Gentiles who know that the early church, a church of Jews and Gentiles, has in fact become a Gentile church, think ourselves back into that earlier perspective? Similarly how can Christians avoid the anachronism of reading first century documents as if Paul and his contemporaries had the advantage of our post-eventum perspective as far as Israel's response to the Gospel is concerned? Too often we resort to such platitudes as -'it was inevitable that the Jews would not respond', despite Paul's apparent openness to another possibility.

A major attempt has been made in the studies contained in this book to try to think one's way back into the situation of Paul's own day and to seek to envisage how what was said and done would be viewed, especially by a Christian of Jewish background. The inclusion of Gentiles in the church as equals with Jews or the assertion that the law is terminated with the coming of Christ, may not seem startling innovations to the modern Gentile, but there is no doubt that they would have been exactly that to a first century Jew. Similarly it would have been no light matter for Paul to advocate that Jewish Christians separate themselves from the synagogue or from their native Judaism.

Associated with this objective is, of course, the attempt to temporarily block out or neutralise my own particular commitments and prejudices. As a Presbyterian who worships in the United Reformed Church, doubtless a certain preference for election and covenant, and a predisposition to believe in a faithful and providential God are still very much part of my personal value system. I hope however that these may sometimes serve to illuminate the text of Paul as well as inevitably getting in the way of my discovering what that text is actually saying.

Because we are historically and culturally conditioned, does not mean that we should be complacent or even pessimistic about the significance of our own interpretive task. On the contrary, precisely because we are conditioned and particularly since history itself is never static and is also always being reinterpreted, we need to be the more careful and exact about the meaning and relevance of the text for our own time. Perhaps we are most fortunate to live at a time in history when Paul's gospel and situation appear to offer useful parallels to, and hence also useful insights into, our pluralist and diverse society.

Chapter 1

Introduction to the Romans Debate: A Personal Perspective

In 1963 when I first began to study Paul's letter to the Romans, the abiding significance of this letter had been marked by a number of recent commentaries, some of which were destined to exert a strong influence on development in the subsequent decades. (1) But despite these significant publications there was as yet little indication of the enormous explosion of interest in the letter that would develop in the early 1970's. Professor F F Bruce kindly directed me to read Johannes Munck's *Paul and Israel* (then available only in Danish and German). (2) It was with Munck that my pilgrimage with Paul in Romans really began. (3) In early research I studied the use of Romans 9-11 in the theology of John Calvin and Karl Barth. This work convinced me of the need to eschew the tendency to view Romans as a compendium of abstract theology with a purported universal relevance but with little real social or historical roots in its first century 'Sitz im Leben.' The experience left me with a deep concern for a historical and theological interpretation of Paul and with a certain wariness of stressing the theological approach in isolation.

What I experienced of the teaching of Romans in the late fifties and early sixties was probably fairly typical. Due to the length of the letter and the brevity of university terms (amongst other things), attention was focused mainly on Romans 1-8. This, combined with C H Dodd's suggestion that Romans 9-11 was an excursus, possibly consisting of an old sermon which Paul decided to incorporate in his letter, had contributed to the neglect of these chapters. (4) Older classical discussions concerning issues such as theodicy or predestination had by now lost much of their appeal. (5) The result was that this section of Romans was seldom regarded as significant and was therefore frequently neglected, particularly in discussions of the purpose of the letter. (6) When chapters 1-8 were interpreted separately it was relatively easy to sustain a dogmatic interpretation of the letter, which then conveniently acted as a summary of Paul's gospel or theology. As Munck noted, 'attempts to understand the author's theological explanations in the context of a timeless systematic line of thought have been given more attention than the discovery of its historical 'Sitz im Leben'. (7)

1. *Introduction to the Romans Debate*

Already in the early nineteenth century, F C Baur had complained that the dogmatic view of Romans had not been allowed to yield one step to the historical lest the Lutheran doctrine of justification should be endangered. [(8)] But by the beginning of the twentieth century Karl Barth was reacting in the opposite direction. Barth rebelled against the analytical historicism in which he had been schooled, claiming that subsidiary disciplines such as archaeology, philology or textual criticism should serve only as a preamble to the true interpretation of 'the Word'. [(9)] Historical exegesis had to give way to 'theological exegesis'. [(10)] The emphasis on eschatology so strongly stressed by Albert Schweitzer was also dominant in Adolf Schlatter's Romans commentary. The latter significantly claimed that righteousness is God Himself at work in that characteristic relationship in which the right is dynamically active. [(11)]

Conceivably Barth's radical revamping of the doctrine of election ought to have contributed to a fresh interest in Romans 9-11. [(12)]But probably because Barth's chief concern was dogmatic theology, his enormous impact on the field of biblical studies didn't immediately arouse the interest in these chapters that might have been anticipated. [(13)]

The Lutheran exphasis on justification by faith was sustained by Rudolf Bultmann as the way to a new self-understanding. [(14)] He saw a close connection in Paul between boasting and the doctrine of justification, the latter being the Gospel's prescription to eradicate the former. This existentialist approach, with its emphasis on the individual, also contributed to a neglect of Romans 9-11. [(15)] Bultmann tended to equate the eschatological dimension in Paul with his own existentialist approach.

However, the existentialist categories which he employed were inadequate as a vehicle for the whole of Paul's thought. [(16)] N A Dahl, in a review of Bultmann's *Theology of the New Testament* in 1954, complained that Bultmann had much to say about Romans 1-8, but practically nothing about Romans 9-11. [(17)] What Bultmann did have to say about these chapters was closely linked with his view of Christ as the end of the law, and was subsumed under the theme, 'Christ the End of History'. [(18)]

In one respect Barth and Bultmann were similar - in various and differing ways their understanding of history had profound significance for their particular expressions of the gospel message. Barth's stress upon divine initiative in the Gospel diminished the significance of the human response whilst Bultmann's stress upon self-understanding left him open to the criticism of being too anthropological. [(19)] Perhaps too they both shared a tendency towards over-realised eschatology inasmuch as they removed the element of futurity from eschatology, emphasising instead the eschaton as the eternal.

The virtue of Johannes Munck's contribution to a fresh understanding of Paul and of Romans was his concentration upon the apostle's eschatological expectations. Building on the work of T W Manson, Munck claimed that the British scholar's essay 'St Paul's Letter to the Romans - and Others', had invalidated the widespread assumption that Romans is a theological presentation, *unaffected by time and history* (emphasis mine). Instead Munck preferred to read Romans as 'a missionary's contribution to a discussion'. (20) The general impact of Munck's approach is evident in Peter Richardson's statement in 1969, 'There is a growing consensus that Romans must be interpreted in the light of Paul's missionary situation'. (21) For Munck, Romans 9-11 is Paul's reconstruction of the order of events in 'Heilsgeschichte' in the light of Jewish failure to believe in Jesus as Messiah and in face of the apostle's own successful Gentile mission. (22)

Munck's contribution, which unfortunately in some quarters gained only a slow and somewhat grudging recognition, (23) contained several significant insights: (1) He emphasised the apocalyptic element in Paul; (2) he related Romans to the context of Paul's mission and work; (3) he noted Paul's corporate thinking - the apostle evangelises an area and sees his converts as representatives of larger groups - Paul is apostle to the nations; (4) he drew attention to the unique contribution which Romans 9-11 makes to our understanding of Paul and of the entire letter, and (5) above all, he challenged the tendency to see Paul always and everywhere engaged in a battle with Jews and Jewish-Christian opponents. (24)

Although I found in Munck the key to a whole new way of thinking about Romans, in one aspect, however, he didn't offer as much insight as I had hoped. His elucidation offered a fresh understanding of Paul and his eschatology, much indeed about Paul's situation at the time of writing Romans but comparatively little on the situation of the Roman Christians. H Preisker was the first in the modern discussion to claim that Romans is a letter that arises out of and is addressed to the actual situation of the Christians in Rome. Preisker convincingly argued that a division had arisen in Rome between Jewish and Gentile Christians, based on the merits of their differing cultural backgrounds, the right understanding of the Old Testament, present and future salvation, and obedience to the state. (25)

In 1968 when I went to Tübingen to continue my research, I was delighted to make the acquaintance of H W Bartsch who had developed a similar approach to Preisker. Bartsch held that because of Claudius's expulsion of the Jews in 49 AD, Gentile Christians were in the majority at Rome. They deprecated the Jewish Christians; so Paul in Romans emphasises the privileges of the Jews to combat this incipient antisemitism. He stressed also the connection between the faith of Christians and that of Abraham. The Gentile Christians are dependent on the Jewish Christian community in Jerusalem - as Bartsch put it - 'as tree and fruit or mother and child'. In other later articles Bartsch claimed that because the Gentile Christians despised the Jewish Christians, no real Christian community had as yet been formed in Rome because each group excluded the other from worship. (26)

From the careful and thorough exegesis of Otto Michel I learnt to look for Paul's roots in Judaism and to discover especially the milieu of rabbinic exegesis and interpretation which Michel demonstrated to be so significant in Paul's own interpretation of the scriptures. (27)

In the stimulating and radical polemic of Ernst Käsemann I found the answer to some of the deficiencies that I had already uncovered in the current understanding of Romans 9-11. Käsemann's critique and modificiation of the existentialist approach of Bultmann, his revered teacher, was fascinating. Käsemann maintained that this approach had caused justification by faith to deteriorate into a theory concerning the rescue of the individual. In a series of essays dating from 1954 onwards, Käsemann argued that Bultmann had reduced Paul's theology exclusively to anthropology, whereas anthropology is only a part of it, being subordinate to the doctrine of God, Christology and cosmology. Salvation cannot be limited to a new self-understanding; the lordship of Christ is expressed not just in terms of personality or self-consciousness, but of one's body and, in terms of the 'extra nos', the entire creation is involved as Romans 8-11 indicate. (28)

God's righteousness for Käsemann is the rightful power with which God makes His cause to triumph in a world which has fallen away from Him and which yet, as His creation, is his inviolable possession. For Käsemann there is an indissoluble connection between power and gift in Paul. By means of this he attempted to give a comprehensive interpretation of Romans 1-11 and not merely of chapters 1-8. Romans 9-11 should be considered under the heading 'The Righteousness of God and the Problem of Israel', thus continuing the theme of the revelation of divine righteousness in the first eight chapters. (29) By emphasising Paul's apocalyptic outlook in order to counteract the weaknesses of existentialist interpretation, Käsemann was instrumental in helping to create a climate of opinion in which Romans 9-11 could attain a fresh significance.

But whilst nothing from historical scholarship that is essential was withheld in Käsemann's study of Paul, his particular emphasis was not to be so much on the 'Sitz im Leben' of Romans as on what Paul meant theologically. (30) In his Tübingen lectures on Romans which crystallised in his 1973 commentary, Käsemann designated the letter, despite the fact that it presents a summary of Paul's theology, as a document of a particular situation. (31) There was suspicion in Rome against both Paul's person and work but Paul wrote to the church there to present himself and his central message because he needed these Christians as a springboard, if not an operational base for his plans in the West. Thus the real problem of the text and therewith the purpose for writing lies in the combination of Rome, Jerusalem, Spain. (32)

Käsemann found in apocalyptic the anti-individualistic and anti-enthusiast emphasis to counteract some of the less satisfactory aspects of Bultmann's existentialist interpretation. He thereby helped relate Romans 9-11 to the central theme of the letter. He also stressed the Jewish heritage of the apostle. (33) Yet Käsemann's emphasis upon justification by faith included the traditional Lutheran antithesis between gospel and law which almost always tends to highlight the discontinuity between the church and Israel.

This tendency was strengthened by the work of one of Käsemann's students. Christian Müller in his book *Gottesgerechtigkeit und Gottes Volk: Eine Untersuchung zu Römer 9-11*, emphasised divine creativity including the right and freedom of God as Creator. (34) God's right is His right to be Creator - to count whom He wills as His seed, thereby loosing the divine election and calling from the physical seed of Abraham. (35) This perfectly correct emphasis is, however, in Romans 9-11, located within a discussion of divine faithfulness to *Israel*, and not just to creation as a whole. The emphasis in Romans 9-11 is not only upon the salvation-creating power of God but also upon His power to restore Israel to her divine destiny. Thus Käsemann's emphasis upon justification and divine righteousness didn't seem, to some scholars at least, to necessitate the relegation of Israel and the law entirely to the old aeon. (36)

It was not Käsemann's intention to concentrate his attention on the situation of the Roman Christians. It was in the study of Paul Minear,*The Obedience of Faith: The Purposes of Paul in the Letter to the Romans*, that a full-blown situational approach to the interpretation of the letter emerged. (37) Basing his thesis mainly on Romans 14-15, Minear outlined a situation in which disputing factions judged or despised one another on account of differences in life-style. He identified five different factions or theological positions and three main Christian groups in the Roman Christian community. In contrast to Käsemann, Minear didn't lay so much stress on the theological aspects of Romans, and once again, minimal attention was paid to chapters 9-11. (38) However, Minear deserves credit for an imaginative and provocative attempt to depict the specific situation that evoked the letter.

The particularity of the situation that led to the writing of each letter was also stressed by Robert Jewett in his 1971 study *Paul's Anthropological Terms: A Study of their Use in Conflict Settings*. (39) Jewett undertook a fully contextual analysis of Paul's anthropological terms by studying the meaning of the terms in each precise context in which they occurred. By this method Jewett sought to identify what is specific in the use of the anthropological terms in each letter and then to go on to draw conclusions about their use in Pauline theology generally. Jewett's methodology indicates his refusal at the outset to presume a standard meaning for a specific term throughout all Paul's letters. He thereby also resists the tendency to generalise from one letter to the other, so that the commonalities of the letters are emphasised rather than their particularity.

The tendency to harmonise is also repudiated. J C Hurd had earlier argued that the precise significance of each letter is best understood when its own distinctive contribution is recognised. He insisted that 'just as the harmonising of the letters with Acts is illegitimate, so too is the harmonising of the letters with one another. Both types of harmonisation are the result of a faulty historical method'. (40)

This approach to the study of Romans had the effect of causing scholars to seek to distinguish in a new way what is distinctive, even unique in the content and argument of the epistle. No more is it legitimate to cross-reference easily from Galatians as if the two letters were identical because of some similarities in content, eg the emphasis on justification by faith.

Another factor aided somewhat the emphasis upon the peculiarity of each Pauline letter. The recent developments in the study of the ancient letter pattern and format, greatly assisted in demonstrating how each letter either agreed with or departed from normal letter patterns and structures. (41)

In the early 1970's a new development in the historical quest of the 'Sitz im Leben' was to arise and prove exceedingly fruitful in some areas. It brought new insights and awareness of Paul's and his converts 'Sitz im Leben'. The sociological approach or sociological exegesis was to enhance the historical approach and give new life to the quest to rediscover the social and cultural milieu of Paul's congregations. (42)

Along with the emphasis upon Paul's conversation partners and the 'Sitz im Leben' to which his letters were addressed, issues dominant at the end of the sixties, other new emphases were to greatly influence the course of interpretation in the next decade. As we have just noted, the sociological approach, particularly when viewed as an extension of the historical, was one such influence which by the mid-seventies was beginning to acquire significance.

We have also already noted the newer research upon the ancient letter patterns and their influence upon Paul's letters. Rhetorical issues raised at the end of the sixties were to remain significant for the next two decades.

But another area of influence had gradually manifested itself in the wake of the Holocaust and Christian reflection upon the role which anti-Judaism may have played in it. Krister Stendahl in particular had drawn attention to Christian interpreters' tendency to wear 'Reformation spectacles' or even to view Paul through 'Augustinian eyes.' In the early seventies this influence was already becoming significant and from the late seventies it was going to bear with considerable force upon the understanding of Paul's theology. Christian-Jewish dialogue offered a new paradigm for Pauline interpretation, though for a scholar such as W D Davies, it was less of an innovation than for many others. (43)

Several major issues remained very much on the agenda of the interpretation of Romans at the beginning of the seventies. The first of these concerned the relative emphasis to be placed upon Paul's situation at the time of writing, and the 'Sitz im Leben' of the Roman Christians. Manson and Munck had stressed the former, Minear and others the latter. But which should have priority?

Another major issue was the relation of Romans to Paul's theology. How do Paul's statements in the letter relate to his theology if they can no longer be considered as his theology 'per se'?. If they are purely situational, ie contingent upon a local situation, then how may his theology properly be derived from them?

A third problem also had become significant. If chapters 9-11 are to be fully integrated into the interpretation of the letter, how are they to be valued in relation to chapters 1-8 and the rest of the letter? Is what comes first of prime significance? Or does the letter progress gradually to a climax in the practical issues of chapters 14-15? Or are chapters 9-11, the kernal out of which the entire epistle emerged? If they were neglected for so long, how can they possibly be regarded as the kernal, or the current or the climax rather than the husk, the backwater or the appendix - to use the images employed by various interpreters? (44)

The following chapters, beginning with my first essay written in 1973, involve a dialogue with many scholars who, in differing ways, have sought to explicate these issues and have thereby made their particular contribution to what has come to be known as 'The Romans Debate'.

NOTES

1. In 1955 Otto Michel's *Der Brief an die Römer*, Vandenhoeck und Ruprecht, Göttingen, was published as the 10th edition of the KEK Series. In 1957 two other major commentaries were published: C K Barrett's *A Commentary on the Epistle to the Romans*, in Black's New Testament Commentaries series; and F J Leenhardt's *The Epistle to the Romans* (E T by H Knight, Lutterworth, 1961). In the same year Otto Kuss published the first of three volumes (Pustet, Regensburg 1957, 1959, 1978). Karl Barth's *A Shorter Commentary on Romans* (1956) was translated into English in 1959 (SCM London). In 1959 the first of John Murray's two volume commentary on Romans appeared (Eerdmans, Grand Rapids, 1959, 1965). In 1962 T W Manson's short commentary on Romans appeared as part of *Peake's Commentary on the Bible*, (ed M Black and H H Rowley, Nelson, London). In 1963 F F Bruce's *The Epistle to the Romans* in the Tyndale New Testament Commentaries series was published, and in German, H W Schmidt's *Der Brief des Paulus an die Römer* (Evangelische, Berlin).
2. Munck's work on Romans 9-11 was completed in 1952 as a prelude to his *Paulus and die Heilsgeschichte* (1954, ET *Paul and the Salvation of Mankind* London, SCM 1959). It was published in German in 1956 and translated into English by Ingeborg Nixon (Fortress, 1967).
3. Cf Krister Stendahl's appreciation of Munck's work in the foreword to the English translation of *Christ and Israel*. Stendahl says 'it was the reading of this book more than twelve years ago which for the first time opened my eyes to Paul and his mission. It was the book that literally lifted hundreds of verses in the Pauline epistles out of a glorious haze of homiletical rhetoric and theological over-interpretation. It gave to the Pauline writings and to Paul the apostle a historical reality which, I hope, has remained with me ever since' (p7). Stendahl also notes Munck's greatest gift as a biblical scholar: 'the ability to read an ancient text with fresh eyes' (p8).
4. *The Epistle to the Romans*, Moffatt New Testament Commentaries, London, 1932, pp 148-9. Dodd did note connections between 3:1-9 and 9:1f, but he was rather unsympathetic to some of the issues Paul raised in chs 9-11, op cit, p44 and pp 148ff.
5. Lorraine Bouttier's *The Reformed Doctrine of Predestination*, Eerdmans, Grand Rapids, 1932, is probably one of the last examples of a traditional

reformed treatment of predestination. But see also E Dinkler's essay, 'The Historical and Eschatological Israel in Romans ix-xi, Journal of Religion, 16 (1956), revised and republished in *Aufsätze zur christlichen Archäologie*, (Tübingen 1967).

6. Even Sanday and Headlam maintained in their otherwise excellent ICC *The Epistle to the Romans* (T & T Clark, Edinburgh, 1895, 1902) in the explication of Romans 9:1f, 'St Paul has now finished his main argument' (p225). But Hans Lietzman in his *An die Römer*, (Tübingen, Mohr 1906, 3 Aufl. Tübingen 1928) emphasised the connection between 3:1f and 9:1f, 'Mit Kap ix beginnt... die Ausführung des 3:1f kurz angeschlagenen Themas', (p89). Similarly Anders Nygren in his 1944 commentary (ET, SCM London, 1952) insisted that chs 9-11 are a consistent development of chs 1-8 and not in any sense a parenthesis or digression (pp 35f).
7. *Christ and Israel*, p5.
8. *Paul: His Life and Works* ET by A Menzies, Theological Translation Fund Library, Edinburgh 1876, p3l3.
9. *The Epistle to the Romans* (6th ed) ET 1933, p15. Cf also R Kroner's comment, 'Analytical historicism kills the soul and retains the corpse', Journal of Bible and Religion, xiv (3) 1946, p132. C H Dodd in his Cambridge inaugural lecture deplored the barrenness of much analytical New Testament scholarship, calling instead for a study of the process which created the parts in order to discover an inner unity in the deeper meaning of the separate parts, *The Present Task in New Testament Studies*, Cambridge 1936, p35.
10. Cf Hugh Anderson, *Jesus and Christian Origins*, Oxford 1964, p22.
11. *Gottes Gerechtigkeit: Ein Kommentar zum Römerbrief*, Calwer, Stuttgart, 1935.
12. Barth's important contribution to the understanding of election is that for him election is 'in Christ' following the insight of the Scot's Confession. Barth realised that he could not simply follow in Calvin's footsteps for if he commenced where Calvin commenced, he would inevitably be led to the same conclusions. Cf *Church Dogmatics*, Vol 2 (2), *The Doctrine of God*, ET, Edinburgh 1957, pp 35f.

13 Cf B Rigaux's comment, 'Pour le théologien suisse, la critique littéraire et historique n'est qu'un premier pas, vite oublié', *Saint Paul et ses lettres*, Paris-Pruges, 1962, p44. This is not to overlook Barth's very real contribution to the understanding of Paul and of Romans; for a fuller evaluation cf R S Barbour, 'Karl Barth: The Epistle to the Romans', The Expository Times, Vol 90, 1979, pp 264-8 and R Jewett, 'Major Impulses in the Theological Interpretation of Romans since Barth', Interpretation 34, 1980 pp 17-31.

14. *Theology of the New Testament*, Vol 1, London 1952, pp 318f.
15. The existentialist view of authentic human existence as composed of broken and unrelated moments of encounter and decision failed to pay proper attention to temporal continuity, cf Hugh Anderson op cit p37. Thielicke rightly points out that the existentialist interpretation denudes

the New Testament of the 'extra nos' dimension, 'The Restatement of New Testament Mythology', in *Kerygma and Myth*, ed H W Bartsch, Vol 2, London 1955, p132.

16. Cf R Schnackenburg, *La Theologié du Nouveau Testament*, Paris-Bruges, 1961, p78 and R H Fuller, *The New Testament in Current Study*, London 1963, pp 72f. Fuller considers that the limitations of the existentialist approach are particularly evident in relation to Romans 9-11.
17. Dahl's substantial review was published in Theologische Rundschau xxii (1954), pp 21-40. Dahl noted that Bultmann's individualistic approach neglected the theme of the people of God in Romans 9-11 and in so doing succeeded only in 'dehistoricising Paul', a tendency Fuller found even more characteristic of Bultmann than 'demythologising', op cit p72.
18. Cf 'History and Eschatology in the New Testament', New Testament Studies, Vol 1, 1954/55, pp 1-16 and Bultmann's 1955 Gifford lectures *History and Eschatology*, Edinburgh, 1957. Cf also 'Christus des Gesetzes Ende: *Glauben und Verstehen*, Vol 2, Tübingen, 1952, pp 32-38.
19. Cf Dahl op cit pp 38-40. Dahl claimed that 'das Gottsein Gottes ist für die paulinische Theologie eine ebenso selbstverständliche Voraussetzung wie das Menschsein des Mensches'. For Dahl God is the Lord of Israel already revealed in the Old Testament, the God of creation, who directs history and who is the goal of history.
20. *Paul and the Salvation of Mankind*, ET, SCM London, 1959, p200.
21. *Israel in the Apostolic Church*, SNTS Monograph Series 10, Cambridge University, 1969, p126.
22. *Paul and the Salvation of Mankind*, p123.
23. Cf K Stendahl's comment that "Munck's 'magnum opus', *Paul and the Salvation of Mankind* has for some reason come to play less of a role in the contemporary discussion of Pauline problems than it deserves", Foreword to Munck's *Christ and Israel* p7. Stendahl thought that part of the reason for this failure is that Munck's larger work has 'the character of a thesis with a distinctive thrust which at points pushes its case quite far'.
24. Munck's opposition to the Tübingen school was very strong and perhaps one of the reasons why his work was not as popular as it deserved to be.
25. 'Das historische Problem des Römerbriefes', Wissenschaftlich Zeitschrift der Friedrich-Schiller Universität, Jena, 1952/53, pp 25-30, pp 25-30. This is not to overlook the important contribution of Wilhelm Lütgert whose valuable study, '*Der Römerbrief als historisches Problem*, Bertelsmann, Gütersloh, 1913, didn't achieve the significance it deserved, possibly because of the war-time situation and the publication of Barth's Romans commentary in 1919.
26. Cf Bartsch's articles: 'Zür vorpaulinischen Bekenntnisformel im Eingang des Römerbriefes', Theologische Zeitschrift, xxii (1967), pp 329-39; 'Die antisemitischen Gegner des Paulus in Römerbrief', in *Antijudaismus im Neuen Testament*? ed W Eckert et al, München, Kaiser: 1967, pp 27-43; 'The Concept of Faith in Paul's Letter to the Romans', Biblical Research 13 (1968), pp 41-53; 'Die Historische Situation des Römerbriefes', *Studia*

Evangelica IV, *Texte und Untersuchungen* 102 (1968), pp 281-291; 'Die Empfänger des Römerbriefes', Studia Theoligica 25 (1971), pp 81-89.

27 Cf Michel's *Der Brief an die Römer* (for details see note 1 above). It is unfortunate that Michel's commentary has not yet been translated into English since it contains such a wealth of solid exegetical detail.

28. Most of these important essays have now been included in the volume *New Testament Questions of Today*, ET, SCM London, 1969. The aspects of Käsemann's interpretation noted here relate particularly to the following essays: 'New Testament Questions of Today' (1957), now in the volume of the same title (henceforth listed as NTQT), pp 1-22, cf espec pp 14- 15; 'The Worship of God in Everyday Life" (1960), NTQT pp 188-95; "The Righteousness of God in Paul,' (1961), NTQT pp 168-82, see espec p181; 'Primitive Christian Apocalyptic' (1962), NTQT pp 108-37. The last two essays are part of Käsemann's debate with Bultmann on the place of apocalyptic in Jesus and Paul. Other important essays such as 'The Faith of Abraham' and 'Justification and Salvation History in the Epistle to the Romans' are included in the other volume of collected essays, *Perspectives on Paul*, ET, SCM London, 1971.

29. Cf Käsemann's *Commentary on Romans* (1973) ET, SCM London, 1980, pp 29f and 253f.

30. Cf the preface to the commentary, p7.

31. Op cit p390. Käsemann, in this and other respects, is more indebted to Barth than is sometimes realised. Cf Jewett op cit pp 26f.

32. Op cit pp 404f.

33. Cf *Commentary on Romans* op cit p254.

34. Vandenhoeck und Ruprecht, Göttingen, 1964.

35. Cf Müller, op cit pp 27-33, Minear op cit pp 8-15 and p45 n8.

36. For a critique on this aspect of Käsemann and some of his pupil's approach, cf K Kertelge, *Rechtfertigung bei Paulus*, Aschendorff, Munster 1967. Kertelge claims that Käsemann and Stuhlmacher overstress God's creative action. The emphasis is always present in Paul but never at the centre. (p308)

37. London, SCM, 1971.

38. Minear claimed that Paul was neither theologian nor historian, op cit p33. Cf my review of Minear's book in The Scottish Journal of Theology Vol 25 (1), 1972 pp 111-113.

39. Published by Brill, Leiden, see espec pp 7-8. Jewett's approach is close to that advocated by R H Fuller. Fuller cites W Schmithals, D Georgi, U Wilckens, and E Güttgemanns as exponents of this new approach to Pauline interpretation (op cit p101). Here we can see already the beginnings of an exphasis upon audience-criticism, including an awareness of Paul's 'conversation partners,' in the attempt to reconstruct the arguments of his opponents. Cf Jewett op cit p7; Minear op cit p7 and H Koester 'Paul and Hellenism' in *The Bible and Modern Scholarship* ed by P J Hyatt, New York, 1965 (p193). Cf also Fuller's review of E Güttgemanns,

Der Leidende Apostel und sein Herr, in Journal of Biblical Literature, LXXVI, 1967, pp 98-101.

40. Hurd's essay 'Pauline Chronology and Pauline Theology', was published in *Christian History and Interpretation: Studies Presented to John Knox* ed W R Farmer, C F D Moule and R R Niebuhr, Cambridge 1967, pp 225-48 (248).
41. Cf O Roller, Das Formular der paulinischen Briefe, Tübingen 1933. Paul Schubert, *Form and Function of the Pauline Thanksgiving*, Beihefte zur Zeitschrift für die neutestamentliche Wissenschaft, 20, 1939; Jack Finnegan, *Light from the Ancient Near East*, 2nd Edition, Princeton 1959; C B Bjerkelund, Parakalo, Form, Funktion und Sinn der parakalo - Sätze in den paulinischen Briefen, Oslo 1967. Much work was undertaken in this area in seminars at the Society of Biblical Literature in the 1970's, cf J L White 'Introductory Formulae in the Body of the Pauline Letter', Journal of Biblical Literature, XC (1971) 1-97 and *Studies in Ancient Letter Writing*, Chico, Scholars Press 1981.
42. E A Judge's study *The Social Pattern of Christian Groups in the First Century* Tyndale 1960, was an early example of this interest but it was only in the mid-seventies that it began to flourish, cf J Gager, *Kingdom and Community: The Social World of Early Christianity*, Prentice-Hall 1975. Abraham Malherbe's Rockwall Lectures on 'Social Aspects of Early Christianity' were delivered in April 1975 and published in 1978. John Gager's comments in a review of several books on this area in 1979 record the rapid rise of interest in the area. 'As recently as five years ago, scarcely anyone would have ventured to predict a revival of interest in the social history of early Christianity. As things stand now, however, the case for the legitimacy and viability of the enterprise is clearly established and accepted.' Gager's review considered Malherbe's book (noted above), G Theissen's *Sociology of Early Palestinian Christianity* (1977) and R M Grant's *Early Christianity and Society* (1977), 'Social Description and Sociological Explanation in Early Christianity: A Review Essay', published originally in Religious Studies Review 5 July 1979 and now included in *The Bible and Liberation: Political and Social Hermeneutics*, ed N Gottwald, Orbis, New York 1983, pp 428-440 (430).
43. Davies had stressed the significance of Jewish background for understanding Paul and also the need for an impartial treatment of Jewish materials; cf his book *Paul and Rabbinic Judaism*, London, SPCK, 1958. Although James Parkes' pioneering writings against antisemitism date from 1930, much of his earlier writing met with little acclaim as he himself notes in the preface to Alan T Davies *Antisemitism and the Foundations of Christianity*, Paulist Press, New York 1979. This volume edited by Davies was a response to the radical work by Rosemary Ruether, *Faith and Fratricide*, Seabury Press, New York 1974. Davies' earlier work *Antisemitism and the Christian Mind: The Crisis of Conscience after Auschwitz*, Herder and Herder, New York 1969, and Roy Ekardt's *Elder and Younger Brothers* 1967, (now published by Schocken Books, New

York, 1973), were also important publications marking the increasing momentum of the scholarly interest in antisemitism. However, it was only in the seventies that biblical scholars took up this theme with full earnestness, and Ruether's study was at least partly instrumental in causing them to do so.

44. The 'kernal'-'husk' imagery originates from F C Baur op cit (see note 8) p315; the current-backwater imagery is from B Noack, 'Current and Backwater in the Epistle to the Romans', Studia Theologia; xix, 1965, pp 155-66; the climax-appendix imagery is found in Stendahl op cit pp 28f; see especially p29 'to the central revelation of these chapters is then appended, so to say, a preface - Romans 1-8'. Leonard Goppelt uses yet another image when he says of chs 9-11, 'It actually is the keystone which closes the arch of Paul's theology and holds it all together', *Jesus, Paul and Judaism*, Nelson, New York 1964, p163: cf my article, 'The Place of Romans ix-xi within the Structure and Thought of the Letter', *Studia Evangelica* Vol VII, ed Elizabeth A Livingstone, Akademie-Verlag, Berlin 1982 pp 121-31.

Chapter 2

Why did Paul write Romans?

In this article I wish to consider several recent views concerning Paul's purpose in writing the letter to the Romans. Drawing on the conclusions of the survey, I will attempt to show that it is only when Romans is understood as a letter to Rome that a solution can be found to the various problems involved in the interpretation of the letter.

1. *Romans as a Letter of Self-Introduction*

Some scholars hold that Paul wrote the letter to the Romans in order to introduce both himself and his gospel to the Christians in Rome. The purpose of the letter is understood to be to prepare for Paul's future mission in Rome and in Spain. (1) The occasion for its composition is understood as follows. Paul had for some time intended to travel to the West but many obstacles, particularly the troubles in the churches at Galatia and Corinth, had hitherto prevented him by hindering the completion of the collection project (cf Rom 1:13, 15:22). But at the time of writing he is on his way to Jerusalem (2) with the collection and now at last he feels free to devote his attention to the West. Romans is written to prepare for his mission there.

This interpretation rightly recognises the strong emphasis in Romans upon the world-wide outreach of the Gospel. (3) The references to Paul's indebtedness to all men, whether Jew or Greek, are clearly in accord with such an understanding. It also gives due significance to Paul's stress on his intention to visit the Roman Christians on the way to Spain (1:10f, 15:22f).

There are, however, several serious objections to understanding Romans as a letter of self-introduction.

Firstly, it is not consistent with what we know of Paul from his other letters that he would feel obliged to outline his gospel for the approval of the Roman Christians (cf Gal 1:8ff). Nor is it conceivable that, after many years as apostle to the Gentiles, Paul would be so unknown to the Roman Christians as to necessitate the sending of a preliminary sample of his gospel in order to win support. (4)

A second objection to this interpretation is that Paul's references to his forthcoming visit are general, almost vague (5); so much so that Marxsen maintains that Paul speaks of his plans only incidentally and that they cannot possibly be taken as the theme of the letter. (6) There is also uncertainty as to what Paul intends to do in Rome. Apparently he intends to evangelise - to reap some harvest among them (1:13). Yet in 15:15, he claims that he writes simply by way of reminder. The latter suggests his intention is to build up an already existing Christian community. We shall discuss this duplicity of motive later.

A third objection is that according to Paul's references to his visit, his plans for Rome are subsidiary to his plans for Spain. (7) Those who emphasise Paul's desire to establish a mission in the capital (8) do not take seriously enough the fact that for Paul Rome is only a stepping-off place on the way to Spain (15:24-28). This makes it unlikely that he would forward to Rome an outline of his gospel in order to win support for his mission there. It would be more reasonable to claim that Paul desires support for a mission in Spain, especially when we take into account the progress of his missionary work at the time of writing. Having just completed his work in the East (15:23), he leaves the 'ecclesiastical province' of Jerusalem. Perhaps Paul's hope is that the Romans will act as a link between the Spanish mission and Jerusalem. (9) Without their support the converts in Spain would be completely isolated and his mission would become a purely individual effort. (10)

Thus it is perfectly legitimate to claim that one reason for Paul's writing to the Romans was to obtain support for his mission in Spain. But whilst this is a reason it ought not to be regarded as *the* reason. (11) This is borne out by the conclusion in 15:30-32. The 'parakalō' with which v.30 begins indicates that Paul is concluding his letter with a sentence which sums up the theme and purpose of writing. (12) In this sentence Paul states that through the prayers of the Roman Christians he hopes the collection will be received by the church in Jerusalem and that he himself will be delivered from unbelieving Jews. Only after this does he mention his forthcoming visit to Rome. It may be argued that since Paul's visit to Rome is subsequent to, and dependent upon the success of his visit to Jerusalem, this is the reason why the reference to Rome comes last. But allowing for this there is still some force in Jervell's contention that the safe delivery of the collection has as much reason to be regarded as the occasion for the writing of Romans as the proposed visit to Rome and Spain. If Paul's chief aim in writing had been to elicit the support of the Roman Christians for his missionary work, doubtless he would have made this more explicit. (13)

2. *Romans as an Assertion of Paul's Apostolic Authority*

Anton Fridrichsen once stated that the letter to the Romans was written to assert, in a discreet way, the apostolic authority and teaching of Paul in the church at Rome. (14) A similar interpretation has been proposed in a recent article by G Klein. (15) Dismissing the opinion of those who hold that Paul is desirous to preach in Rome because it is the capital, Klein maintains that Paul writes not because of what he wants *from* the Romans, ie in the way of support etc, but because of what he has *for* them, ie his apostolic authority as apostle to the Gentiles. (16)

Klein bases his interpretation on a certain ambivalence which he believes is discernible in Paul's approach to the Romans. Sometimes they are addressed as full members of the Christian community, as brothers etc. Yet Paul also speaks of his intention to preach the Gospel in Rome. Klein holds that no one has so far provided a satisfactory explanation of the apparent contradiction that exists between Paul's boast not to build on another man's foundation (15:20) and this expressed desire to preach the Gospel in Rome (1:11).

Klein's solution is as follows. The Roman Christians may be accurately described as Christians inasmuch as they have believed the Gospel etc, but they are not yet a properly founded church since they lack Paul's apostolic signature. This explains why Paul feels free to visit them even though they are already believers. It is also the reason why the designation 'ekklēsia' is missing in the prescript and throughout the letter. (17) Romans is unique since there is no real parallel to this situation where a church existed without a proper apostolic founder. Paul's concern is that the church in Rome should be fully established. When Romans is understood in this way, a certain equivalence between the purpose of the letter and Paul's proposed visit to Rome is discerned. In both he stresses his gospel and his apostolic commission as apostle to the Gentiles.

A basic criticism of Klein's opinion is that it is difficult to discover exactly what is lacking in the Christians at Rome. Klein does not claim that any specific problem exists, hence his view that the Romans are in some sense deficient is difficult to accept. The logical implication here is that Paul had a very officious and authoritarian understanding of his apostleship. It should also be noted that whilst Klein's interpretation accounts for the absence of the word 'ekklēsia' it fails to give due consideration to 1:6ff and 15:14ff, where Paul describes the Romans as full of knowledge, capable of instructing one another, and having a faith that is universally acclaimed. (18) He writes to them on some points simply by way of reminder (15:15). But if they were entirely lacking in apostolic foundation, how could Paul claim that he writes to them simply by way of reminder. (19)

The view that Paul wrote Romans to assert his apostolic authority lacks conviction. The fact that there is no reference to 'ekklēsia' can be explained other than as Klein does. If some of the Roman Christians had been converted elsewhere and then migrated there at a later date, (20) it is possible that being of diverse origin, they may have been unwilling to unite with one another or with local Christians, and problems may have arisen within the Christian community between those of Jewish and those of Gentile origin. (21) Thus their actual deficiency could have been that they were unwilling to form a united Christian church, hence Paul's avoidance of explicit reference to 'ekklēsia'. There is no need to dispute Klein's assertion that in Romans Paul emphasises and asserts his apostolic authority. What is in doubt is the reason why Paul does so and, in any case, it is questionable whether this represents his main purpose in writing.

3. *Romans as a Letter to Jerusalem*

Recently several scholars have shown a tendency to locate the occasion for the letter to the Romans in the circumstances of Paul rather than in those of the Roman Christians. As Paul sets out for Jerusalem, his mind is dominated by major issues such as wide-scale Jewish rejection of his gospel, the maintenance of the link between the Gentile congregations and the 'Urgemeinde' in Jerusalem, and the unity of Jew and Gentile in the Church (symbolised by the collection). Thus the themes with which Paul deals in the letter and his approach to them are determined by the prospect of his imminent arrival in Jerusalem. (22)

This interpretation helps to explain why Paul in Romans takes up again issues such as justification by faith which he has already discussed in earlier correspondence. Exponents of this view believe that it helps to explain why these issues are now dealt with in a manner different from that of the other Paulines. The altered character of the polemic is to be explained by the fact that now, unlike their treatment in earlier letters, the themes are divorced from a specific situation in a particular congregation. (23) Thus Bornkamm considers that 14-15 are lacking in concreteness in comparison with the similar discussion in 1 Cor 8. (24)

Inasmuch as it is both legitimate and necessary to keep in mind the Jerusalem context in which Romans originated, we agree with the emphasis of those who view it as a letter to Jerusalem. But we cannot agree with Jervell's assertion that it is wrong to attempt to discover in the letter itself the historical situation that led to its being written. (25) There is no letter of Paul's, apart possibly from Romans, of which it can legitimately be claimed that it was written more for the sake of Paul than for those to whom it was addressed. Nor is Romans merely a discussion of Paul's own problems. At some points it is clear that Paul is simply asking a rhetorical question; (26) at others it seems probable that he is re-using older material, hammered out in endless discussions with Jews or Judaizers. (27) But it would appear well-nigh impossible to achieve a consistent interpretation of the whole letter if one insists that all Paul's questions are purely rhetorical or that the objector is always of Jewish origin. (28)

Again it should be noted that although there is much in Romans that is polemical, on a straight-forward reading of the letter the attitude of self-defence, whether in relation to Paul himself or his gospel, is not so dominant as some interpretations suggest. Lütgert rightly notes that Paul's statements are not so much protests made in self-defence against those who reproach him for holding certain opinions, as exhortations and warnings directed against those who actually hold such views. (29) W G Kümmel believes that Paul replies to objections which he anticipated would come from the Roman congregation. (30)

As to Bornkamm's opinion concerning the concreteness of 14-15, it would appear that this is a very subjective judgment since other scholars hold an entirely opposite understanding of the same section. (31) When we study 14-15, we do not get the impression that Paul is discussing purely hypothetical issues; the discussion concerning the 'weak' and the 'strong' suggests, on the contrary, that he has in mind a division within a specific Christian community such as that which may have existed in Rome. As Kümmel states, 'We repeatedly get the impression that Paul is polemizing against false views being advocated in the Roman congregation'. (32)

A corrective to the approach of those who stress the similarity between the content of Romans and Paul's other letters is to devote more attention to those parts of the letter which are unique in Paul's writing, particularly 9-11. The content of these chapters must be given appropriate significance in any interpretation of the letter. The preoccupation with the theme of the failure and apparent rejection of the Jews would appear to support a Jerusalem address for the letter. Paradoxically, however, one of the most decisive arguments against the view that Romans is secretly addressed to Jerusalem is the fact that Paul's discussion of Jewish rejection of his gospel is specifically addressed to Gentile Christians and not to Jewish. (33)

The weakest point in the view that Romans is a letter to Jerusalem is that although this interpretation enables us to establish some connections between the writing of Romans and Jerusalem, it fails to provide any conclusive reason why the letter should actually have been addressed to Rome. We are left with a letter secretly addressed to Jerusalem, its contents having been principally determined by the problems Paul will face there. But the letter is not really sent to the place to which it is supposedly addressed and becomes in the end a sort of monologue or private confession of Paul (34) as he reflects in advance on the issues that lie ahead of him at Jerusalem.

Jervell makes a vague statement to the effect that the letter was sent to Rome because 'Paul needed the Christian community' there. (35) But this is not a sufficient reason. Despite the omission of the references to Rome in 1:7 and 1:15 in some manuscripts, this cannot be taken as proof that the original place of address was not Rome. (36) Probably the best explanation of the manuscript evidence is that the original reference to a particular place was later deliberately excised in order to give the document a wider sphere of reference. (37)

4. *Romans as a Circular Letter*

In an attempt to take into account the evidence which indicates that Romans was actually sent to Rome, some scholars maintain that while Rome may have been a destination for Paul's letter, it was by no means the only one. If Romans is regarded as a circular letter the necessity of making a choice between Jerusalem and Rome is removed. This interpretation owes much to the work of T W Manson. Arguing chiefly on the basis of the textual evidence, Manson came to the conclusion that Romans is best interpreted as a letter from Paul 'to the Romans - and Others'.

Romans is to be understood as a summing up of the positions reached by Paul and his friends at the end of the long controversy the beginnings of which appear in I Corinthians and in Philippians 3. Paul sends copies of this statement to Ephesus for the information of the churches of Asia, whilst he himself intends to inform the Christians in Corinth as well as those in Syria and Palestine by word of mouth. At the same time he decides to send a copy of his summing up and an outline of his future plans to the Christians in Rome. Romans is essentially 'a manifesto setting forth Paul's deepest convictions on central issues'. (38)

Despite its attractiveness, Manson's interpretation does not provide an adequate explanation for the sending of the letter to Rome. Suggs focuses attention on this weakness when he asserts that the article should have been entitled 'St Paul's Letter to Others - and the Romans'. (39)

Suggs prefers to regard Romans as a 'brief' drawn up by Paul in anticipation of the renewed necessity of defending his gospel in Jerusalem - a 'review of areas of prior dissension and a projection of solutions to possible future conflicts'. (40) He holds that the apparent 'Jewishness' of the letter is due to the fact that Paul has Jerusalem in view as he writes to the Gentile churches. For this reason he is at pains to develop a defence of his gospel which provides minimal offence to the Jews. Only thus may Paul hope to achieve the unity between the Jewish and Gentile wings of the Church symbolised by the collection.

Suggs has succeeded in explaining the Jewishness of a letter which is addressed to Gentile Christians. But has he overcome the weakness noted in Manson's interpretation? According to Suggs the content of the letter relates to all the Gentile churches and therefore Rome is included as one of the areas on the 'mailing list' to which Paul's 'brief' is despatched. A decisive reason for sending the letter to Rome is, we submit, still lacking.

A similar criticism may be levelled at Bornkamm's designation of Romans as 'Paul's last Will and Testament'. The letter represents Paul's final summary of his theology, although he himself did not write with this aim consciously in view. It became this only incidentally because of Paul's imprisonment and subsequent death. Bornkamm overcomes the problem of harmonising the destination of the letter with its contents by relating it both to Paul's visit to Jerusalem and to his intended visit to Rome. The message which Paul has to defend in Jerusalem and that which he intends to preach in Rome are one and the same. (41) Here again we have a letter which is addressed in the first instance to Gentile Christians in Rome, and yet its contents have been largely determined by Paul's relationship to the Jewish Christian community at Jerusalem. It would appear that only a very arbitrary connection between the two cities has been established.

Bornkamm could have avoided this criticism had he allowed, as Marxsen does, that part of Romans relates directly to a particular situation within the Christian community at Rome. The latter holds that the discussion in 12-15 is not purely hypothetical. A problem has arisen in Rome concerning the significance of Jewishness for the Church and in these chapters Paul attempts to solve the problem. (42) Marxsen thus acknowledges a real connection between part of Paul's letter and the Roman Christian community. Although from the point of view of this article, Marxsen's interpretation is an advance on that of Bornkamm, it is beset by another difficulty. Is it consistent to allow, as Marxsen does, that 12-15 relate directly to Rome, whilst 1-11 are held to speak only of an 'indirect situation' of which 'we cannot be certain that it did actually obtain in Rome, but which Paul nevertheless envisaged on the basis of his experiences at Jerusalem'? (43) In our opinion it is preferable to relate the whole of the letter to Rome.

5. *Romans as a Letter to Rome*
From the survey of various opinions it would appear that Romans is best understood as a letter written to Rome on account of a specific problem. (44) A division had apparently arisen because the liberal-minded Gentile Christian majority (the strong in faith) were unwilling to have fellowship with the conservative Jewish Christian minority (the weak in faith). In the letter which is primarily addressed to the former (45) since they were chiefly to blame for the dispute (cf 15:1), Paul undertakes an exposition of the righteous purpose of God both for Jew and Gentile as realised in Jesus Christ and revealed in the Gospel.

In order to counteract the animosity between the two groups, Paul stresses the equality of Jew and Gentile in sin (3:20), and in the Gospel (10:12). He claims that God's purpose was to make Abraham the father of all believers, both Jews and Gentiles (4:11-12). Since he is 'the father of us all' (4:16) the implication is that there should be no division within the church.

The covenant with Abraham gave to the Jews a privileged place as recipients of the divine revelation. But Paul is careful to stress that this priority (1:16, 2:9f) has a religious and not a racial basis (2:28f, 3:9). In acknowledging a certain advantage to the Jew, he denies any intention of setting one group above another (cf 3:1-9). (46) And yet God's gifts to Israel are not to be lightly dismissed (cf 3:1-2, 9:4-5). Although God is free to choose his own people both from within (9:6-11) and from without (9:22ff) the nation of Israel, in his freedom he has chosen to make his gifts and calling irrevocable (11:29), so that his purpose still includes the Jews.

Paul's response to the Gentile Christians' misunderstanding of 'Heilsgeschichte' and their resulting presumptuous pride is to remind them that they have been grafted into the trunk of Abraham (11:18) and that the salvation of Jew and Gentile is interdependent in the purpose of God (11:28-32). (47) The Christ whom Gentiles worship is none other than the goal, 'telos', of the Law of Judaism (10:4). Election properly understood is not a question of Jew or Gentile but of Jew *and* Gentile. Thus there can be no foundation for the Gentile Christians' assumption that they have simply replaced the Jews in the Divine purpose. That this is unwarranted is evidenced by the fact that Paul sees his mission (11:13f) like that of Jesus (15:8f) as directed to both Jews and Gentiles. Paul aims a final blow at Gentile Christian conceit by claiming that the hardening of Israel is both partial and temporary (11:25f), and that in any case the ways of God are beyond human comprehension (11:33f). Highmindedness is therefore ruled out (48) (11:25, 12:3f) and Jewish and Gentile Christians ought to accept one another freely as Christ has accepted them (15:7).

In conclusion it should be noted that this interpretation meets certain requirements the fulfilment of which our survey of recent opinions has shown to be necessary for an adequate understanding of the letter. The disunity provides a definite reason for Paul's writing to Rome. The harmful effects that reports of anti-Judaism among Gentile Christians in Rome would be likely to have upon the reception of Paul's collection in Jerusalem (and hence upon the unity of the entire church) explains why Paul should send such a letter to Rome at this time; it also establishes the connection between Romans and Jerusalem which some scholars have recently emphasised.

The fact that Paul deals with such a comprehensive subject as the purpose of God accounts for the recurrence and the somewhat different treatment of certain themes in this letter. In Romans, particularly 5-8, these themes are not discussed separately but in their mutual relationship within the Divine economy, eg the Law and the Spirit in 7-8. This is probably the reason why some scholars have regarded Romans as a treatise of Pauline theology. The vastness of the subject (the purpose of God) also helps to explain why some parts of the letter are less obviously related to Rome than others. These are stages in an argument, the full thrust of which finally becomes plain only in 11-15.

This interpretation also accounts for the absence of 'ekklēsia' in the letter. The omission is understandable if this was a delicate issue in Rome due to the division within the Christian community.

Finally this interpretation has the merit that it gives an integral place to chapters 9-11 within the argument of the letter. They are not viewed merely as an appendix to 1-8 but are seen to be closely related to 1-4, 12:1ff and 14-15. It also explains why Paul's discussion of the Jews in 9-11 is addressed to Gentile Christians.

NOTES

1. Eg C H Dodd, *Romans*, MNTC (1932), p7.
2. Cf T M Taylor, 'The Place of Origin of Romans', JBL, LXVII (1948), p281f.
3. Cf G Bornkamm, 'Der Römerbrief als Testament des Paulus', *Geschichte und Glaube,* 2 (München 1971), p135.
4. Cf J Jervell, 'Der Brief nach Jerusalem: Über Veranlassung und Addresse des Römerbriefes', Studia Theologica, XXV (1971), p66.
5. Cf C K Barrett, Romans, BNTC (London 1957), II.
6. *Introduction to the New Testament* (ET Oxford 1968), p92.
7. Cf Jervell, op cit, p66.

8. Eg Dodd, op cit, p7.
9. Cf F J Leenhardt, *The Epistle to the Romans* (ET London 1961), p13f.
10. Cf Bornkamm on 'propemphthēnai' (xv:24), op cit, p123.
11. Cf D Georgi, *Die Geschichte der Kollekte des Paulus für Jerusalem* (Hamburg Bergstedt 1965), p81 and P Minear, *The Obedience of Faith: The Purposes of Paul in the Epistle to the Romans* (SCM, London 1971), p5f.
12. Cf C B Bjerkelund, *Parakalo. Form, Funktion und Sinn der parakalō Sätze in den paulinischen Briefen* (Oslo 1967)
13. Op cit, p66f.
14. 'The Apostle and his Message', Uppsala Universitets Aarsskrift, III (1947), p7.
15. 'Der Abfassungszweck des Römerbriefes', *Rekonstruktion und Interpretation* (ges Aufs München 1969), p129ff.
16. Op cit, p135.
17. Ibid The word occurs only in ch 16 and there 'only in a purely episodic way', cf Leenhardt, op cit, p16.
18. See also Bornkamm's criticism of Klein's interpretation of 15:20, op cit, p138, n47.
19. Cf H W Bartsch, 'The Concept of Faith in Paul's Letter to the Romans', Biblical Research, XIII (1968), p44.
20. Cf E A Judge and G S R Thomas, 'The Origin of the Church at Rome: A New Solution', The Reformed Theological Review, XXV (1966), p81ff.
21. Cf W Wiefel, 'Die jüdische Gemeinschaft im antiken Rom und die Anfänge des römischen Christentums: Bemerkungen zu Anlass und Zweck des Römerbriefs', Judaica, XXVI (1970), p65ff.
22. E Fuchs, (*Hermeneutik*, Bad Canstatt 1954, p191) suggested that the secret address of Romans might be the church in Jerusalem. On the connection with Jerusalem cf also Marxsen, op cit, p95, Bornkamm op cit, p130ff, Jervell, op cit, p66f and M J Suggs, 'The Word is Near You: Rom X:6-10 within the Purpose of the Letter', in *Christian History and Interpretation: Studies Presented to John Knox,* ed W R Farmer, C F D Moule and R H Niebuhr (Cambridge 1967), p289ff.
23. Cf Suggs op cit, p294f and 312, Jervell op cit, p68.
24 Op cit, p135.
25. Cf op cit, pp62-64.
26. Cf R Bultmann, *Der Stil der paulinischen Predigt und die kynisch-stoische Diatribe* (Göttingen 1910) II, p62f.
27. Cf J Jeremias, 'Zur Gedankenführung in den paulinischen Briefen', *Studia Paulina*, ed J N Sevenster and W C van Unnik (1953), p148f.
28. Cf W Lütgert, Der Römerbrief als historisches Problem, BFChTh, 17 (1913), pp69-79. It seems unlikely that in part of Romans Paul addresses Jewish Christians and in other parts Gentile, cf Hort as quoted by Sanday and Headlam, *Romans*, ICC (Edinburgh 1902), p324.
29. Cf op cit, pp74-76.
30. *Introduction to the New Testament* (ET SCM, London 1966), p220ff.

31. Eg Marxsen op cit, p95ff.
32. Op cit, p221.
33. Cf H W Bartsch 'Die antisemitischen Gegner des Paulus in Römerbrief', *Antijüdaismus im Neuen Testament? Abhandlung zum christlichen-judischen Dialog,* Bd 2 (München 1967), p27ff.
34. O Michel understands Romans as the exegetical demonstration that Paul's preaching confronts both Judaism and paganism in the proper way with the truth of the Gospel. *Der Brief an die Römer* , 12 Meyer KEK (Göttingen 1963) p4
35. Op cit, p64.
36. Cf T W Manson, 'St Paul's Letter to the Romans - and Others', *Studies in the Gospel and Epistles*, ed M Black (1962), p235ff.
37. Cf N A Dahl, 'The Particularity of the Pauline Epistles as a Problem in the Ancient Church', *Neotestamentica et Patristica, Eine Freundesgabe, O Cullmann zu seinem 60 Geburtstag überreicht* (Leiden, 1963), p260ff.
38. Op cit, p241.
39. Op cit, p295.
40. Op cit, 312.
41. Op cit, p138.
42. Op cit, p95f
43 Op cit p101
44. As Minear rightly notes (op cit, 7ff), though he fails to do justice to 9-11.
45. Contra Minear's view that Paul addresses several groups or factions, op cit, p43f.
46. Cf F C Synge, 'The Meaning of "proechometha" in Rom III:9', ExpT LXXXI (1970), p351.
47. Cf P Richardson, *Israel in the Apostolic Church* (Cambridge 1969), p127.
48. E Käsemann holds that Paul stresses the admonition in 12:3, *New Testament Questions Today* (ET SCM London 1969), p192.

Chapter 3

Romans III as a Key to the Structure and Thought of the Letter

Numerous and varied suggestions have been proposed by scholars in recent years concerning the occasion and purpose of Paul's letter to the Romans. (1) Though not all are sceptical as to the outcome, some scholars feel that the varying conclusions witness to an increasing confusion rather than clarity in the interpretation of the letter. (2)

One reason for this diversity of opinion may be the actual structure and content of Romans itself. Chs 1:1-17 and 15:14f function as brackets around the 'body' of the letter. (3) Since these chapters deal with Paul's travel plans and his concern for the Roman Christians, it is inevitable that they will be at the centre of any discussion concerning the situation to which the letter is addressed or out of which it emerged. Consequently these passages tend to receive undue attention from scholars concerned with the occasion and purpose of the letter. (4) Other scholars, however, who lay more stress on the theological significance of Romans, tend to concentrate on the body of the letter - usually chs 1-8, sometimes 1-11 (5), and, less frequently, 9-11 (6).

The way to a comprehensive and more generally acceptable interpretation of the letter must lie, therefore, in a proper combination or unification of these two emphases; ie in seeking an explanation of the occasion and purpose of Romans which is consistent with, and adequately related to, the content of 1:18-11:36. Any interpretation which makes good sense of only part of the letter is automatically, by definition, excluded. A coherence must be established also between 1:18-11:36 and 12-15 (16). (7) In the search for a comprehensive interpretation of the letter, some light, we believe, may emerge from a closer study of ch 3.

Scholars have frequently drawn attention to the great extent to which ch 3 is composed of questions which are answered at a later point in the letter. (8) The chapter begins with a series of questions in vv 1-8 and ends with another series in vv 27-31. The remainder consists of a summary-conclusion (to 1:18-2:29) in v 9a - also introduced by a question - and supported by a catena of Old Testament citations demonstrating the utter sinfulness of all men whether Jew or Gentile (vv 10-18), Paul's commentary upon these (vv 19-20) and a statement concerning his understanding of the revelation of God's righteousness in Jesus Christ (vv

21-26). Since the latter passage is generally regarded as being of crucial significance both in the letter and in Paul's theology, it is to it that we will give first consideration.

I. *Ch 3:21-26 as the Centre of Paul's Theology in Romans*

This section differs from the diatribe (9) style of the question-answer sections (such as 3:1-8); it differs also in content. It is characterised by a kerygmatic or declaratory style similar to that of ch 5 and, to a lesser extent, of ch 8. (10) In contrast to the diatribe style sections, punctuated by frequent questions and interjections, here Paul is not asking questions or addressing real or imagined opponents, but expounding the meaning of the Christ-event as he understands it in the light of earlier Christian traditions. (11) Already in the statement of the theme of the letter in 1:16f. Paul has stressed three elements in his gospel: (i) the Gospel is not something of which he is ashamed but that which puts Paul in debt to all men and which therefore demands universal proclamation; (ii) in the Gospel the righteousness of God has now been revealed as a power which through faith in Christ leads to salvation, and (iii) the Gospel is to the Jew first but also to the Gentile.

In 1:18-2:29 Paul has shown that, in the light of the Christ-event, the former distinctions among men whether as Jews or Gentiles, have now (cf 'nuni de' in 3:21 and 'en tō nun kairō' in 3:26) been rendered obsolete by the new aeon that has dawned with the Gospel. (12) The only distinctions that are now valid are those which God, the judge of all the earth, makes on the basis of the Gospel. The unbelieving Jew in the old aeon is now no better than the unbelieving Gentile. (13)

In 3:21f Paul interprets the meaning of the Christ-event as the present eschatological activity of God which has transformed the relationship between Jew and Gentile. We note the emphasis on the eschatological present in 3:21 and 3:26, and again in 5:9,11 and 8:1. The similarity in style and content between these sections suggests that the latter sections are a development and a continuation of the former. It is significant that in 3:24-26, as already in 1:3-4, Paul uses a Jewish-Christian credal formula to expound his gospel. (14) His intention, it would appear, is to demonstrate that the Gospel which he preaches, which Gentiles believe, is none other than the good news of the fulfilment of God's promises to Israel. (15) Paul's gospel did not originate in a vacuum, it has a pre-history. Although it proclaims the power of God as 'creatio ex nihilo', (16) it is not itself of this nature. It is based on the redemption that has now taken place in Christ, the Christ-event being understood as the explanation, revelation and culmination of the divine purpose in the world for which God first entered into covenant with Israel.

If Käsemann is correct in his understanding of Paul's additions to, and modification of, the Jewish-Christian formula in 3:21f, (17) it is legitimate to take v 26 as indicative of Paul's own theology and distinctive emphasis. To a certain extent this is also true of vv 24-26a, in that we presume that what Paul quotes he intends to endorse and that v 26b-c modifies rather than corrects vv 24-26a. (18) According to 3:26, Paul considers that the Christ-event has a two-fold outcome (a) to demonstrate that God is righteous and (b) to demonstrate that he rectifies (19) him who has faith in Jesus. Here we have what may, with some justice, be termed the theological centre and basis of Paul's argument in Rom 9-11. We stress that there are two emphases. (20) It has been the tradition in Protestant, particularly Lutheran, theology to concentrate on the second of these, ie the justification or rectification of the ungodly. But both must be stressed simultaneously and the one certainly not at the expense of the other.

That God in Christ has revealed Himself as righteous and self-consistent means that He keeps faith with His people, that He keeps his promises to Israel. It follows that any consideration of righteousness as the rectification of the ungodly must also necessarily involve a consideration of righteousness in relation to God's promises to Israel - His faithfulness to the covenant. This is in fact demanded by the scope of Paul's gospel which is universal not in opposition to Jewish particularism, as has often mistakenly been believed, (21) but precisely on the basis of that Jewish particularism which, through the fulfilment in Christ of the promises to Israel, is now opened up to include Gentiles also. (22)

This means that Rom 1-8 should not be considered in isolation from 9-11. The history of post-Reformation interpretation reveals that the contrary has in fact been the case. (23) In the discussion of the righteousness of God there has been a consistent failure to take into account chs 9-11 with the result that in Bultmann's exegesis, justification has tended to deteriorate into a theory concerning the rescue or the new self-understanding of the individual. (24)

This could have been avoided by a more consistent interpretation of Rom 1-11 where the rectification of the individual is set in the context of the promises and the people of God. Michel rightly emphasises that chs 9-11 are the criterion by which one may judge whether 3:21f has been rightly understood. (25) Only when the rectification of the ungodly is viewed in relation to the historic people of God is there any compelling necessity for chs 9-11 to succeed chs 1-8, but when the motif of the constitution and continuity of the people of God is seen as central, then it is the theme of 'Rechtfertigungslehre' which provides a unified interpretation of chs 1-11. (26) This demands that due regard must be paid to both chs 1-8 and 9-11; neither may be considered as either supplementary to, or simply an elaboration or illustration of the other, otherwise a one-sided interpretation will result. As Marxsen notes, 'Taken out of context, passages (in Romans) could be interpreted in an anti-Jewish sense; but taken out of context, chs 9-11 could be interpreted in a pro-Jewish sense. But Paul's concern is neither with the one nor the other but with peace in the new aeon'. (27)

It is noteworthy that when the twin themes of the righteousness of God as self-consistent and as rectifying the ungodly, are emphasised together, then a strong connection is established between chs 1-4 and 9-11. Chs 5-8 then become the problem (28) or to use terminology suggested by Noack, what used to be regarded as the 'current' turns out to be the 'backwater'. (29) The theme of Jews, Gentiles and the Gospel prevalent throughout chs 1-4 and 9-11 points to a similar conclusion. (30) But, as we shall see later, different patterns may be discerned in the letter when it is viewed from different perspectives. What is significant is that throughout chs 3:21-26, 5 and 8, the theme is the eschatological present viewed as the time of fulfilment in Jesus, the son of David, of the messianic promises.

In a synopsis of 5:1-11 and 8:1-39 Dahl has demonstrated a parallelism between these two sections of the letter; almost all the major themes of 5:1-11 reappear in ch 8. The vocabulary of 5:1-11 however, differs from that of ch 8 in that in it the vocabulary is that of chs 1-4 whereas that of ch 8 is set against the background of 5:12-8:25. (31) Thus chs 5 and 8 are a continuation and development of the themes of 3:21-26. (32)

In a high point of his argument in ch 8, Paul reminds the Roman Christians that they have not received the spirit to fall back into fear but the spirit of sonship whereby they can call 'Abba, Father' (v15). This, in turn, means that they are children and heirs of God, joint-heirs with Christ (v17) and, provided they share in Christ's sufferings, God will deliver His elect to their full redemption in the consummation of the new creation (vv 18-31). (33)

It is not surprising that post-Reformation exegesis has stressed the centrality of justification by faith in Romans (and therefore also in Paul's theology). But Paul's emphasis in ch 8 is not simply on the safe conduct of believing (or elect) individuals to their eventual glorification. What prompted Paul in the first instance is more likely to have been a concern to stress the actualisation in the church composed of both Jews and Gentiles (34) of the promises given to Abraham. God's word or promise has not failed in that the eschatological blessings are now being realised among believers. This part of ch 8 is already a partial answer to the problem of the Jewish rejection of the Gospel with which Paul will deal in 9:6f. In spite of the failure of the Jews to accept the Gospel, God has vindicated Jesus as Messiah, the heir and fulfiller of the promises to Abraham which are thereby guaranteed to be fully realised in the revelation of the sons of God in the consummation of the new creation. Paul's interest here is primarily in the promise and its realisation, whereas Protestant interest has centred on the recipients of the promise and has therefore showed little concern for the Jews who through rejection of the Gospel have excluded themselves.

Thus the doctrine of justification by faith is the presupposition and basis on which Paul approaches the failure of his fellow Jews to accept the Gospel. (35)

We will find also that Rom 8 is not his only or last word on the subject. (36) He has yet to deal with the faithfulness of God which demonstrates that He himself is righteous, even in His relation to the disobedient. What he has to say on this in chs 9-11 runs a great risk of being misunderstood if the emphasis of 3:21f, ch 5 and ch 8 is not kept in view. (37) In order to clarify further the relationship between chs 1-8 and 9-11, we must look again at ch 3 in order to get a clearer picture of the structure of the letter.

2. *Chapter 3 as the Structural Centre of the Letter*

In the search for clues to the organisation of the letter, the question-answer sections especially 3:1-8, offer useful guidelines for discerning the structural centre out of which the entire letter is developed.

The quest for a fresh understanding of Romans which has recently culminated in what we may term 'The Roman Debate' was inaugurated by T W Manson in 1948. (38) Manson viewed Romans primarily as a summing up of Paul's missionary controversies, a circular letter which set forth his deepest convictions on central issues. Munck took up Manson's suggestions claiming that the new approach had invalidated the widespread assumption that Romans is a theological presentation unaffected by time and history. The letter may now be regarded as 'a missionary's contribution to a discussion'. (39)

One result of relating Romans to Paul's missionary context was that a 'Sitz im Leben' was thereby provided for the questions and objections in the letter. Jeremias, rejecting the view that Romans is a dogmatic treatise, viewed it as an epistle which had developed from Paul's frequent dialogue with Jews. (40) The dialogue style of the letter has been a subject of debate in much subsequent research. In one of the more recent commentaries,

3. *Romans III as a Key to the Structure and Thought of the Letter*

M Black describes the letter as a Jewish-style rhetorical discourse which owed much to the rhetorical practices of the Stoic diatribe of the period, especially as adapted by Jewish controversalists. (41)

It would seem preferable in view of the deliberate literary style of the letter to modify Jeremias' view by stressing that the objections need not always or necessarily be of Jewish origin.

Paul may simply be speaking as a Jewish Christian, or asking a rhetorical question to further the progress of his argument or even taking up positions adopted by the Roman Gentile Christians. (42) If, as seems likely, the letter is the written equivalent of the oral presentation which Paul would have delivered to the congregation had he himself been present, (43) then in the majority of cases he would have been addressing a predominantly Gentile congregation and this ought to be reflected in his letters; this does not however preclude the possibility of Paul speaking personally and apologetically either as an apostle or as a representative of believing Jews. (44)

Jeremias provided a useful insight in his observation that the thought sequence of Rom 9-11 is determined largely by these questions and objections. The answers to them occupy the greater part of these chapters. (45) Again, the fact that the interruptions have the effect of making some sections of the letter appear as digressions (46) must not be allowed to mislead us as to Paul's real intention. Since the questions-objections frequently serve as the heading for a new section as in 6:1-15; 7:7; 9:14,30; 11:1,11, or as the conclusion of one section and the commencement of another, as in 3:31-4:1, it is clear that these introduce major issues which Paul wishes to discuss in the letter.

It is significant that the common diatribe style provides a link between 6-7 and 9-11. We have already noted how the theme of Jews, Gentiles and the Gospel links 1-4 and 9-11, thereby somewhat isolating 5-8. (47) But when stylistic considerations are uppermost we find that chs 5 and 8 share a common kerygmatic declaratory style with 3:21-26 whereas 6-7 and 9-11 are linked by that of the diatribe. (48) The structure of the letter will become clearer when we observe the relationship between the questions Paul asks and the answers he gives to them.

The first question with which ch 3 commences is not in fact really answered here - the answer is not fully developed until 9:4f. It is only then that Paul continues the list of the advantages of the Jew, the first of which is given in 3:2 - 'they were entrusted with the word (promises) of God.' (49) Following this initial question comes a list of questions extending to 3:8. In 3:3 the question is put ,'What if some (Jews) were unfaithful? Does their faithlessness nullify the faithfulness of God?' The answer to this - that God's word has not failed, is provided in 9:6f. Again in 3:5 the question is put that if the unbelief of the Jews serves God's good purpose (in allowing the Gospel to go to the Gentiles) is God not in fact unjust in judging the wicked (Jews)? The answer to this question is likewise provided in ch 9 in vv 14f in terms of God's freedom to use nations as He wills for his own glory. God is committed to Israel but His commitment is in keeping with the glory of His great name so that His covenant faithfulness may mean the salvation of only a remnant of Israel at the present time. (50)

One unanswered question remains. 'Why not do evil that good may come?' (3:8). (51) This is in fact answered in 6:1-7:6 and may also account for Paul's discussion of the Law in 7:7f. The second series of questions in 3:27-31 arise out of Paul's exposition of the Christ-event in 3:21-26 and provide an outline for Paul's treatment of the Abraham tradition in ch 4. (52)

From this survey of Paul's questions and of his answers to them in subsequent chapters, we have arrived at a conclusion similar to that in the discussion of the diatribe style. The questions in 3:1-8 link this section with 6-7 and 9-11 whilst those in 3:27-31 link 3:21f with ch 4. The issue which must now be considered is whether the diatribe style sections, in spite of their appearance as digressions, do not, in fact, constitute the real theme of the letter and, if so, then how do they relate to the kerygmatic, declaratory sections.

3. *Romans as Witness to the Historical Situation to which the Letter is Addressed*

The fact that the questions in 3:1-8 precede Paul's exposition of the Christ-event in 3:21f is significant. This indicates that Paul looks to the Cross for an understanding and solution of the problems he faces. It could reasonably be argued that the questions in Romans are purely rhetorical, - literary devices to draw out the practical consequences of doctrines such as baptism. The sequence in ch 3 points, we submit, in the contrary direction. Our suggestion is that Paul faces real issues in Rome as outlined in 3:1-8 and that his exposition of the Christ-event in chs 3:21-26, 5 and 8 is particularly designed to answer these problems. (53)

The latter chapters deal with the eschatological present whereas the questions put may sometimes refer to the pre-Christian era - the place of the Law or the election of Israel, ie items in Heilsgeschichte, the significance of which has been radically transformed by the coming of Christ. The question of continuity between Judaism and Christianity was a real issue among the Roman Christians. (54)

3. *Romans III as a Key to the Structure and Thought of the Letter*

Our contention is therefore, that Rom 3 provides an insight into the existential centre or focus of the letter. F C Baur rightly claimed that 'it certainly appears that he (Paul) cannot have devoted so large a part of his epistle to answering this question (the relation of Judaism and heathenism to each other, and the relation of both to Christianity) without some special reason prompting him to do so, such as might have arisen out of the circumstances of the church at Rome'. (55) Our contention is that the issues with which Paul deals in Romans are not simply the outcome or development of previous missionary disputes, nor hypothetical questions to draw out the significance of Christian doctrines, but problems within the Roman Christian community about which Paul is informed and with which he intends to deal. If we take the example of Paul's use of the Abraham tradition in ch 4, this will illustrate our thesis.

The outcome of Paul's discussion of Abraham is found in 4:16f. (56) 'That is why it depends on faith, in order that the promise may rest on grace and be guaranteed to all his descendants - not only to the adherents of the law but also to those who share the faith of Abraham, for he is the father of us all...' The grammatical structure here with its concentration on the purpose and intention of God's dealings with Abraham - particularly the reference to Abraham being intended to be 'the father of us all', (57) ie of Jewish and Gentile Christians, show us that Paul intends to use Abraham as a uniting figure in the church composed of Jewish and Gentile Christians, and probably also as a model of 'the strong in faith'. (58) Not only this, but it is presupposed in 4:1 that what Abraham found was grace. Thus the concern in Rom 4 is not merely with Abraham as an example of a man of faith, the prototype of the believer, or simply as scriptural proof of what is already asserted in ch 3. David or Moses could not have served Paul's purpose here. Abraham is chosen as the one who found grace, the bearer of the promise who is replaceable by no other figure, the one with whom God first entered into covenant to bless the nations. (59) In the time of fulfilment the covenant is opened up to include Gentiles also so that Jewish and Gentile Christians may both regard Abraham as father.

Ch 6:1f is an even better example to show that Paul's questions are not merely rhetorical and that the objector is not necessarily Jewish. According to 3:8 some people slanderously report that Paul preaches the doing of evil that good may ensue and grace abound. In 6:1f, Paul repudiates such suggestions with a strongly ethically orientated exposition of the Christian's union with Christ's death and resurrection in baptism. (60) The catechetical teaching associated with baptism is continually evoked in Paul's reply, eg 6:3,9,16; 7:1. (61) It is significant that in 6:3f Paul addresses directly the

Roman Christians using the second person plural and in 6:11-13 he becomes even more precise in his use of the imperative. This is clear proof that the suggestion - that continuing in sin in order that grace may abound represents a Jewish parody of Paul's gospel - is a mistaken opinion. Paul is addressing baptised Christians and exhorting and commanding them not to live an antinomian existence. This suggests that those who slanderously reported Paul in 3:8 may be Gentile Christians who mistakenly attributed their own antinomianism to Paul's gospel of grace. (62)

Further support for the view that Paul's questions represent real issues in the church at Rome is found in 9-11. In 11:13f Paul after a long discussion begun in 9:1, addresses himself pointedly to the Gentile Christians and specifically warns them not to boast over the fate of the unbelieving Jews. 'If you do boast remember it is not you that support the root, but the root that supports you' (v 18). Again he warns 'do not become proud, but stand in awe' (v 20). This is no hypothetical situation and the dialogue style gives no reason to believe that Paul does not address himself to a real situation in Rome where current anti-Judaism was threatening the unity of the church. (63) Paul's carefully constructed conclusion in 11:30-32, his exhortations in 12:1f and in 14-15 support this interpretation of ch 11. (64)

An even clearer indication in support of the above is the concluding scripturally substantiated imperative in 15:7f, 'Welcome one another, therefore, as Christ has welcomed you, for the glory of God'. Here is clear evidence that Paul commands two groups to accept each other as equal and full members of Christ and his church. The succeeding two-fold emphasis upon Christ's ministry - (i) 'He became a servant to the circumcised to show God's faithfulness, in order to confirm the promises given to the patriarchs and (ii) in order that the Gentiles might glorify God for his mercy', shows that Paul wishes to demonstrate that the Gospel concerns both Jews and Gentiles. This is further substantiated by a number of Old Testament citations which speak of Israel and the Gentiles respectively enjoying the salvation of God.

In view of the direct connection of 15:7f with 14:1f, it is clear that the division between the weak and strong is one along Jew-Gentile lines and it is then easy to read back via 12:3 and to relate chs 9-11 with 4:16f and 6:11f to a particular set of circumstances in the Christian community at Rome.

4. *Conclusion*

In the letter to the Romans, differences in style and content are indications of the manner in which Paul addresses himself to the situation of the

Roman Christians. The source of his answers to the problems of Christian life or doctrine is his 'Kreuzestheologie' in which the doctrine of justification by faith is central. In Romans the Christ-event is depicted as the inbreaking of the new aeon in which the righteousness of God is revealed. In the letter Paul's gospel is presented as the fulfilment in Christ of the promises made to Abraham and his descendants. This form of presentation is to be expected in view of Paul's reminder to the Gentile Christians 'it is not you that supports the root but the root that supports you' (11:18) The emphasis upon Jewish-Christian tradition, the fulfilment of the promises, the goodness of the Law and the advantage of the Jew indicates that the question of the constitution and continuity of the people of God was a crucial issue among the Christians at Rome. Without appearing to be unduly specific we maintain that Paul faced two main issues in Rome (1) anti-Judaism on the part of Gentile Christians which was a cause of division among the Christian groups and (2) antinomianism - also on the part of Gentile Christians - some of whom were possibly former proselytes. (65) The latter problem may in fact, through the issue of the place of the Law, have been related to the first and major problem. The outlook of the Roman Christians had marked similarities with that which later came to expression in Marcionism.

If Robinson is correct in his claim that Christian experience in Romans is deliberately depicted in terms of the justified Jew who has entered on his inheritance in Christ, (66) then the reason for this form of presentation could be that Paul wished to oppose 'marcionite' tendencies in the Roman Christians. It might also have the aim of assuring the Jewish Christian minority that God's promises to Israel had not failed. If one of Paul's aims in the letter is to show Gentile Christians how their hope rests on Israel's Messiah, in order to achieve this it was necessary for Paul to demonstrate the righteousness and faithfulness of God to Israel. As a compromise with Cranfield's view that the logic of the Gospel partially determines the structure and argument of the letter, (67) we would suggest that it was because of the needs of the Christians in Rome that Paul felt compelled to demonstrate the fulfilment in Christ of the promise to Abraham.

It was not simply that Paul prepared a summary of his gospel because for various reasons he wished the Roman Christians to be better informed as to its content. Paul's interest is in the divine activity that derives from the covenant with Abraham and culminates in the saving event of Jesus Christ and the proclamation of the Gospel to both Jew and Gentiles. But where the Gospel is too individualistically interpreted Romans has sometimes been understood mainly as depicting the progress of the Gospel in the lives of individual Christians, ie in terms of justification, sanctification and glorification. But in Paul's theology justification and the people of God are themes which belong inseparably together.

For Paul it is the logic of the Gospel as the outcome and fulfilment of the hope of Israel that he presents to the Romans because this is for him the only adequate response to an incipient Marcionism. Our thesis is however that the raison d'etre of Romans is the needs of the Roman Christian community and that it was the nature of these that incidentally caused Paul to write a letter which, in some respects at least, reads like an abstract summary of his gospel or theology. The centre of Paul's argument in the letter is 3:21-26 and its climax is chs 9-11; but the actual situation that determines both how he argues and the themes of his arguments is the circumstances of the Roman Christians. Paul's own situation as he heads for Jerusalem, and his commission as apostle to the Gentiles are also relevant for a full understanding of Romans but these play a secondary role.[(68)]

We conclude that despite its careful structure, and the length of its sustained arguments Romans must still be regarded as a letter addressed to a specific situation in Rome. There is also evidence in the letter that Paul is acquainted, in outline, at least, with the circumstances of the Roman Christians. The fact that he had not yet visited Rome cannot be regarded as an adequate reason for viewing the letter simply as an outline of his theology or as a summary of his gospel unrelated to any particular issues in Rome. The onus rests on those who disregard Paul's specific exhortations and commands in the body of the letter and in chs 12-16 to explain why these should not be interpreted in the same way as those in Galatians or Corinthians.

The fact that the doctrinal sections in Romans were written for the sake of a particular historical situation in no wise denigrates them as witness to Paul's gospel or theology. But we must be careful to distinguish between what is central in Romans and what is central to Paul's theology. It may be that by a fortunate coincidence, these may actually be similar, possibly even identical, but it would be difficult to prove this is in fact the case. This means that Romans must play its part in helping us to construct the theology of Paul; but until we are clear what that theology is, we must be cautious and not give way to the tendency to use this letter *alone* as the measuring line for all that constitutes genuine Pauline theology. However it may be interpreted, there is no doubt that this letter wil continue to play a major role in the development of Christian theology. We have no need to defend its position even for the best of those dogmatic reasons which F C Baur deplored in his day.

'The dogmatic view is not to yield one step to the historical, lest the position of an epistle such as that to the Romans should be impaired, and the Lutheran forensic process of justification, which is of such moment to maintain in its integrity, suffer from the shaking of its great buttress.' (69)

NOTES

1 Cf the most recent discussion in CEB Cranfield, *The Epistle to the Romans* Vol II, ICC, ed J A Emerton and C E B Cranfield (Edinburgh 1979), 814-823 and U Wilckens, *Der Brief an die Römer I*, Evangelisch-Katholischer Kommentar zum Neuen Testament (Benzinger-Neukirchen 1978), 33-52, cf also the collection of essays in *The Romans Debate* (Minneapolis 1977) and my critique of some of these essays in 'Why did Paul write Romans?', Expository Times 85 (1973-74), 264-69, Chapter 2 in this volume.

2 Luz's verdict, after a survey of the literature, sums up the reaction of some scholars - 'Eine eindeutige Lösung drängt sich aus dem Studium der Sekundärliteratur nicht auf', 'Zum Aufbau von Röm 1-8', Theologische Zeitschrift 25 (1969), 165.

3 'Body' is used loosely in this instance only - normally we take it to refer to chs 1-11, cf C J Roetzel, *The Letters of Paul* (Atlanta 1975), 28. Cranfield warns of the danger of regarding the introduction and conclusion, ie 1:8-16a and 15:14f as detachable from the rest of the letter (op cit 816). Although he takes the view that Paul sends to the Romans a summary of the Gospel as he understood it, Cranfield rejects as 'quite unacceptable' the view 'that the structure and contents of 1:16b-15:13 were determined simply and solely by the logic of the Gospel' (ie entirely without reference to the situation in Rome), op cit 818f.

4 Eg P S Minear, *The Obedience of Faith: The Purposes of Paul in the Epistle to the Romans*, (SCM 1971). Only half of the contents of Minear's study is devoted to the body of the letter; cf also Cranfield's criticisms, op cit, 820-21.

5 In his review of Bultmann's *Theologie des Neuen Testaments* in Theologische Rundschau 22 (1954), 21-43, now published in English in *The Crucified Messiah* (Minneapolis 1974), 90-128, N A Dahl criticised Bultmann for his gross neglect of Rom 9-11; this tendency in the Bultmann school has not yet been entirely overcome, cf C Müller, *Gottes Gerechtigkeit und Gottes Volk. Eine Untersuchung zu Römer 9-11*, (Göttingen 1964), 5-27.

6 K Stendahl, *Paul Among Jews and Gentiles* (SCM 1977) 4, represents what might loosely be termed a Scandinavian interest in Rom 9-11 which comes to full expression in J Munck, *Christ and Israel* (Philadelphia 1967). Cf also B Noack 'Current and Backwater in the Epistle to the Romans', Studia Theologica XIX (1965) 155-166. L Goppelt, *Jesus, Paul and Judaism* (New York 1964) 153, sees Rom 9-11 as the keystone of Paul's theology and F C Baur regarded these chapters as the kernal out of which the entire letter

emerged, *Paul: His Life and Works*, ET by A Menzies, Theological Translation Fund Library (1876) 315.

7 The most recent research supports the view that ch 16 was a part of the original letter, cf H Y Gamble, *The Textual History of the Letter to the Romans* (Eerdmans 1977) and U Wilckens, op cit (see note 1), 24-27. For a contrary opinion cf E Käsemann, *An die Römer*, HNT, (Tübingen 1973) 400f. The view taken here is that ch 16 should not be used as a basis for any interpretation of the letter but only as supporting evidence for interpretations arrived at on the basis of chs 1-15.

8 Cf H Lietzmann, *An die Römer*, HNT, 8 (1933) 89, A Schlatter, *Gottes Gerechtigkeit* (Stuttgart 1959) 122, Luz, op cit (see note 2), 169.

9 The reference here is only to a dialogical or diatribe style. H Thyen maintains that Paul's letters are closer in style to the synagogue homily than the diatribe, *Der Stil der jüdisch-hellenistischen Homilie*, Frlant 47 (Göttingen 1955) 59f. On the diatribe style see also N A Dahl 'The God of Jews and Gentiles' in *Studies in Paul* (Minneapolis 1977) 188-9; K P Donfried, 'False Presuppositions in the Study of Romans' in *The Roman Debate*, (see note 1), 132f, and R Scroggs, 'Paul as Rhetorician. Two Homilies in Romans 1-11' in *Jews, Greeks, and Christians: Religious Cultures in Late Antiquity*, Essays in Honour of W D Davies, ed by R Hamerton- Kelly and R Scroggs (Leiden 1976) 270f.

10 O Michel notes that vv 21-26 are distinguished from their immediate context by 'einen proklamatorischen Stil' whereas vv 27-31 have 'einen aufgelockerten, dialogisch-rhetorischen charakter', *Der Brief an die Römer*, KEK IV, 14. Auflage (Göttingen 1978) 146-7. H E Stoessel, by charting the number of questions, divides Rom 1-11 into two types of passages, those in declarative and those in an argumentative style, 'Notes on Romans XII 1-2', Interpretation XVIII (1963) 168.

11 We take the view here that Paul is deliberately using earlier traditions to show that he recognises the Jewish origin of his gospel and the (temporal) priority of Jewish- Christianity; where he quotes or uses the tradition we presume that he does so with approval; the argument in this paper is not dependent on whether certain verses are pre- Pauline. On Paul's use of credal formulations cf H Conzelmann, *An Outline of the Theology of the New Testament* (ET SCM 1969) 166f; G Eichholz, *Die Theologie des Paulus im Umriss* (Neukirchen 1977) 123f and 189f; also Hans Jürgen van der Minde, *Schrift und Tradition bei Paulus* (Paderborn 1976) 38f and 190. E Käsemann argues that while Paul's theology is based upon tradition generally, it is not based on credal formulations in particular, 'Konsequente Traditionsgeschichte', Zeitschrift für Theologie und Kirche (1965) 143.

12 Cf C K Barrett's excellent treatment of the theme of judgement in 1:18-3:20, *A Commentary on the Epistle to the Romans*, BNTC (London 1962) 31-71. On the contrast between the old and new aeon cf Käsemann, *An die Römer*, 8f, Luz, op cit (see note 2), 171-2, Müller, op cit (see note 5), 50.

13 W Marxsen, *Introduction to the New Testament* (ET Oxford 1968) 105.

14 According to Käsemann Paul cites here 'ein hymnisches Fragment' (*An die Römer* 88). Cf also H J van der Minde, op cit (see note 11), 58-67. For a fuller discussion of righteousness, see E Käsemann, *'The Righteousness of God in Paul'*, in *New Testament Questions of Today* (ET SCM 1969) 168-82 and M T Brauch, 'Perspectives on God's Righteousness in recent German Discussion', included as an appendix in E P Sanders, *Paul and Palestinian Judaism* (SCM 1977) 523-42; G Klein's article 'Righteousness' in *The Interpreter's Dictionary of the Bible* (Abingdon 1976) 750-52 and several essays on this theme in *Rechfertigung*: *Festschrift für Ernst Käsemann zum 70 Geburtstag*, (Tübingen and Göttingen 1976).

15 'The aim of Romans is to show the Gentiles how their hope rests on Israel's Messiah', D W B Robinson 'The Priesthood of Paul in the Gospel of Hope', in *Reconciliation and Hope NT Essays on Atonement and Eschatology* presented to Leon Morris on his 60th birthday, ed R J Banks (Paternoster 1974) 231-45 (232).

16 Cf Käsemann, op cit 114-117. Cf also Käsemann's essay 'The Faith of Abraham in Romans 4', *Perspectives on Paul* (ET SCM 1969) 91-93.

17 Käsemann regards 3:26b and c as Paul's commentary upon an earlier Jewish-Christian fragment, *An die Römer*, 92. Cf also the dissertation of J W Williams, *The Interpretation of Romans 3:21-26 and its Place in Pauline Soteriology*, (Manchester 1973) 251f.

18 Contra Käsemann, op cit 94. Cf P Stuhlmacher, 'Zur neueren Exegese von Rom 3:24-26' in *Jesus und Paulus*, eds E E Ellis and E Grässer (Göttingen 1975) 331, O Kuss, *Der Römerbrief* (Regensburg 1957) 160 and Cranfield, op cit vol 1 (1975) 199 Müller, like Käsemann, claims that Paul thinks in terms of God's faithfulness to the whole creation rather than to the covenant people, but he acknowledges that God acts are still oriented towards Israel since Israel remains the secret centre of history, op cit 112-3.

19 L E Keck suggests the term 'rectification' instead of the traditional 'justification', *Paul and his Letters*, Proclamation Commentaries (Fortress 1979), 120.

20 Cf Barrett's comment 'Righteousness... has two aspects represented by the two clauses in v 26', op cit (see note 12), 73, and Müller's criticism that Bultmann identified 'dikaiosynē' and 'dikaiosynē theou' with 'dikaiosynē ek pisteōs', op cit (see note 5), 25.

21 Cf Sundkler, 'Contributions à l'étude de la pensée missionaire dans le Nouveau Testament', Revue de l'Histoire et de Philosphie Religieuses, 16 (1936), 462-99 and Munck's discussion of same in *Paul and the Salvation of Mankind*, 258f. Cf also Dahl's criticisms of Käsemann on this point, 'The God of Jews and Gentiles', *Studies in Paul*, 191.

22 Cf Peter Richardson, *Israel in the Apostolic Church* (Cambridge 1969), 133.

23 Cf Müller, op cit (see note 5), 14-18. Müller here follows Käsemann contra Bultmann, cf Käsemann's comments in this respect in several essays in *New Testament Questions of Today*, 14-15, 131f, 181, 191.

24 Cf Müller, op cit 21-27, Müller praises Lohmeyer's attempt to avoid an individualistic view of justification - 'Gottesvolkfrage und Recht–fertigungslehre gehören für ihn zusammen. Wenn die Auslegung beide Voneinander isoliert, erfasst sie beide falsch' (op cit 15).

25 Op cit (see note 10), 307.

26 Käsemann includes the term 'Gerechtigkeit' in the title of each of the five main sections of his commentary on Romans. In this emphasis he has followed Schlatter, op cit (see note 8), 292, 302, 329.

27 Op cit (see note 13), 103.

28 Cf Luz, op cit (see note 2), 162.

29 Op cit (see note 6), 155f.

30 This is well argued by Scroggs who concludes that 'Romans 1- 4 and 9-11 are united in theme, structure and use of scripture', op cit (see note 9), 281.

31 'A Synopsis of Romans 5:1-11 and 8:1-39', in *Studies in Paul*, 88-90.

32 Cf J Jeremias, 'Zur Gedankenführung in den paulinischen Briefen', in *Studia Paulina in honorem Johannis de Zwann*, (Haarlem 1953), 148 and Michel's illuminating discussion of the structure and content of the letter, op cit (see note 10), 43-54.

33 Since 'ti eroumen' in Romans usually introduces Paul's answer to an objection as in 3:5, 4:1, 7:7, 8:31, 9:14, 30, Jeremias considers that the section 8:18f may be the answer to an objection that suffering contradicts the assurance of salvation claimed in 8:1-17, op cit, 146-8, similarly Michel, op cit (see note 10), 45.

34 D W D Robinson claims that the theme of ch 8 is 'the liberty of the Jew who has entered his inheritance in Christ and his hope of glory according to promise and election'; the positive Christian experience and the expectation of final glory are 'set forth deliberately as the experience of the justified Jew, indeed of Israel itself in the person of the servant and apostle of the Lord', op cit (see note 15), 244- 5.

35 We do not mean to imply that Rom 9-11 is simply an illustration of Paul's application of this doctrine. Dahl asserts in this respect 'we express ourselves more correctly when we say that from the beginning Paul's view of the relation to Israel of the Gentiles profoundly shaped his doctrine of justification. Only later, especially in the thought of Augustine and Luther, did the doctrine of justification become fundamentally important apart from the problem of Israel and the Gentiles'. 'The Future of Israel' in *Studies in Paul*, (156). Cf also the essay on 'The Doctrine of Justification' in the same volume (95-120). Stendahl, op cit (see note 6), 129-32) expresses similar views but disagrees with both Dahl and Käsemann that it is polemical. 'It has not grown out of his struggles with the Judaistic interpretation of the law - it is not "a fighting doctrine, directed against Judaism"' (130) - as Käsemann has asserted; cf 'Justification and Salvation History' in *Perspectives on Paul*, 63-78, for Käsemann's defence of the centrality of the doctrine in Paul's theology. Recently Sanders has also claimed that justification is part of Paul's polemics and not the centre of his theology which he describes (following Schweitzer) as

'participationist eschatology', *Paul and Palestinian Judaism*, 434-47, 483-96, 502-8.

36 We must also take into account 11:29 'The Gifts and the call of God are irrevocable' in determining the meaning of justification in Romans. This, rather than 8:39 represents the climax of Paul's argument.

37 Stendahl's view that Rom 11 is non-christological and that there is a God-willed separate existence for unbelieving Jews fails to take into account 3:21-4:25, op cit 4 and 129f. Cf W D Davies, 'Paul and the People of Israel', New Testament Studies 24 (1977), 15-16, 33, n1 and my article 'Salvation for Jews and Gentiles; Krister Stendahl and Paul's Letter to the Romans', *Studia Biblica III* (findings of the VIth International Congress on Biblical Studies), Sheffield 1980.

38 'St Paul's Letter to the Romans - and others', in the Bulletin of the John Rylands Library 31 (1948) 224-40, now included in *The Romans Debate* (see note I), 1-16 and earlier in T W Manson, *Studies in the Gospels and Epistles*, ed M Black (Manchester University Press, 1962), 225-241.

39 Cf *Paul and the Salvation of Mankind* (200).

40 Op cit (see note 32), 147.

41 *New Century Bible* (London 1973), 29-30.

42 Cf Robinson, op cit (see note 15), 245, W Lütgert maintained that in 6:1f Paul is addressing antinomian Gentile Christians and not protesting in self-defence against the views of Jews or Jewish-Christians who criticise him. *Der Römerbrief als historisches Problem*, BFChTh 17(2) (Gütersloh 1913), 76-79.

43 Cf J L White, 'New Testament Epistolary Literature in the Framework of Ancient Epistolography', a paper at the 1979 SBL meeting in New York now published in *Aufstieg und Niedergang der römischen Welt*, ed H Temporini, Berlin 1976-, Vol II 25. 2 (1984) 1730-56.

44 On this cf Robinson as in note 15. Wilckens still regards the objections as Jewish in origin, op cit (see note 1), 18.

45 Op cit (see note 40), 147. Cf also J Dupont, 'Le problème de la structure littéraire de l'êpitre aux Romains', Revue Biblique 62 (1955), 365-97.

46 Cf N A Dahl, 'Two Notes on Romans V', Studia Theologica 5 (1951) 41.

47 Scroggs holds that the material in chs 1-4 and 9-11 is completely self-consistent and demonstrates a continuous development of thought and use of scripture, chs 5-8 being so different that they cannot be said originally to have belonged to that homily. Scroggs argues that Rom 1-11 comprises two homilies - an exegetical homily in 1-4 and 9- 11 having as its model the narrative of 'Heilsgeschichte' found in Jewish homiletic tradition, whereas in chs 5-8 Paul 'speaks out of a diatribe structure perhaps remoulded by the Hellenistic Synagogue', op cit (see note 9), 297.

48 This is a strong argument against Scroggs' view that Rom 5-8 is a different homily from that in 1-4 and 9-11.

49 The plural 'ta logia' in 3:2 may also be taken in the wider sense of God's self-revelation, cf Cranfield, op cit (see note 1), 178-9. Despite the use of the

singular in 9:6, the recurrence of the same term denotes the connection between the two chapters, cf Luz, op cit (see note 2), 169.

50 Israel is not a title that belongs indiscriminately or inalienably to all the descendants of Abraham, cf P Richardson, op cit (see note 22) 126-46.

51 Whether 3:7-8 should be regarded as one objection or two is unclear. Dahl op cit (see note 46), 42, n2 and Jeremias op cit (see note 40), 148 take them as one objection. If v 7 is taken separately from v 8 then the content of v 7 relates back to the objection in v 5 and provides a transition to the objection in v 8; cf Cranfield's discussion, op cit (see note 1), 183-87.

52 Cf Dupont, op cit (see note 45), 372, n3. Wilckens relates the objection in 3:31 to 7:1-8:11, following Käsemann in stressing the unity of 7-8 but differing from him in that he sees 8:12-30 and 8:31-39 as two sections separated from 8:1- 11, which take up again themes from 5:3-5, op cit (see note 1), 18-19.

53 Cf Michel's suggestion that it might be possible to reconstruct a simple outline of Paul's message from chs 1-2, 3:21-30, 5 and 8:1-17, op cit (see note 10), 45. Cf also Luz on kerygmatic formulations in Romans, op cit (see note 2), 225f.

54 W D Davies claims that 'throughout his treatment of circumcision and the Law... Paul was concerned with a central question: the nature or constitution of the people of God - its continuity and discontinuity with the Jewish people of history', *The Gospel and the Land* (University of California, Berkeley 1974), 171.

55 Op cit (see note 6), 316.

56 C H Dodd, *The Epistle to the Romans*, MNTC (London 1932), 69.

57 Despite his useful discussion of Abrahamskindschaft in ch 4, Michel claims that Paul's aim is to show that Abraham is primarily father of Gentile Christians, op cit (see note 10), 170; contrast Barrett, op cit (see note 12), 96.

58 Cf Minear, op cit (see note 4), 53-6 and Wilckens, op cit (see note 1), 261-85, especially 283.

59 Cf E Käsemann, 'The Faith of Abraham in Romans 4, *Perspectives on Paul* (98) and Wilckens, op cit (see note 1), 261-85, especially 283.

60 Cf H Frankemölle, *Das Taufverständnis des Paulus: Taufe, Tod und Auferstehung nach Röm 6*, Stuttgarter Bibel-Studien 47, (Stuttgart 1970) 24.

61 When Paul uses 'oidamen de' he is referring to commonly accepted traditions, cf G Bornkamm, 'Baptism and New Life in Paul', *Early Christian Experience*, (ET SCM 1969) 85 n5; cf also Michel, op cit (see note 10), 200-268 n13; N A Dahl 'Anamnesis: Memory and Commemoration in Early Christianity', Studia Theologica I (1947), 69-95, now in *Jesus in the Memory of the Early Church* (Minneapolis 1976), 11-29; D W Burdick '"Oida" and "ginōskō"' in the Pauline Epistles' in *New Dimensions in New Testament Study*' ed R N Longenecker and M L Tenney, (Grand Rapids 1974) 344-56.

62 Cf W Lütgert, op cit (see note 42), 78-9.
63 W D Davies, 'Paul and the People of Israel', New Testament Studies 24 (1978), 4-39, see 13f, 36.
64 Cf H W Bartsch, 'Die antisemitischen Gegner des Paulus im Römerbrief', *Antijudaismus im Neuen Testament*, (München 1967) 27-43.
65 Cf Marxsen op cit (see note 13), 98, and W Schmithals *Der Römerbrief als historisches Problem* (Gütersloh 1975), 83f.
66 See note 15.
67 See note 3.
68 On this see Chapter 2.
69 Op cit (see note 6), 313

Chapter 4

The Freedom and Faithfulness of God in Relation to Israel

1. *Introduction*

Since no-one today would wish to maintain that Paul writes theology in a vacuum, it is recognised that the proper exegesis of a letter can only be carried out in the light of some probable context which the exegete envisages on the basis of the text before him. (1) A basic problem in the interpretation of the letter to the Romans is the lack of explicit reference to the concrete issues to which Paul responds in the letter. Nowhere is this more obvious than in chs 9-10 (ch 11 does have a specific address to Gentiles in vv 13f). However, the peculiarity of Romans ought to be regarded more as a difference in degree than in kind. In all of Paul's letters we face the same hermeneutical circle. In order to interpret a letter we need to know the background or situation out of which it arises and to which it is addressed; this background however can only be defined through the letter. The exegete must move in a circle of inference and deduction from the letter to the situation and back. In this respect Romans is no different from Paul's other letters; (2) but to the degree that it is less explicit it is correspondingly more difficult to be precise about its interpretation.

Since those sections of the letter, ie chs 1 and 12-16, from which we might expect to derive most background information, do not of themselves provide sufficient clarification of the letter's purpose to enable us to interpret its statements in any meaningful context, (3) we are compelled to look to the body of the letter; then on the basis of our perception of what is the thrust of its main argument, we must proceed as it were in reverse order back to the situation to which such a letter is likely to have been addressed. Ideally this requires to be done for each chapter or main section of chs 1-11. (4) As this is impossible within the compass of a short study, we will devote our attention to ch 9 and its function within chs 9-11. There is now widespread agreement that chs 9-11 should be seen as an integral part of Paul's argument and given at least equal weight with the rest of the letter. (5) The view taken here is that when chs 9-11 are seen as integral, they then in fact become the climax of the argument extending throughout 1-11 (6) If this presupposition is granted then by a careful study of this section it should be possible to decipher the central theological issue in Paul's argument in Romans. From that we can then deduce what is the most crucial issue to which the letter as a whole was directed.

A further methodological presupposition is that the reconstruction of the situation to which the letter is addressed must be based primarily on Romans - the other Paulines, deutero-Paulines etc may also be taken into account, but if we take the particularity of each letter seriously then Romans itself must be the main witness. [7]

2. *Paul's Argument concerning Israel in Romans 9:1-29*

The chapter begins with the strongest possible assertion of Paul's grief and concern for his Jewish kinsmen. Possibly his own mission to the Gentiles had raised doubts as to whether he any longer had any real concern or hope for the salvation of Israel. [8] To obviate such suggestions, Paul designates them not as Jews, but calls them by the honoured title Israelites; [9] as such they are seen as heirs of the promised inheritance - the sonship, the glory and the covenants, the giving of the law, the worship and the promises, and to them also belong the patriarchs (v 4f). That Paul intends here to stress the election privileges of Israel becomes evident both in the assertion of his own solidarity with Israel - 'my brethren, my kinsmen by race' (v 3) and also by his climactic conclusion that the Christ of the Gospel is the promised Messiah of Israel (v 5). [10] Paul's dilemma is highlighted by the sharp contrast between the privileges of the Jews and his own acknowledged grief at their disobedience to the Gospel - implied throughout ch 9 but not explicitly stated until 9:30f.

The expression of Paul's grief is not to be interpreted as a tacit admission that God's declared purpose - his word of promise (cf vv 6 & 9) in the election of Israel has come to nought (v 6a). This half verse, as many commentators have noted, is the sign under which the whole of 9:6-29 stands. [11] Thus whatever Paul says, however critical he may be of Israel, his primary aim is to demolish any assertion that God has cast off Israel (cf 11:1, 11).

In v 6b Paul proceeds to explain his understanding of election. God's word of promise (v 9) is to Israel and He remains faithful to Israel. But the term 'Israel' is not simply an ethnic or national title, it is the title of the chosen people of God. To demonstrate this, Paul proceeds to take examples from the scriptures to show that God has always exercised His sovereign freedom in making selections *within* the covenant people. Paul's thesis is that 'not all are children of Abraham because they are his descendants' (v 7). Children of natural descent (ta tekna tēs sarkos) are not necessarily identical with children of promise (ta tekna tēs epangelias). Abraham's seed (sperma) are not co-extensive with his children (tekna). Children of God are those who are both descendants of Abraham and children of promise. This is Paul's exegesis of Gen 21:12 - 'It is thy descendants through Isaac that shall be called thy seed.' (12) - a text chosen among other reasons because it referred back to Israel's beginnings.

Paul has already discussed Abraham's faith in ch 4; Isaac typifies the children of promise in that the scripture says that he was born to aged parents because God promised Abraham a son (Gen 18:10,14). To this supplemental text Paul again adds another, Gen 25:23. Since it could be argued that the reason why Isaac was chosen as the bearer of the promise (and not Ishmael) was because the former was the son of Abraham's wife and the latter of his handmaid, Paul cites Gen 25:23 - 'The elder shall serve the younger', in order to prove that divine election is not determined by human ancestry or achievement. Since scripture says that before Rebecca's twin boys were even born, the younger was chosen, this proves that God's electing purpose (hē kat' eklogēn prothesis tou theou) v 11, is determined only by the freedom of the divine choice. This is the only principle of selection. Therefore no one can make any claims upon God on grounds of ancestry or other qualification. (13)

We note in passing Paul's method of argument; he has expounded the story of Rebecca's twins in his own vocabulary and then crowned his argument with a citation from the Torah (Gen 25:23) and another from the Prophets (Mal l:2-3, 'Jacob I loved, but Esau I hated') v 13. (14) The former citation contains in the same verse the words - 'Two nations are in your womb'. Thus Paul is clearly not thinking of Jacob and Esau as two individuals (15) but as nations - of Israel and of Edom and their role in salvation history.

That a watershed in the argument has been reached is indicated by Paul's use of the recurring phrase, 'Ti oun eroumen'. This indicates, we believe, the commencement of a new subsection of the argument and also that Paul is here taking up a specific issue of relevance in the situation at Rome. In ch 3 in a series of questions concerning the topics he intends to deal with later in the letter (16), Paul has asked virtually the same question as here - 'Is there injustice on God's part?' and here as there it is instantly repudiated by the formulistic phrase, 'mē genoito', (v 14). In demonstrating the independence of the divine election, Paul has left himself open to the charge that it is entirely arbitrary and in fact basically unjust. It is to repudiate this charge that Paul quotes Ex 33:19 - 'I will have mercy on whom I have mercy, and I will have compassion on whom I have compassion'.

Cranfield suggests that Paul no less than Barth, thought of these words as parallel to and an explicatory paraphrase of Ex 3:14 - 'I am who I am'. They are thus seen as affording a specially significant revelation of the innermost nature of God. [17] We believe that Paul's meditation on Ex 33:19 provided the basis for his understanding of the freedom and faithfulness of God to Israel in Romans 9. A T Hanson sees in the citation of this text evidence that Paul was not indifferent to the historical setting of his scripture citations. God's revelation of his character as mercy in the theophany to Moses is all the more significant because it occurred at an important point in the story of Moses' part in the wilderness sojourn. [18] Leenhardt makes a similar comment. Instead of punishing the Israelites with the severity which their infidelity in the fabrication of the idol demanded, - 'He gave them a new revelation of His grace and at the same time displayed its basic principle: "My grace is utterly free..." Thus the rebellion of Israel did not have the effect of revoking the election'. [19]

It is essential to keep in mind the reason why Paul cites Ex 33:19. These words are intended not as proof that the divine election is abitrary but as proof to the contrary. If as suggested they offer a true parallel to Ex 3:14, then Paul sees election as evidence of the innermost character of God as revealed through Moses and, in his own time, in Jesus Christ. The impossiblity of divine injustice is the main theme of vv 14-18. The words 'ara oun' in v 16 indicate that Paul now gives his exegesis of the Exodus citation. [20] 'So it depends not upon man's will or exertion, but upon God's mercy.' As a supplementary citation in support of this assertion Paul turns to the account of Pharaoh in Ex 9:16.

The variations from the LXX text suggest that Paul wishes to focus on the sovereignty of the divine purpose in relation to Pharaoh's role in history. [21] Even in his rebellion as the enemy of God's people, Pharaoh is shown in scripture to have served two functions. He is raised up so that the divine power may be shown at work and the divine name proclaimed in all the earth. The latter function, especially the reference to the divine name revealed to Moses in Ex 3:14, reminds us that Pharaoh, no less than Israel, was used to reveal God's power and proclaim his character of mercy. Paul's exegetical comment on Ex 9:16 - 'So then he has mercy upon whomever he wills, and he hardens the heart of whomever he wills' (v 18), indicates why he refers to the case of Pharaoh. If the latter as well as Israel may be used in God's electing purpose then the divine action is not predetermined by anything in the human situation. But though Paul in v 18 insists on the absolute freedom of God, this verse is supplementary to the key citation in v 15. Thus God's positive or negative use of nations and their leaders is still governed by His free mercy. There is nothing that does not come under this control.

4. *The Freedom and Faithfulness of God in Relation to Israel*

Verse 19 marks a subdivision in which Paul turns to another scriptural passage. The emphasis is on the authority of the creator over his creatures; the diatribe style with the references to man serves to stress the transcendence of the creator and to develop this, Paul take up the image of the potter. In this image we find echoes of several passages, (22) eg 'Shall the thing formed say to him who formed it, thou hast not made me wisely?' (Isa 29:16f) and Jer 18:1f where the potter remoulds a spoiled vessel. In the latter the word of the Lord is, 'O house of Israel, cannot I do with you as this potter has done?' (v 6). God's ways with Israel are not fixed but flexible, being conditional upon her obedience to the divine purpose. The image of the potter stresses the constructive creativity of God (and not the destructiveness). Whereas the story of Pharaoh illustrated the divine power to use even unwilling subjects, the image of the potter points to the interaction of the Lord with Israel for the eventual achievement of His design.

It is only with v 21 that Paul begins to reveal the relevance of his scriptural arguments. In vv 21-23 he combines aspects of his two illustrations to explain God's dealings with Israel in the eschatological present. (23) In v 22f Paul takes up again separate phrases of the citations concerning Pharaoh and the potter, giving his commentary upon them in view of contemporary events. (24) Just as the hardening of Pharaoh at the time of the Exodus served God's purpose in the liberation of Israel, so now it is possible for the non-believing Jews, (though they may be both targets of God's wrath and instruments of it, like Pharaoh), still to have a teleological function in the purpose of God. (25) The obvious parallels between vv 17 and 22 indicate that the twofold divine purpose in relation to Pharaoh - to reveal God's power and to make known His name - is now also considered in respect of Israel. But a third element is here introduced 'to make known the riches of his glory upon the vessels of mercy' (v 23). This represents the climax of the construction, (26) but the point of v 22, that the divine purpose may include the demonstration of both wrath and power, must not be overlooked, even though all is encompassed within the goal of mercy.

The strange structure of vv 22-24 - a conditional clause without any independent clause, indicates more the nature of the problem than Paul's lack of clarity in thought. Paul is tentatively putting forward an interpretation of the divine purpose for Israel who is at present disobedient. to the Gospel. (27)

The clause commences with 'What if God?' but the 'if' here should be taken, as Barrett suggests, 'What if it were the case, as in fact it actually is?' (28) Now Paul makes explicit the goal of his argument 'what if God chooses to bear with unbelieving Israel in order to reveal His wrath and power and to make known the riches of His glory in the vessels of mercy?' These vessels Paul forthwith identifies, in a brief parenthesis in v 24, as the Christian community composed of both Jews and Gentiles. The words 'not from the Jews only' show how alien it would be to Paul's way of thinking to suggest a simple transfer of Israel's promises to Gentiles. Although he came close to speaking of a 'true Israel' in v 6f, Paul does not think of the Church as a new Israel. (29) Nor does his view allow the Church to be described as 'eschatological Israel' or any other such title that contains within it the germ of a threatened disinheritance of the Jews. (30) Paul regards Israel as the historic people of God to whom the promises were given.

Up to this point in the discussion Paul has spoken only of selection *within* Israel. Implicit in his argument is the assumption that all the children of promise were also all descendants of Abraham. It is only in vv 23-24 that Gentiles (almost in an aside) come on to the scene. Two scriptural citations from Hosea are offered as proof that the 'not-people', the 'not-beloved' are destined to become the people of God, sons of the living God. In vv 27-29 two further citations from Isaiah are added to show that God will also save a remnant of Israel. (31) Small though this remnant may be, were it not for divine grace it would not exist at all. Only divine grace has prevented Israel from the fate of Sodom and Gomorrah. Paul consciously sets out these citations as proof also that it is God's will that the Church should be composed of both Jews and Gentiles; (32) Schoeps is wrong to interpret this to mean that Paul implies the replacement of Israel by another people. (33)

It is also unlikely that Paul intends to replace the concept of God's faithfulness to the covenant with that of faithfulness to the creation. (34) Paul universalises God's redemptive action, but this does not mean the transfer of His faithfulness from Israel as if particularism and universalism were absolutely antithetical in his theology. (35)

The argument in Romans 9 suggests the opening up of the covenant promises to include Gentiles also. If the covenant concept is regarded as somehow inadequate to include God's new revelation in Christ, (36) it may be preferable to think in terms of God's faithfulness to His own revealed name or character. Judgement as well as mercy has its place within the concept of faithfulness to the divine name, and includes the emphasis upon the preservation and display of the divine glory (37) in which Israel and her future is inextricably involved.

3. *Summary of the Argument of Ch 9:1-29*

The section ends as it began, in stressing God's continuing grace towards Israel. Using the scriptures Paul has pointed to a pattern in God's dealings. Selection has always taken place within Israel, but even wrath and hardening have their function within the overarching theme of God's electing purpose. In His selection only one factor is determinative - that of the divine mercy acting in freedom. Thus no one, not even Israel, can make claims upon the God of Israel; conversely no one, and especially not Christians, can presume that God is determined even by Israel's disobedience - 'He remains free as regards the disobedient just as He is free towards the obedient'. [38]

We saw that in vv 22f, Paul began to relate his scripturally based argument concerning divine freedom in unconditional election to the contemporary situation. He denoted his solidarity with Israel in the opening verses of the chapter and throughout we get the impression that Paul is speaking to the church of Rome about a third party (cf the reference to 'us' in 9:24). The purpose of Paul's argument would appear to be to persuade the Romans to interpret the facts of the contemporary situation, ie Gentiles responding to the Gospel but Jews by and large disobedient to it, in the same way as he understands it. God has, in fact, retained a believing remnant in Israel, and scripture shows that He can also use the disobedient for His glory. This indicates that Paul's aim is to show that God's promises are still valid for Israel, that she still serves His purpose even in disobedience, and that Israel (and the Church) owe their existence entirely to the grace of God. The unstated presupposition of this chapter is that a situation exists, whether in Paul's mission work or, as is more likely, within the Roman Christian community, where it is both relevant and necessary for Paul to argue for God's continuing grace to Israel.

We shall now look briefly at the continuation of Paul's argument in chs 10-11, to see whether the content of these chapters upholds this hypothesis.

4. *Paul's Argument concerning Israel in Chs 9:30-11:36*

In a concluding summary in 9:30f, Paul gives the reason for his anguish over Israel. The Gentiles have responded to the Gospel, but Israel with a zeal similar to Paul's Pharisaic zeal and equally lacking in understanding, stumbles over Christ. She fails to see that He is the goal of the law (10:4). [39] Here a number of lines of argument concerning the law at last converge. The references to unconditional election in ch 9, to 'works' in 9:32, and 'their own righteousness' in 10:3, have traditionally been interpreted in association with the doctrine of faith and works in chs 3-4. In this the legalistic tendency of Judaism's meticulous observance of the law has been emphasised. Recently, Sanders has charged some scholars with reading back into the New Testament a post-Reformation understanding of faith and works. (40) What Paul is actually opposing is the Jewish view that accepting and living by the law is a sign and condition of a favoured status. Paul's 'not by works of law' shows that he held a different view of 'Heilsgeschichte' from that of Judaism. It was never, he says, God's intention that one should accept the law in order to become one of the elect. Abraham is proof of this since he was chosen without accepting the law. Paul attacks the traditional understanding of covenant and election, according to which accepting the law signified acceptance of the covenant. (41) That Sanders is basically correct in this view is borne out by the references to the remnant in 11:2f; (we will not look further at ch 10 at this point since the main argument concerning God's faithfulness to Israel is continued in ch 11).

In answer to the question as to whether God has cast away His own elect people (11:1), Paul gives himself as first proof to the contrary. He is an Israelite. Moreover, Christians ought to be aware (42) that Elijah was wrong to feel that he alone was loyal - God's grace had maintained a righteous remnant of seven thousand.

Paul then applies the remnant theme to the current situation 'So too at the present time, there is a remnant chosen by grace' (v 5). The proper context of Paul's discussion of faith and works is seen in his comment in v 6, 'but if it (the chosen remnant) is by grace, it is no longer on the basis of works, otherwise grace would no longer be grace'. As the remainder of ch 11 will demonstrate, Paul's concern is to show that grace and the making of claims are mutually exclusive. Israel's failure results not from seeking to do enough good works to earn righteousness, but in failing to understand her own election.

To keep the course of his argument explicit, Paul pauses to give another summary to the effect that the elect obtained the goal of salvation but the rest were hardened. In v 11, he introduces another objection or devious conclusion concerning Israel - perhaps Israel was destined to fail irretrievably from God's salvation. This meets with the customary rebuff - 'by no means'; their hardening was instrumental in the salvation of the Gentiles. But this is not of itself the final goal. (43) The Gentiles and their faith is not the only goal of Paul's own ministry (v 13). As an apostle to the Gentiles his mission has, as an indirect outcome, the salvation of some of the Jews. In a twice repeated emphasis (vv 12 and 15) Paul suggests that if the unbelief of the Jews had the beneficial result of bringing faith to the Gentiles, their full inclusion can mean nothing less than life from the dead.

One is conscious at this point that Paul wishes to stress the likelihood of Israel's eventual salvation, as if he were aware that this was in doubt in some quarters. But for Paul, as the reality of the first fruits points to the sanctification of the total harvest, and the holiness of the roots determines the sanctity of all the branches, so Israel's salvation is something wholly to be expected and not in the least to be doubted. (44) It is not without significance that Paul now pointedly turns again to the Gentile Christians in Rome; he warns them that, as wild olive shoots grafted into the tree of God's people, they have no right to boast over the unbelieving Jews who have been excluded through lack of faith. Doubtless too, the branches analogy is designed to remind Gentile Christians that branches of themselves do not constitute a living tree.

The Gentiles are specifically commanded not to be proud but to stand in awe - 'It is not you that support the root but the root that supports you'. (vv 18-21) There could be no clearer indication that Paul is upholding the special place of Jewish Christianity and hence possibly also the links with Jerusalem. (45) That Gentiles have equal access with Jews and that there is equality within the Church is Paul's central message but this does not usurp the place of Israel to whom belongs the promise of election. Presumption of superiority on the part of Gentile Christians will lead to the same result as in the case of unbelieving Jews - they too will be broken off, (vv 21-23). Likewise the disobedient who do not persist in their error will be grafted back again because God has the power to do so (vv 23-24).

As a final blow to Gentile Christian conceit, Paul in v 25f reminds them that the hardening of Israel is both partial and temporary. God will save Israel because 'the gifts and the call of God' (as gifts of grace) are irrevocable (v 29). The Jews are still beloved on account of the election of the patriarchs even though some may have proved to be the enemies of the Gospel.

Paul takes it for granted that eventually Israel will be saved - but Dahl is probably correct in his claim that the emphasis here is on *how* Israel is to be saved. (46) What was hinted in ch 10 and elaborated in 11:11-14 is now described as the unveiling of a mystery. Paul is doubtless referring to the expected pattern of events in salvation history. The Gospel goes firstly to the Jews, the Jews believe and then the Gentiles will share in their blessings. But things have not turned out as the first Christians had expected and Paul is here describing the reversal of the sequence of events in which he had played such an important part. (47)

'To the Jew first' for Paul does not mean a mission to Jews only until such times as Israel is won over to the Gospel. 'To the Jew first' for Paul indicates much more than this temporal priority. Paul in his evangelism possibly did go first to the synagogues, but what is much more important, Paul expects Gentiles to recognise the inalienable position of Jewish Christianity as the root on to which they, as branches, are grafted. 'To the Jew first' for Paul means a recognition of the abiding election of Israel. Presumably where the election of Israel is not recognised or in some way misunderstood, then the Gentile Christians would be failing in their function to make Israel 'jealous', and Paul as the apostle to Gentiles, appointed by the Messiah of Israel (cf 1:3f), would have a responsibility to counteract such a mistaken opinion.

The conclusion of ch 11 consists of a very precise drawing of parallels between Jews and Gentiles. (48) Just as the Gentiles were once disobedient to God but have now received mercy through the failure of the Jews to respond to the Gospel, so too the Jews will be won from their disobedience by the faith of the Gentiles. A true correspondence between the two has been established - God has consigned all men to disobedience, so that He could have mercy upon all (v 32). In sin and in God's grace to sinners, Jew and Gentile are truly equal.

In chs 10-11 we have found confirmation of the situation envisaged from our interpretation of ch 9. Paul's concern for Israel and his confidence in the validity of her election and eventual salvation have been further elaborated. Those to whom he addresses his apology for Israel are clearly designated as Gentile Christians. They show a marked tendency to boast over Israel's downfall, regarding themselves as having replaced Israel in God's favour. (49) But the faithfulness of God to Israel is established in that 'the gifts and the call of God are irrevocable' (11:29). The mystery revealed to Paul, which he uses to admonish Gentile Christian pride, shows that the hardening of Israel is temporary and that the salvation of Jew and Gentile is inextricably interconnected. The references to the law and works are found to be best explained as part of a discussion concerning the meaning of election. Throughout the entire section we found that Paul sought to stress the positive continuity, through God's grace, of the people of God in history. (50) By this he apparently intends to oppose any separation of the Gentile Christian Church from its Jewish Christian roots and Jerusalem. We find no sign in ch 11 of a confrontation or even a dialogue between Paul and Jews or Judaism. (51) The dialogue takes place between Paul and the Roman Gentile Christians concerning Israel's role in salvation history and the attitude of the Gentiles to Israel. (52) Paul's warning to Gentile

Christians not to boast over Israel clarifies one issue left open in our summary of ch 9. Was it Paul's situation, ie his mission work, or the situation of the Roman Christians that evoked the apology for Israel? Ch 11 is evidence that it was primarily the situation of the Roman Christians. (53)

5. *The Theme of Rom 9-11 in Relation to the Purpose of the Letter*

It now remains for us to ask how the situation which we have envisaged from the study of chs 9-11 can help us to be more precise about the purpose (or purposes) of the letter. A major problem in the history of the interpretation of Romans lies in its dual character - it is apparently addressed to Gentiles, but discusses Jewish themes in a Jewish type of argument. (54) Scholars from Luther to Barth have noted the emphasis which it lays on the proper understanding of the Old Testament. Recently Black has claimed that its main theme is 'Gospel and Law'. (55) Black and many of the older commentaries seek to explain the 'Jewishness' of the letter by reference to Judaisers or a Jewish Christian majority. Schmithals explains this aspect of the letter by positing that its audience is primarily Gentile Christian God-fearers attached to or recently separated from the synagogue. (56) This is why chs 1-11 have the character of a debate with the Jewish synagogue. In this view he has been followed closely by J C Beker who sees the primary audience as those 'Gentiles' who recently abandoned the synagogue as 'God-fearers or proselytes'. They with their Jewish Christian brethren must understand that the Gospel both confirms and abolishes Israel's privilege. It is significant that Beker includes the statement that 'they are also warned against backsliding to the synagogue'. (57) Käsemann regards the combination of Rome, Jerusalem and Spain as vital to understanding the purpose of Romans. Paul presents himself and his central message to the as yet unknown Roman congregation. If he could win over the Roman Church and especially its Jewish Christian minority, or at least dispel their existing suspicions he would get rearguard protection in relation to Jerusalem too.

The latter factor explains why Paul stresses the course of salvation-history and the salvation of all Israel, why he is so mild and accommodating to Jewish Christian concerning observance of days, and why he bases his gospel so firmly on scripture, from which too he derives his world mission. (58) Schmithals rightly questions how Paul, in a letter directed to Gentile Christians, can hope to win a Jewish-Christian minority. This, he says, remains Käsemann's secret! (59)

A weakness in several of these interpretations is that a Judaising Jewish-Christian minority or back-sliding Gentile Christian God-fearers have to be introduced (without any concrete evidence) to explain the Jewishness of the letter. It appears that Paul still tends to be seen as the opponent of all things Jewish. (60) But when a number of the factors noted above are related to the situation which we envisaged for chs 9-11, then a much more consistent picture can be drawn.

The dual character of the letter is explained by the fact that it is addressed to a predominantly Gentile Christian community about the role of Israel in salvation history and in relation to the Gospel. There was probably debate among the Romans about the significance of 'Jewishness' for the church; (61) this suggests that there was also a group of Jewish-Christians or Jewish-influenced God-fearers who may have needed Paul's protection against the arrogance of the strong (chs 14-15). (62) The boasting of the latter suggests they were numerically and/or theologically in the ascendency. The 'weak' may have had some doubts as to the viability of life outside the sphere of the law and the synagogue. (chs 5 and 8). (63) The theme of election necessitated by the misconceptions of the Romans appears throughout the letter. Ch 3:21f establishes the equality of two peoples, Jews and Gentiles, by virtue of God's act in Christ. Paul views this both as the means of access to salvation for Gentiles and the confirmation of God's faithfulness to the Jews. (64) Equality of status for Jew and Gentile contradicts 'covenantal nomism' but Paul's aim in Romans 1-4 is not to refute this, but primarily to establish the full equality of Jew and Gentile in terms of divine grace. (65) Abraham in Rom 4 is thus not simply an illustration of 'the justified sinner' but stands as the first of the people of God, (66) one who is proof that the law is not necessary for salvation. Abraham is a uniting figure who can be seen as a father of Jewish, proselyte and Gentile Christians (cf the olive tree in ch 11). Ch 8:31f may be interpreted as Paul's setting forth of the Christian understanding of election in Christ in advance of his discussion of the election of Israel so as to prevent any misunderstanding of his own position. (67)

Another feature of Romans may enable us to be more specific about the problems Paul faced in Rome. We noted the parallel between 3:5f and 9:14f. It is clear also that 3:1-2 is taken up again and developed in 9:4f. We believe this indicates that Paul in 3:1-8 sets out a list of issues in Rome which he intends to discuss later in the letter. There are three questions: what is the advantage of the Jew? (vv 1-2); does the unbelief of the Jews mean that God is unfaithful or unjust? (v 3f); and why not do evil in order that good may come? (v 8). (68) The first two questions are discussed in chs 9-11 and the third in chs 6-7. Traditionally 3:7-8 are taken as Jewish or Jewish-Christian caricatures of Paul's doctrine of justification by faith. (69) But only in Paul's theology of the Gentile mission is there any real basis for the belief that 'through my falsehood God's truthfulness abounds to his glory'. (v 7). We conclude, therefore, that the problems among the Roman Christians focused on a debate about the place of the Jews in the light of Paul's Gentile mission. It is also possible that the beneficial outcome of Jewish unbelief for the Gentiles may have encouraged the suggestion in 3:8 and 6:1f that sin is the necessary prerequisite for grace to abound. Such thinking is typical of Gentile Christian 'enthusiasts' rather than of Jews or Jewish Christians. (70)

The total picture points to a misconception of the doctrine of grace for daily Christian life and for the future of Israel. (71) The tendency to view the Church as the successor of the old Israel suggests a radical doctrine of the two aeons. Jews and all things Jewish, including the law, are relegated to the old aeon as the sphere of sin and judgement in contrast to the new aeon where grace abounds. (72) Hence Paul's emphasis of judgement according to works in chs 1-2, and his demonstration in chs 9-11 that grace and judgement are not two mutually exclusive spheres.

Paul had to become involved in the discussion at Rome because his gospel and mission were at stake. So too was the unity of the church and the link with Jerusalem. Gentile Christians needed to understand God's grace to Israel in order to understand his grace to them. Paul's law-free gospel does not lead to a life without obligation (73) but places him under obligation to Greeks, barbarians and all men, including unbelieving Jews.

This understanding of the situation in the Roman Christian community helps to explain both Paul's use of early Christian traditional formulae (cf 1:3f, 3:22f, 4:25 etc), and his continuous dialogue with scripture in the letter. Both of these emphasise continuity, the former with Jewish Christianity and the latter with Judaism. In the scriptures and the traditions, Paul has a common basis of belief which he shared with the Romans; (74) but he uses these not to give them proper apostolic foundation nor merely to commend himself to an unknown community but to prevent them from cutting themselves off from their roots. (75) The scriptures witness to the reality and pattern of God's election in history. As such they are not simply the record of past events but a witness to the freedom and faithfulness of God in his ways with men. (76) As such they are essential for the Church's self-understanding and unity.

We have attempted on the basis of chs 9-11 to reconstruct the situation which Paul may have addressed in Romans. As Käsemann says of his own reconstruction, 'Naturally, this is a reconstruction. But history is the field of reconstruction, and whether these are right or not depends on how far they overcome the problem posed. This hypothesis does so to a very high degree'. (77)

This contribution is offered in gratitude for the teaching and publications of A T Hanson, whose scholarly insights have enabled me to see more clearly the unity of the scriptures of the Old and New Testaments.

NOTES

1 Cf G Eichholz, *Die Theologie des Paulus im Umriss* (Neukirchen-Vluyn 1977) llf.

2 Cf H Gamble, *The Textual History of the Letter to the Romans, Studies and Documents*, Vol 42, ed I A Sparks (Grand Rapids 1977) 132.

3 Paul Minear's study, *The Obedience of Faith: The Purposes of Paul in the Epistle to the Romans* (SCM 1971) has been criticised by C E B Cranfield for attempting to interpret the entire epistle on the basis of chs 14-16, *Romans: International Critical Commentary*, Vol II (Edinburgh 1979) 820-22.

4 See my doctoral dissertation 'The Purpose of Paul in the Letter to the Romans: A Survey of Romans 1-11 with Special Reference to Chapters 9-11', presented to the University of Edinburgh 1972.

5 Cf Cranfield op cit 446f. See also E Käsemann, *Commentary on Romans* (ET, SCM 1980) 253-256.

6 See Chapter 2 'Why Did Paul Write Romans?' Similarly J C Beker, *Paul the Apostle: The Triumph of God in Thought and Life*, (Fortress, Philadelphia 1980) 87.

7 See H D Betz, *Galatians: Hermeneia Series*, (Fortress 1979) p5.

8 Cf W D Davies' comment 'Over-conversion was a common phenomenon. Other Gentiles..., like many Jews who heard him and to whom he wrote, took Paul to demand a complete rejection of the ways of Judaism and to invite messianic licence', 'Paul and the People of Israel', New Testament Studies, 24. (1979) 22.

9 'Ioudaios' occurs only at 9:24 and 10:12 in chs 9-11.

10 On this see N A Dahl, *The Crucified Messiah and Other Essays*, (Augsburg, Minneapolis 1974) 37-47 and W D Davies op cit 4f and 15 n3. ('The centre of gravity for Paul was the messiahship of Jesus and its implications'). Contra cf Sanders, *Paul and Palestinian Judaism*, (SCM 1977) 514.

11 Cf Cranfield op cit p473.

12 This is Cranfield's translation - except where otherwise stated the RSV text is quoted.

13 'Paul did not deny the importance of ancestry, but only man's right to use it in making claims upon God', J Munck, *Christ and Israel*, (ET Fortress 1967) 138.

14 Although Paul exploits Hellenistic forms and literary genres, he takes seriously the scriptures of his people and seeks to deal with the problem in their terms - employing rabbinical and other methods to do justice both to

this new emergence, the Christian community, and its matrix, the Jewish people; W D Davies op cit p14.

15 See F J Leenhardt, *The Epistle to the Romans* (ET Lutterworth 1961) 249f, and Munck op cit 42, 48.

16 See Chapter 3, 'Romans 3 as a Key to the Structure and Thought of the Letter'.

17 Op cit 483.

18 Hanson shows that Paul is often wrongly criticised on this score, *Studies in Paul's Technique and Theology*, (SPCK 1974), 157-8.

19 Op cit 253.

20 See also v 18 and 'tout estin' in v 8 and 10:7. E E Ellis regards 9:6-29 as a good example of the 'proem' midrash which when used in the synagogue was developed around the Pentateuchal text for the day with additional supplemental texts to interpret it. There are sufficient similarities to rabbinic discourses to suggest a common milieu. *Prophecy and Hermeneutic*, (Mohr, Tübingen 1978) 155f and 218f.

21 Paul's text has four changes from the LXX, cf Cranfield op cit 485-88.

22 See B Lindars, *New Testament Apologetic* (SCM 1961) 242, also Munck op cit 58f.

23 Cf G Bornkamm, *Das Ende des Gesetzes: Paulusstudien*, Ges. Aufs. I (München 1958) 90-92.

24 Cf C Müller, *Gottes Gerechtigkeit und Gottes Volk. Eine Untersuchung zu Römer 9-11*, (Göttingen 1964) 33n38; N A Dahl op cit 144f.

25 Cf Dahl op cit 144f.

26 Cranfield op cit 498.

27 Cf Bornkamm as in n23 above.

28 *A Commentary on the Epistle to the Romans, Blacks New Testament Commentaries* (London 1957) 189.

29 Cf P Richardson, *Israel in the Apostolic Church* (Cambridge 1969) 126-47 esp 131.

30 Contra E Dinkler, 'The Historical and Eschatological Israel in Rom 9-11: A Contribution to the Problem of Predestination and Individual Responsibility', Journal of Religion, 36 (1956) 109-27.

31 Lindars notes that the text of 9:25 has been adapted from the Hebrew. The remnant theme is the link between the texts from Hosea and Isaiah. Paul probably used an existing group of texts - what is new is the application to the Gentiles, op cit 243.

32 Cf Richardson op cit 133.

33 Paul: *The Theology of the Apostle in the Light of Jewish Religious History*, (ET London 1961) 240. Cf A T Hanson op cit 154, 234.

34 Contra Käsemann op cit 79f. Cf K Kertelge's criticisms in *Rechtfertigung bei Paulus*, (Munster 1967) 308 and M Brauch's appendix in Sanders' book, op cit 539f.

35 Cf Munck, *Paul and the Salvation of Mankind*, (SCM 1959) 154, 234.

36 Sanders criticises W D Davies' view that Paul carried over into his interpretation of the Christian Dispensation, the covenantal conceptions of Judaism, op cit 514.

37 Cf J Piper, 'The Demonstration of the Righteousness of God in Romans 3:25, 26', Journal for the Study of the New Testament, 7, (1980) 2-32.

38 *A Shorter Commentary on Romans* (SCM 1959) 127.

39 Cf Cranfield's most recent suggestion on Christ as the goal of the Law in 10:4, op cit 519.

40 Op cit 33-59, 442f.

41 Sanders has developed his views and replied to some of his critics in a paper given at the SNTS meeting in Toronto 1980 entitled 'Paul and the Law: Different Questions, Different Answers'. Cf also H Hübner, *Das Gesetz bei Paulus*, (Göttingen 1978) 44f, 93f, 118f.

42 On Paul's use of common Christian catechesis see N A Dahl, *Jesus in the Memory of the Early Church* (Augsburg, Minneapolis 1976) 11-29 and H J van der Minde, *Schrift und Tradition bei Paulus*, (Paderborn 1976) 120f.

43 Cf Munck, *Christ and Israel*, op cit 123.

44 Cf Munck, *Paul and the Salvation of Mankind*, op cit 259.

45 Cf Beker op cit 330.

46 Op cit 152. Cf also O Betz 'Die heilsgeschichtliche Rolle Israels bei Paulus' Theologische Beiträge, 9 Jahrgang 1, 1978, 1-21; contra cf S Kim, *The Origin of Paul's Gospel*, (Mohr Tübingen 1981) 83f.

47 Cf Munck op cit 276f.

48 Cf Barrett op cit 224, Richardson op cit 127.

49 In Justin Gentile exclusivism almost replaces former Jewish exclusivism Richardson op cit 127.

50 Cf W D Davies, *The Gospel and the Land*, (Berkeley 1974) 171.

51 Contra Beker, op cit 75-91.

52 Paul's intention is not 'israelkritisch' but 'kirchenkritisch', Eichholz op cit 290f.

53 This is where we differ from Munck's interpretation, and also from Dahl, 'The Future of Israel', op cit 78f.

54 Cf W Sanday and A C Headlam *A Critical and Exegetical Commentary on the Epistle to the Romans*, ICC (5th Ed Edinburgh 1902) XXXII; Schmithals op cit 9, 83f; W G Kümmel *Introduction to the New Testament*, (1975), 309.

55 *Romans. New Century Bible* (London 1973) 23.

56 Op cit 22-24, 83f Schmithal's theory of two letters to Rome has no real textual foundation, cf A G M Wedderburn, 'The Purpose and Occasion of Romans Again', Expository Times, 90, (1978-79) 137-41.

57 Op cit 91. Beker refers to Rom 11:20 here, but he does add a question mark!

58 Cf Käsemann op cit 405.

59 Op cit 50n40.

60 Cf M Barth's criticism of Käsemann's view 'Paul and Israel', *New Testament Questions of Today* (SCM 1969) 183f, that 'the apostle's essential

adversary is the pious Jew'. Barth also criticises U Wilckens' claim in *Rechtfertigung als Freiheit*, Neukirchen 1974, p7) that 'Paul was an irreconcilable enemy of all "Judaism" in Christianity'. 'St Paul - A Good Jew', Horizons in Biblical Theology, An International Dialogue, I (1979) 7f.

61 Cf W Marxsen, *Introduction to the New Testament*, (ET SCM 1968) 95f.

62 Cf H W Bartsch, 'Die antisemitischen Gegner des Paulus im Römerbrief', *Antijudaismus im Neuen Testament* ? hrsg W Eckert etc (München 1967) 40.

63 Cf E Trocmé, "L'Epître aux Romains et la Méthode missionaire de l'Apôtre Paul", New Testament Studies, 7, (1960-61) 151f.

64 Cf Dahl, *Studies in Paul*, op cit 123.

65 Cf Sanders op cit 488-91.

66 Cf U Wilckens, *Der Brief an die Römer*, Evangelisch- Katholischer Kommentar zum Neuen Testament, Neukirchen-Vluyn (1978) 280-85.

67 'What is the nature of the discontinuity and continuity between the Jewish people and those 'in Christ'? Cf W D Davies 'Paul and the People of Israel' op cit 14.

68 Here we follow Käsemann, op cit 84-85.

69 Käsemann sees these as actual (not hypothetical) objections, but attributes them to Paul's (Jewish) adversaries, op cit 84.

70 Cf Käsemann on ch 12:3, op cit 332f, 359. It *is* possible that opponents of Paul were troubling the Christians at Rome, cf ch 16:17-20.

71 'Charis' is central in Romans, cf 4:16, 5:2, 5:15-6:23, 11:5-6, 12:3, Eichholz op cit 292, D J Doughty, 'The Priority of Charis', New Testament Studies, 19,(1973) 163f.

72 Cf ch 7:7 'ho nomos hamartia'.

73 Cf Eichholz op cit 5.

74 Cf H J van der Minde op cit 190-197.

75 Paul's warning is all the more serious if Christ is (also) intended in the reference to the root, cf 15:12 (Isa 11:10); the Gentiles hope is the root of Jesse who comes to rule over them. O Betz has shown that the source of Paul's thought in Rom 9-11 is Isa 6, especially v 13, Isa 11:1,10 Gen 49:10, and Gen 17:7 linked with 2 Sam 7,12f. R Clements notes that in the case of 'themes' such as that of the remnant the concept itself is in many respects more important for understanding the development of thought than the particular occurrence of the term, 'A Remnant Chosen by Grace', (Romans 11:5, *Pauline Studies: Essays Presented to F F Bruce*, ed D A Hagner, (Paternoster Press 1980) 107f.

76 Cf Hanson op cit 154 and B F Meyer, *The Aims of Jesus*, (SCM 1979) 202.

77 Op cit 406.

Chapter 5

Christ the End of the Law: Romans 10:4

1. *Introduction*

If there is any one good reason for choosing to write about this verse, it is because there is such widespread disagreement about its meaning. As C F D Moule says, 'It is one of the most hotly debated passages in the Pauline epistles'. .(1) An unfortunate feature of this verse is that its interpretation tends to be determined more by the understanding of Pauline theology that one brings to it than by what the text actually says.

We draw attention first of all to the wider context in which the verse is set, ie the letter to the Romans. This is extremely significant because Paul's attitude to the Jew and to the law is so much more conciliatory in Romans than in Galatians. (2) Moreover, since Romans is the later and more thorough document, wherever there is a divergence of view I consider it advisable to put more weight on Romans than Galatians. As W D Davies says, 'Paul's criticisms of the law were not uniformly negative - they fluctuated with the conditions which he faced. For example, in Romans he abandoned the unqualified dismissal of the law expressed in Galatians'. (3)

We should also note that this letter includes such favourable references to the law as 7:12, 'So the law is holy, and the commandment is holy and just and good', and 13:10, 'Love is the fulfilling of the law', and 8:3-4, 'God sent his son... in order that the just requirement of the law might be fulfilled in us'. The more immediate context, ie ch 10 also supports a positive understanding of the law. (4) What Barth says of 10:6f can be extended to cover the entire chapter - 'All that we read... is one invitation to participate in the law's fulfilment'. (5) Ch 10 presupposes the situation outlined by Paul at the end of ch 9; despite the fact that the Gospel has been taken to the Jews, the majority of them are still unbelieving in the Gospel - the mission to the Jews has met with only slight success. Paul is here simply describing and assessing this contemporary situation. As at the beginning of chs 9 and 11, he speaks sadly and with deep concern for his unbelieving brethren. His diagnosis is that though it must be granted that they have a zeal for God, it is in fact unenlightened.

This ignorance can also be described in terms of the law and of righteousness. The Jews sought to achieve righteousness by way of the law, ie by using the law as a means to legal righteousness, but they did not succeed in fulfilling the law and so failed to find righteousness. (6)

5. *Christ the End of the Law; Romans 10:4*

Bring has drawn our attention to the fact that law and righteousness are virtually synonymous here (7) - a strong indication of Paul's positive intention concerning the law in this section. It is also noteworthy that the description of Jewish unbelief as failure to fulfill the law is the opposite of what Paul claims for believers in 8:4, where it is said that the just requirement of the law is fulfilled in those who walk according to the Spirit. (8) They missed the goal of the law - true righteousness, because they sought a righteousness of their own achievement and did not submit to God's righteousness (as revealed in Jesus Christ) (10:3). This is the dark background of Jewish unbelief which is presupposed in 10:4. This verse marks the beginning of Paul's exposition of Christ as the 'telos' of the law, rather than a continuation of what the law and self-righteousness Jews could not do. .(9) M J Suggs suggest that by identification of Christ-Wisdom-Torah in 10:6-10, Paul sought to resolve the tension between Gospel and Law and thereby rescue his gospel from the stigma of absolute opposition to the law. (10)

2. *The Meaning of 'Telos' in Romans 10:4*

This leads us to the problem of the interpretation of 'telos' in 10:4. The basic issue in the text is whether 'telos' has the temporal sense of 'end' or 'cessation' (11), or whether it has the final sense of 'goal' or 'outcome' (12), or possibly combines both these meanings. (13) The contrasts between faith and works in 9:30-31, between God's righteousness and a righteousness of our own (10:3), and the righteousness of the law and the righteousness out of faith (10:5-6), have been regarded as ample evidence for the temporal sense and Christ is thus considered as the end of the law as a means to righteousness. (14) This is the meaning preferred by the New English Bible which gets rid of the ambiguity of 'end' (which could be used both in the sense of termination or of goal), and translates 'For Christ ends the law', thereby actually strengthening the negative emphasis of the verse by using a verb instead of the Greek noun, whereas with strange inconsistency, the same word is translated 'end' in 6:21-22. We feel that this translation does less than justice to the original text. 'Paul is not saying that Christ destroyed or ended the law "teleutē" or that He is the "cul-de-sac" "teleutan" thereof'. (15) If this is what Paul says it means that he allows that prior to Christ the achievement of righteousness by works was a perfectly valid activity. It would also mean that Christ is the end of a false principle which, as a matter of historical fact, He was not, since law-righteousness continued to be the aim of the Jews. (16)

5. *Christ the End of the Law; Romans 10:4*

Our modern distinction which regards the Old Testament as 'the Law' (in a legalistic sense) in contrast to the New Testament as 'the Gospel' tends to encourage such a view, particularly evident among Lutherans. [17] It is most unlikely however, that Paul, who argued so strongly in Rom 4 that Abraham was justified by faith, would allow that anyone at any time could be justified by works of law ('...by such shall no flesh be justified.' 3:20).

This problem is often overcome by the argument that Paul is not thinking of the Old Testament use of the law, but rather of the legalistic use by the Judaism of his own time. He is not so much criticising the law as what the Jews were doing with the law. [18] If we bear in mind the fact that the Greek language which Paul used has no word-group to denote legalism, legalist or legalistic, [19] then we can appreciate the great problem Paul faced when he sought to distinguish between a good Law and the bad use of it by some Jews. There is no doubt that this fact helps us to clarify some texts where Paul's language concerning the law is rather ambiguous, but it is doubtful if it is of any help in this text. The 'eis dikaiosynēn' is best understood as expressing purpose so that we should translate the verse 'For Christ is the completion of the law that everyone who has faith may be justified'. [20]

But what law is intended here? We do not regard the law in this section as the Old Testament law misused, [21] or as the Mosiac Law which is only part of the total revelation of God, or even as a reference to the promises contained in the law but 'as the law in its fulness as a revelation of God's promise and righteous demands which were fulfilled in Christ and therefore reached their end in Him'. [22] That this interpretation of the law is justified is confirmed by the fact, which we have already noted, that in ch 9:30-32 Law and righteousness were virtually interchangeable and also that in 10:6-8 not only is the law quoted but Christ himself is understood by Paul to stand in the place of 'this commandment' in Deut 30:11. [23] Karl Barth gives a useful interpretation of 'telos' in this verse when he understands it as 'anakephaliōsis', the sum or totality of all that Law stood for - as expressed in the rabbinic concept of the 'kelal'. [24] If we interpret law in this verse in its fullest sense and bear in mind the normal Jewish revulsion against any suggestion that the law should be abolished, it is unlikely that the statement here means simply that Christ is the termination of the law. [25]

If there is any suggestion of termination in the verse, this negative sense cannot be primary, as Du Plessis suggests, [26] but at best secondary. This is more in accord with its normal meaning in the New Testament according to Du Plessis' own investigation. Du Plessis found that 'the New

Testament revealed a unique use of the word "telos". In this application the creative appropriation of New Testament writers manifested itself conspicuously; "telos" received at their hands its messianic and eschatological connotation and this motif provided the fundamental theme of New Testament kerygma'. (27) For the New Testament writers Christ himself determined the meaning of 'telos' and all the separate uses of the word were determined by a christological basis. (28) When we consider the messianic and christological emphases surrounding the word 'telos' these are more likely to have fulfilment rather than abrogation as their primary sense. The investigation of secular and biblical use of 'telos' by Flückiger supports this interpretation. He found that at every place in biblical Greek where 'telos' can be translated by 'end' (Ende), the basic meaning of 'goal' (Ziel) is also in the background. (29) Another factor gives additional evidence that the primary meaning of 'telos' in v 4 is goal or completion. The 'diōkōn' in 9:31 means striving after a goal (cf Phil 3:12, 14). The Jews were running or striving after a goal but did not achieve it. This goal of righteousness is, in 10:4, declared to be Christ. (30) Bring gives as a meaning for "telos" 'the winning post in a race, the completion of a task, the climax of a matter'. (31)

If we accept the final sense of 'telos' as fulfilment or completion, as primary in 10:4, it may be allowed that the secondary sense of end or termination may also be included. As Leenhardt suggests 'Christ puts an end to the law because the law finds in Him its goal and its crown'. (32) In any case it is not a static abrogation of the law that Paul intends by the word 'telos' because 'telos' itself is a dynamic concept embodying the idea of one phase ending, coinciding with the inception of another. Christ as the 'telos' of the law is not so much abrogation of the law, but 'an act of transition, of transformation of its (the law's) servitude from death to life'. (33) Moreover, the final sense of 'telos' fits in better with 'eis dikaiosynēn' and also gives a better understanding of the 'gar' at the beginning of vv 4 and 5.

3. *Romans 10:4 in Context*

The context of 9:30f shows that Paul is not attacking the Jews but simply outlining their failure to find salvation. In view of this we think it more fitting that Paul in 10:3, instead of proceeding to contrast the way of Christ with the error of the Jews should proceed instead to explain that because the Jews did not understand the real meaning of the law (9:31) they could not appreciate Christ as the positive fulfilment of that Law. We conclude then that the 'gar' in 10:4 means a continuation of the argument in 10:3 and that it refers to Christ not to emphasise the distance of the Jews from salvation but to so present Christ in Jewish terms (34) as the completion of their relevation, that their failure to recognise Him becomes all the more surprising. By virtue of the fact that Christ has fulfilled the law, life and righteousness are now freely available for the people of the law, and likewise on the same terms, to those without the law. (35) The immediate context is in keeping with this interpretation of 10:4 as is also the contents of chs 9-11 when viewed as the climax of an argument extending throughout chs 1-11 and having its practical application in chs 14-15. (36)

Despite traditional exegesis, even 10:5-6 is not to be seen as conflicting with this interpretation. The 'gar' in v 5 and the 'de' in v 6 have traditionally been regarded as plainly denoting a contrast between law-righteousness and the righteousness of faith, and as such were basic to the argument for the temporal sense of 'telos' in v 4. But neither of these words need necessarily mean that this contrast is intended. If it is correct to maintain that v 4 sets out not what men cannot do, but what Christ has done, ie His fulfilment of the law, then the 'gar' of v 5 may be regarded as introducing the explanation of *how* Christ is the goal of the law. (37) He is the completion of the law by virtue of the fact that He lived it and practised it. (38)

It may legitimately be argued that Christ is not necessarily intended by the words from Lev 18:5, 'the man who practises the righteousness which is based on the law shall live by it'. Ridderbos holds that 'What Paul means to say is this, that he who strives after the righteousness that is by the law is then bound to the word of Moses, that is, to do what the law demands.... In that sense it can be said that Moses (or the law itself) defines the righteousness that is of the law. This is not an appeal to Moses in support of 'a false position', but a binding of this position to its own point of departure; he who seeks righteousness in the law faces, as appears from the law itself, the requirement of doing'. (39) It should be noted however that Ridderbos' view does not necessarily rule out the interpretation of 10:4 advocated in this paper, despite his opposition to it.

Again the 'de' of v 6 is only an insurmountable obstacle to our argument if taken as adversative as is normally done. But this is not necessarily the only possibility and it is quite legitimate to interpret it as having only a transitional or explanatory function (40) and so vv 6f as well as v 5 may be properly understood as a continuation of v 4, of Christ as the goal of the law.

This interpretation avoids the problem which we would otherwise have of holding that Paul in v 5 quotes Moses (Lev 18:5) as an example of the wrong kind of righteousness - law-righteousness, whereas in v 6 he quotes Deut 30:12f (also from Moses) in support of faith-righteousness. Given Paul's view of the Old Testament, it is unlikely as Bring asserts, that Paul himself would set scripture against scripture in the course of his own argument. (41) Instead of setting out a contrast between law-righteousness (v 5) and faith-righteousness (v 6), Paul intends both quotations to support his claim that the righteousness now realised in Christ is that to which Moses also pointed. The righteousness 'ek tou nomou' (v 5) is thus seen to be equivalent to the righteousness to which the Old Testament witnesses, ie the righteousness of faith (and not law-righteousness).

Although it is not feasible within the scope of this chapter to deal with the remainder of ch 10, it is fair to assert that several factors, namely the Neofiti Targum, our increasing knowledge of Paul's use of the Old Testament, (42) and of Palestinian Judaism, along with a greater awareness of the particularity of the Pauline letters, are combining to point towards a fuller understanding of the development of Paul's argument in Rom 10. In view of this a fresh look at the interpretation of v 4 may prove both necessary and fruitful. (43)

NOTES

1 'Obligation in the Ethic of Paul' in *Christian History and Interpretation: Studies Presented to John Knox*, Ed W R Farmer, C F D Moule, R R Niebuhr, (Cambridge 1967), p401.

2 Cf C E B Cranfield, 'St Paul and the Law', SJT XVII, (1964) pp 43ff, and W D Davies, 'Paul and the People of Israel', NTS, XXIV, (1977), pp12ff.

3 Op cit p19.

4 Ch 10 is not merely a recapitulation from another angle of what has already been stated in ch 9. Ch 10 has a transitional function - between the emphasis upon God's freedom in relation to Israel in ch 9 and that upon his commitment to Israel in ch 11; cf J Munck, *Christ and Israel*, (Philadelphia 1967), p78.

5 *A Shorter Commentary on Romans*, (London 1959), p127.

6 It is not the activity of doing the Law that is wrong but that this leads to the wrong end. Paul fundamental critique of the Law is that following the Law does not result in being found in Christ. Cf E P Sanders, *Paul and Palestinian Judaism*, (London 1977), pp550-1.

7 'Paul and the Old Testament: A Study of the Ideas of Election, Faith and Law in Paul with Special Reference to Rom 9:30-10:21'. Studia Theologica, XXV, (1971), p46.

8 Cf F F Bruce, *The Epistle of Paul to the Romans*, (London 1963), p198.

9 Cf A J Bandstra, *The Law and the Elements of the World*, (Kampen 1964), p104. This interpretation is based on a comparison between Rom 10:4f, and Phil 2:7f first proposed by Schlatter. Cf also Munck, op cit pp88-9.

10 'The Word is Near You: Rom 10:6-10 within the Purpose of the Letter', in *Christian History and Interpretation*, op cit p311. The significance of this view is that it shows Paul trying to make a positive link between the law and the Gospel. E J Epp argues that Torah, according to the rabbis created before the world, should have been Paul's logical link between the Gentiles and God ie via Israel, so Paul had to redefine Torah's proper place and role, "Jewish-Gentile Continuity in Paul: Torah and/or Faith?" (Rom 9:1-5)", *Christians among Jews and Greeks*, pp 80-90, (see n.6, Ch11)

11 This view with minor variations is held (among others) by Sanday and Headlam, *The Epistle to the Romans*, ICC, (Edinburgh 1902), p284; Gutbrod, *Theological Dictionary of the New Testament*, trans. by G W Bromiley, vol IV, pp 1068f; H Lietzmann, *An die Römer*, (Tübingen 1928), p96; Bultmann, 'Christus, des Gesetzes Ende', in *Glauben und Verstehen*, ii, (Tübingen 1952), p48; E Bammel, 'Nomos Christou', *Studia Evangelica*, III, (1964), pp 123f; and Käsemann, *An Die Römer*, (Tübingen 1973) p270.

12 In general support of this view we find - K Barth, *The Doctrine of God. Church Dogmatics*, II(2), (Edinburgh 1957), p245; M Barth, *Jesus, Paulus und die Juden*, (Zurich 1957), pp 60f; H W Bartsch, 'The Concept of Faith in Paul's Letter to the Romans', Biblical Research, XIII, (1968) pp51-2; R Bring, *Christus und das Gesetz*, (Leiden 1969), pp35-72; C E B Cranfield, op cit pp 48-53; F Flückiger, 'Christus, des Gesetzes "Telos"', Theologische Literaturzeitung, X, (1954), pp153-4.

13 Others allow that both emphases are legitimate, while differing as to which is primary, cf PJ Du Plessis, *'Teleios': The Idea of Perfection in the New Testament*, (Kampen 1959), pp 142f; C F D Moule, op cit pp 401f and 'Fulfilment-Words in the New Testament: Use and Abuse', New Testament Studies XIV, (1967/68), pp301f; and C K Barrett, 'The Interpretation of the Old Testament in the New', *The Cambridge History of the Bible*, I, pp408f

14 Cf Sanday and Headlam, who hold that the 'principle of work righteousness' was brought to an end by Christ, op cit pp283f.

15 Du Plessis, op cit p142.

16 Cf Barrett, *A Commentary on the Epistle to the Romans*, (London 1957), p198.

17 Luther never intended to drive a wedge between the Old Testament and the New - his lectures on Genesis show that he considered the chief content of the OT to be the promise that Christ would come. Cf Bring, op cit p23.

18 Cf H N Ridderbos, *Romeinen*, (Kampen 1959), p233, as quoted by Du Plessis, op cit p123.

19 Cf Cranfield, op cit p55, and Moule, op cit pp389f.

20 Cf Bring's translation of this verse, op cit p45.

21 Cf Du Plessis's view - 'The primary sense is a negative one: termination of the profound fallacy that the fulfilment of the Law is a method of redemption at all', op cit p142.

22 Cf Bandstra, op cit p106.

23 Cf Bandstra, op cit p106; Bring, op cit p49. Lietzmann notes that Paul has substituted the personified 'righteousness' for the original phrase in Deuteronomy 'this commandment', op cit p96.
24 *The Doctrine of God, Church Dogmatics*, II(2), p245.
25 Cf Moule, 'If anything is superseded, it is not Torah as such but a temporary covenant; and thus the finality, paradoxically, is the beginning of a new era'. 'Fulfilment Words in the New Testament', op cit p302.
26 Op cit p242.
27 Ibid.
28 Ibid. See also p135.
29 Op cit p154.
30 Cf Bring, *Christus und das Gesetz*, pp 35f, 'Paul and the Old Testament' p47, n22; Flückiger, op cit pp 154-6; and Moule, op cit pp 301f. Contra, cf Käsemann, op cit p370.
31 'Paul and the Old Testament', op cit p47.
32 *The Epistle to the Romans*, (London 1961), p266.
33 Cf Du Plessis, op cit p142. See also the remainder of this section 'Christ, Conversion of the Law', (pp142-6).
34 Paul's apologetic intention, ie not to give needless offence to Jews or Jewish Christians in Jerusalem, but to make his position as palatable as possible, is rightly noted by Suggs (op cit p298), though he tends to put too much stress on Romans as a 'brief' to Jerusalem rather than to Rome.
35 Cf R Bring, 'The Message to the Gentiles', Studia Theologica, XIX, (1965), pp36-7.
36 Cf W S Campbell, "The Place of Romans 9-11 within the Structure and Thought of the Letter", *Studia Evangelica*, VII, ed E A Livingstone, Akademie-Verlag, Berlin 1982, pp121-31. See 'Why did Paul write Romans?' (Chapter 2 in this volume).
37 Cf Cranfield, op cit p49.
38 Bandstra, op cit p104.
39 *Paul. An Outline of His Theology*. Trans. by J R De Witt, (London 1977)
40 Cf Bandstra, op cit p104, n133.
41 Op cit p49, Suggs, op cit p301.
42 Cf A T Hanson, *Studies in Paul's Technique and Theology*, (London 1974), pp136f, and M Black, 'The Christological Use of the Old Testament in the New Testament'. NTS, XVIII, (1971), pp1-14.
43 Stuhlmacher advocates a reconsideration of the relationship between Law and Gospel in Paul's theology. 'Das Ende des Gesetzes'. ZTK, 1 XVII, (1970), pp14f.

Chapter 6

Christianity and Judaism: Continuity and Discontinuity

The relationship between Christianity and Judaism is a vast theme. Some of the most significant developments affecting the relationship have originated from historical events such as the Jewish-Roman war and the eventual destruction of Jerusalem; the Holocaust is a more recent example. In this study we shall confine ourselves to theological issues in three key topics: covenant, Paul's conversion-call, and the use of the title 'Israel' The aim is to demonstrate that continuity as well as discontinuity between Christianity and Judaism is basic to the New Testament understanding of all three.

1.*New Covenant or Renewed Covenant?*
The ambiguity concerning the understanding of 'covenant' in the New Testament is illustrated by the variation both in the meaning and in the frequency of the term. Of the thirty-three occurences, eight are in the undisputed letters of Paul, seventeen are in Hebrews, with four occurences in Luke/Acts, and one each in Mark, Matthew, Ephesians, and Revelation.

Paul first uses the adjective new (kainē) in connection with covenant (diathēkē) in the reference in 1 Corinthians 11:25 to the institution of the Lord's Supper. Mark simply refers to 'my blood of the covenant' (14:24). In the earliest and best manuscripts of Matthew and Mark, 'new' is not included. Luke 22:17-20 includes two traditions - a shorter one that does not mention 'covenant' at all, and a longer one that mentions 'the new covenant.' The sole reference to 'the old covenant' is found in 2 Corinthians 3:14 where Paul speaks of reading the old covenant. It is probable that behind the references to 'new covenant' in the New Testament is the passage in Jeremiah 31:34 where the prophet says, 'Behold, the days are coming, says the Lord, when I will make a new covenant with the house of Israel and the house of Judah'. The significant feature of this covenant, which will distinguish it from that made at the Exodus, is that the Lord will put his law within them: 'I will write it upon their hearts'. If Jesus did actually use the phrase 'new covenant', probably he had this prophecy in mind.

'Covenant' in Hebrews
This epistle cites the Jeremiah passage in full (from the Septuagint) in Hebrews 8:8-12. The author has more than one meaning for the word

'diatheke'; he can use it as meaning a 'testament', associated with the death of the testator (9:16f). Hebrews offers a clear contrast between the old and the new, but, unlike Paul or Jeremiah, its author finds the essence of the two 'diathēkai' in the cultic aspect. This approach is doubtless to be understood in light of the purpose and the audience for which the document was originally written. The interpretation of Hebrews will differ depending on whether the author is seen as contrasting Christian faith with Judaism or with some Jewish-Gnostic heresy.

In his recent *Introduction to the New Testament*, H Koester suggests that the author of Hebrews, addressing the whole Christian church, enters into a critical theological controversy with Gnosticism in refuting the Gnostic understanding of both the redeemer and the process of salvation by means of a Christological and ecclesiological interpretation of Scripture. (1) In his commentary on Hebrews, Robert Jewett notes the close parallels between Colossians and Hebrews; the key argument in both is that Christ has overcome the elemental forces of the universe. He takes up the proposal of Charles P Anderson that the lost Laodicean letter, written probably by Epaphras, is in fact the Epistle to the Hebrews (cf Col 4:16). (2)

The fact that the most recent scholarship considers the purpose of Hebrews as being essentially to oppose a Jewish-Gnostic type of heresy means that we must be extremely careful not to read this letter simply as a stark contrast between Judaism ('the old') and Christianity ('the new') as symbolised by two distinct covenants. Koester in fact warns that parts of Hebrews may be completely misunderstood if the letter is interpreted as a criticism of the Jewish cult. He states: 'To be sure, the material and temporal limitations of the sacrificial cult are pointed out (9:9-10), but the actual point of the argument as a whole is to prove that the heavenly reality of the path that the redeemer took led through his death; only for that reason does the new covenant stand (9:15-17). The author does not argue against Judaism, but against the gnostic denial of the salvatory significance of Jesus' death'. (3)

The Particularity of the Pauline Epistles

To interpret Paul's letters as abstract and timeless theological treatises, as if they had originated in a historical vacuum, is entirely to misunderstand them. It is clear that the major and undisputed letters are addressed to individual churches about specific problems encountered at a particular period in their history. The genius of Paul is that he was able to write coherent and consistent theology while translating it into the contingent particularities of each local church.

Thus the theology of the cross, Paul's unique apocalyptic interpretation of the death and resurrection of Jesus, constitutes the dogmatic centre and core of his gospel. (4) But this is continuously reinterpreted and restated to relate to differing local problems. To understand Paul aright is not merely to take note of what he has written but to interpret his written words in the context out of which they arise and to which they are addressed. Thus in acknowledging Paul to be a consistent theologian, we will insist on distinguishing him from the systematic theologian. Often the failure to interpret Paul historically as well as theologically has resulted in gross exaggeration of Paul's views, especially on the theme of Judaism.

'Covenant' in Paul

Paul, as we have already noted, refers to 'the new covenant' in 1 Corinthians 11:25. In 2 Corinthians 3:6 he also refers to apostles being qualified 'to be ministers of a new covenant, not in a written code but in the Spirit'. There is a reference to two covenants in Galatians, but the references in Romans - 'to them belong... the covenants' (9:4) and 'this will be my covenant with them' (11:27) - present a more positive understanding of God's covenantal relationship with Israel. The problem with most of these references is that very often they are incidental or secondary to the main theme in hand. Nowhere do we have as a central theme in any of Paul's letters a stark contrast between Christianity and Judaism in terms of old and new covenant. Paul does not think so much in terms of static abrogation - of the replacement of one covenant by another - but rather, in terms of dynamic transformation. Thus Christ is the *'telos'* or goal, of the law rather than its termination (Rom 10:4). (5) It would seem unwarranted therefore to make the allegorical reference to two covenants in Galatians the basis for an important New Testament doctrine. In any case Paul does not use the terms 'old' and 'new' here. This is doubtless because both covenants are in fact traced back to the figure of Abraham. Again the reference in 1 Corinthians 11:25, though ambiguous, has no immediate contrast with Judaism in its context.

The unique reference to 'the old covenant' in 2 Corinthians 3:14 is more problematical. But the actual theme is a contrast between forms of ministry which itself originates from a reference to the Corinthians as Paul's letter of recommendation, 'a letter from Christ... written not with ink but with the Spirit of the living God, not on tablets of stone but on tablets of human hearts' (2 Cor 3:3). This contrast reminds us of a basic contrast that Paul sometimes uses, between the 'outward' and 'inward' Jew (Rom 2:28f), and between the spirit and the letter (Rom 7:6).

Part of the problem of 2 Corinthians is that we are unclear as to the identity of Paul's opponents. Both Ernest Käsemann (6) and Dieter Georgi (7) hold that Paul may have a polemical intention in this passage, which may be directed against Jewish or Jewish-Christian opponents. C K Barrett considers that these opponents regarded themselves as preeminent Christian apostles. They carried letters of authority from Jerusalem but they refused to recognise Paul's apostolic status. They also accommodated themselves to the Hellenistic or gnosticising criteria employed by the Gentile Christians in Corinth. (8)

Moreover, there is a real possibility that Paul is here making use of his opponents' slogans and reversing their opinion that spirit and letter are directly linked in the interpretation of the Old Testament. Perhaps this is one reason why Paul takes up a pre-Pauline midrash on Exodus 34:30. (9) For a clear understanding of 2 Corinthians 3-4, we require a more precise knowledge of the beliefs of Paul's opponents and also of the first century midrashic understanding of Exodus 34. Only then can we base important doctrines upon it. In any case we cannot agree with Käsemann's conclusion in his essay 'The Spirit and the Letter', that 'the phenomenon of the true Jew is eschatologically realised in the Christian who has freed himself from Judaism'. (10)

Käsemann does warn against any absolute identification of the Old Testament as letter or any simplistic depreciation of the law simply because it was written down. He points out that behind the reference to 'written... with the Spirit... on tablets of human hearts' lies an assertion of the fulfilment of Jeremiah 31:33, and that Paul has in mind here both the reference to stone tablets and the contrast of Ezekiel 11:9 and 36:26 where Israel's stony heart is to be replaced by a heart of flesh. The implication is that the new covenant of which Jeremiah speaks has become a reality. Käsemann, however, sees here two contrasting covenants so that Paul 'has to decide between the old and the new covenants, instead of seeing both as a historical continuity in the light of the concept of the renewed covenant'. (11)

Despite the fact that, in his recent book *Paul and Palestinian Judaism*, E P Sanders deplores the implicit anti-Judaism in much German Pauline scholarship earlier in this century, he himself concludes that Paul's religion is far removed from the covenantal nomism that essentially constituted Palestianian Judaism. He concludes that the idea of the covenant was not a central one for Paul, for whom 'participation in Christ', a way of salvation that by definition excludes all others, was basic. (12) Sanders goes on to argue that 'Paul in fact explicitly denies that the Jewish covenant can be effective for salvation.' In an essay on 'Paul and Covenantal Nomism', Morna Hooker points out that Sanders is correct only if by 'Jewish covenant' he means the covenant on Mount Sinai, which Paul regards as an interim measure until the promises are fulfilled. While allowing that it may be pure chance that Paul never described God's promises to Abraham as a 'covenant', Hooker suggests that this may be because Paul prefers to speak of it in terms of promise, and to use the term 'covenant' for what happens in Christ. (13) God's promises to Abraham relate to the future and it is only in Christ that the promised blessing becomes effective.

W D Davies has drawn attention to the fact that the word 'new' can be used both of Jeremiah's new covenant and also of the new moon. He writes: 'The ministry of the old covenant, and by implication the old covenant itself, had its glory (2 Cor 3:7). Moreover, just as the new covenant conceived by Jeremiah, Jubilees and the sectarians at Qumran did not unambiguously envisage a radical break with the Sinaitic covenant but a re-interpretation, so Paul's new covenant. Thus Jer 31:33 does not look forward to a new law but to 'my law', God's sure law, being given and comprehended in a new way. The adjective 'hadasah' in Jer 31:33, translated 'kainē' by Paul, can be applied to the new moon, which is simply the old moon in a new light. The new covenant of Paul, as of Jeremiah, finally offers re-interpretation of the old.'.(14)

This conclusion concerning the meaning of covenant in Paul should not be regarded as confusing Judaism and Christianity. We are not advocating any theory of two covenants - whether it is one in absolute contrast to the other, as Käsemann suggests, or two covenants for two distinct peoples, as some modern scholars propose. Rather, the object of our study has been to emphasise that there is real continuity between Judaism and Christianity.

If we minimise the differences between these, we fail to account adequately for the origin of Christianity, though we do thereby acknowledge God's revelation of himself in Judaism. Alternatively, if we exaggerate the element of discontinuity, we can then stress the uniqueness of the Christian revelation at the expense of calling into question the faithfulness of God. For if one covenant can fail, so too can another; moreover, if Christianity claims to be an absolutely new revelation of God, how then do we see ourselves in relation to Islam, or to any subsequent religion appearing on the stage of history?

Käsemann claims that whereas Abraham is, for Paul, a prototype of the Christ, Moses is the antitype. (15) If we accept this designation, it would appear that in relation to Moses and Sinai, Paul would speak of a *new* covenant. But if Abraham is a true prototype, then surely we must speak in terms of a *renewed* covenant, in terms of fulfilment and affirmation, rather than purely in terms of stark contrast.

2. *Paul's Conversion-Call*

W D Davies has long insisted that a proper understanding of Paul's attitude to the law is attained only in the light of his understanding of Jesus as Messiah. (16) Whatever else is in dispute concerning Paul's Damascus experience, one thing is clear: it involved a messianic or Christological content. Krister Stendahl argues that a proper interpretation of Romans 7 shows that Paul, as a loyal Jew, had experienced no struggle or guilt feelings that would have led him, through dissatisfaction with the law, to turn to Christ. Paul's concern, as distinct from that of Luther, was not 'How can I find a gracious God?' Neither did he suffer from an introspective conscience. Instead of speaking of Paul's conversion, Stendahl prefers to regard him as someone who did not abandon his Jewishness for a new religion but, rather, as a Jew who was given a new vocation in service of the Gentiles. (17)

R P Martin agrees that Paul as a Jew was probably not consumed with guilt and inner conflicts. But Martin takes issue with Stendahl because Stendahl fails to note that the intermediate term between Paul the persecutor and Paul the apostle is Christ himself. 'The central link acting as a hinge to connect the old and the new for Paul, was *a revelation of Christ in his glory as the image of God*.' It is the Christological dimension of Paul's conversion, strangely missing from Stendahl's exposition, which for Martin turns out to be the indispensable factor in explaining it. (18) We believe that Martin is correct in this emphasis and that Paul's attitude to the law is more intelligible in the light of it. Paul's reassessment of the law resulted from the revelation of Jesus Christ. As Davies notes, 'To isolate the criticism of the Law from the total messianic situation, as Paul conceived it, is both to exaggerate and emasculate it. The criticism of the Law was derivative, a consequence of the ultimate place Paul ascribed to Jesus as Messiah'. (19)

E P Sanders has recently drawn attention to the fact that, since the Reformation, there has been a tendency to read back the struggles of the sixteenth century into Paul's experience and theology. He deplores the tendency to caricature Judaism as a 'religion of works'. We agree with him and with W D Davies that the precedence of grace over law in Israelite religion persisted, despite some neglect, in Judaism. (20) In deference to

Sanders it should be acknowledged that the boasting that Paul opposes is perhaps better understood as the making of claims rather than as the achievement of good works. This making of claims consisted in regarding the mere possession of the law as a badge of election. But for Paul the recognition of Jesus as Messiah, and its corollary - the admission of Gentiles as Gentiles - means that such a view of the law is precluded.

Yet even the assertion that Jesus is Messiah was not for Paul tantamount to a rejection of Judaism, or the founding of an entirely new religion but, rather, expressing the profound conviction that the final expression and intent of Judaism had been born. For this reason we believe that it is inadequate to speak only in terms of Paul's conversion - as if he were moving from one religion to another; and likewise only in terms of his call - as if he were continuing in an unaltered faith. The conversion-call combination emphasises both continuity and change.

3. *Paul and Israel*

a) Paul and the Israel of God (Gal 6:16)

Peter Richardson has maintained that the designation of the church as 'the new Israel' did not occur until the time of Justin. It was only by AD 160 that the church was identified with the 'Israel of God'. (21) His thesis has yet to be disproved. Though there may be signs in the New Testament of an implicit adaptation and application of titles and roles that point already in the direction of this identification, there is not so much *explicit* evidence as one might expect. Thus in Hebrews, even though the concept of Christians as the 'Israel of God' underlies much in the letter, this is never actually explicitly expressed.

We need to distinguish clearly between those features that point to Gentile Christians as elect or as now being included within the people of God, and those that might tend toward the idea of the displacement of Israel by the Christian church. Galatians 6:16 might possibly qualify as an explicit identification of the church with 'the Israel of God'. The Revised Standard Version renders it: 'Peace and mercy be upon all who walk by this rule, upon the Israel of God'. This might be taken to mean that the latter phrase is simply in apposition to the former and that Paul's benediction is applied to all those Christians, who, like him, regard circumcision as unessential. This would also mean that Paul, already at this period in history, identifies the Christian church as 'the Israel of God' in opposition to the historical people Israel. This interpretation is unlikely for several reasons.

Although Paul does distinguish between Abraham's two sons - one is born 'according to the flesh' and the other 'through promise' (Gal 4:22f) -

his main aim is not to show a contrast between the Israel of God and fleshly Israel (*Israēl kata sarka*). He writes to discourage Gentile Christians from accepting circumcision and (possibly) the bondage of keeping the whole law. Paul asserts that Jesus became accursed so that 'in Christ Jesus' the blessing of Abraham might come upon the Gentiles (3:14). But there is no suggestion that the inclusion of Gentiles necessarily involves the exclusion of Jews. Moreover, since apart from Galatians 6:16 there is no other evidence until AD 160 for the explicit identification of the church as 'the true Israel', this isolated instance would be hard to explain by itself. Why was it that no one in the next hundred years used this verse to identify the church as 'the new Israel' if it was accepted that Paul had in fact already done so?

It is better to take Peter Richardson's translation as indicating the proper sense in which this verse should be understood: 'May God give peace to all who will walk according to this criterion, and mercy also to his faithful people Israel.'.(22) Thus Paul's benediction also includes the faithful in Israel, although this group is not coextensive with 'all Israel'. The New English Bible translation offers a similar understanding: 'whoever they are who take this principle for their guide, peace and mercy be upon them, and upon the whole Israel of God'. Our approach to Galatians 6:16 has naturally been coloured by the meaning of 'Israel' in Romans 9-11 and it is to this that we must now turn.

(b) Paul and Israel in Romans 9-11: Paul Opposes Anti-Judaism within the Christian Community

In the interests of clarity and brevity, we shall set out in note form the main emphases of these chapters.

a) What Paul acknowledges:
1 The continuing rejection of the Gospel by the majority of Jews (9:30-10:3).
2 The influx of a large number of believing Gentiles (9:30).
3 The reason for Israel's failure - an unenlightened zeal 10:2). Christ, or possibly the law itself, (23) has become a stumbling stone to the Jews (9:33).

b) What Paul affirms:
1 His deep personal concern for his fellow Jews (9:1-3; 10:1).
2 The abiding election privileges of the Jews - 'they are Israelites... to them belong the sonship', etc (9:4-5).

3 The freedom of God in election - it depends only upon God's mercy (9:15); God is free to admit Gentiles and to retain Jews within his purpose as he wills.
4 No one, and especially not the Jews, is beyond the reach of the gospel call (10:12).
5 God has the power to graft in again those now disobedient (11:23).
6 The unbelieving Jews, though now 'enemies of God as regards the Gospel', are still beloved by Him for the sake of the patriarchs (11:28).
7 The gifts and call of God are irrevocable (11:29).

c) What Paul denies:
1 That the word, ie promises of God, has failed: there is a remnant chosen by grace although not all descended from Israel belong to Israel (9:6).
2 That God is arbitrary or unjust: He is both free and compassionate (9:15).
3 That God has rejected His own people: Paul and the remnant prove this not so (11:1-5).
4 That God has destined Israel to ultimate rejection: God over-ruled their unbelief for the good of the Gentiles and Israel remains central in God's plan (11:11-16).

d) What Paul warns against:
1 Gentile Christians must not boast over unbelieving Jews (11:17f).
2 Gentile Christians must not forget that it is the (Jewish) root that supports them; branches of themselves are not a tree - they *share* the richness of the olive tree (11:17f).
3 Gentile Christians must not become proud or presumptuous but must stand in faith and awe (11:20)
4 Gentile Christians must not presume to know the mind of the Lord; they are not to become 'wise in their own conceits', since Israel's hardening is only partial and temporary (11:25f).

e) What Paul hopes for:
1 That the success of his ministry among Gentiles will lead to some Jews being saved (11:14).
2 That the eventual outcome of the Gentile mission will be that the Jews will be provoked to obedience, so that 'all Israel will be saved' (11:11, 25f).
3 That Gentile Christians, Jewish Christians, and Jews will realise that they are inseparably linked through God's saving purpose for the world (11:28-32).

6. *Christianity and Judaism: Continuity and Discontinuity*

From this review we can see that Paul opposed the proud Gentile Christians by refusing to allow any absolute separation between the church and Israel. (24) This is not surprising because it is unlikely that the church existed as a completely separate entity before AD 70. Gentile Christianity can never be complete by itself: Paul describes it as a branch dependent on the Jewish Christian root. By this he hoped to prevent the dissociation of Gentile Christians from their Jewish roots, and possibly also from Jerusalem to which he was about to set out with the collection; this collection was intended to help bind together the two wings of the church.

It is likely that Paul wanted the Roman Gentile Christians to see both the ministry of Christ and his own ministry as examples for them to follow. In Romans 15:8 Paul states that Christ has become (gegenēsthai) a servant (*diakonos*) to the Jewish people. J Koenig suggests that the natural and proper meaning of this perfect-tense verb is that Christ has become, and still is, a servant or minister to the Jewish people, namely, that Paul has the ongoing post-resurrection effect of Christ's servanthood in mind and is not merely thinking of his life and death. (25) The Gentile Christians may have concluded wrongly that Paul's Gentile mission signified that he had given up hope for Israel. Koenig argues that Paul is really still aiming to influence Israel by making them jealous (11:-1f). This means that both Paul's ministry and that of Jesus may be described as having Jews *and* Gentiles in view; cf 15:8 where Christ is described as a minister of the circumcision to confirm the promises to Jews, and that Gentiles might glorify God for his mercy. If Paul and Jesus desired the salvation of both Jew and Gentile, then it would follow that the Roman Christians should not see their salvation as separate from the destiny of Israel. The solidarity of both Jew and Gentile in salvation is what Paul intends to stress. This emphasis is relevant to our contemporary scene and it is to this that we must now turn.

4. *The Relationship between Christians and Jews Today*

We have found from our study of covenant, Paul's conversion-call, and the title 'Israel' in the New Testament that there is evidence of both continuity and discontinuity between Christianity and Judaism. We have suggested that in the past there has sometimes existed a tendency among New Testament scholars to depreciate Judaism. Although we do not wish to promote an exaggerated reaction in the contrary direction, we believe that it is now time for a balanced but positive appreciation of Christianity's continuing debt to Judaism, and for an end to all implicit anti-Judaism within Christianity.

This will not mean that Christians will cease to witness to Jews. Witness and dialogue are demanded not because Jews are either similar to Christians or differ radically from them but because it is the Christian's duty to witness to all persons simply because this is of the essence of being in Christ. Any serious-minded Christian will seek to know and understand those with whom we are in dialogue - but especially our Jewish neighbours with whom we have a special bond in a shared history and scripture. In this we disagree with Stendahl's view that it dawned on Paul that the Jesus movement is to be 'a Gentile movement - God being allowed to establish Israel in his own time and place!' Stendahl finds it significant that Paul omits the name of Jesus Christ from the whole section of Romans 10:17-11:36. (26) We think Stendahl makes too much of this argument from silence. Paul *does* speak of seeking to save some of the Jews through his Gentile mission (11:14). The reference to 'the deliverer' in 11:26 can legitimately be taken to refer to Christ. Also the form of argument of 11:12-24 can most naturally be located within the normal scope of Pauline eschatology, that is, the 'how much more' is based on the surpassing grace of Christ's redemptive work. Even the concluding doxology is implicitly Christological. (27)

We oppose any view of Christianity and Judaism that proposes a theory of purely separate development. If we have read Paul aright, he has stressed the continuity of divine revelation and the resulting need for solidarity even when, because of disobedience on *either* side, there may be wide differences between Christians and Jews. The problem of leaving 'the salvation of all Israel' until the final consummation of human history is that this view suggests that in the meantime Jews and Christians can lead a separate existence.

We agree with Thomas Torrance that the relation of the Christian church and its mission to Israel must be quite unlike that to any other people or religion. But we are unhappy when he claims that 'the Gospel can hardly be brought *to* Israel, for it derives *from* Israel... Jews cannot be treated by Christians as unbelievers but only as brother believers with whom they are privileged to share a common faith in God and the same promises of salvation'. (28) Torrance stresses so much the commonality of our heritage - the continuity between Christianity and Judaism - that he has omitted the element of discontinuity and so slurs the genuine distinction that actually exists between them. Because of the element of discontinuity between Christianity and Judaism, there will inevitably be some tension between them. But it is part of genuine Christian witness to ensure that there is no more tension than our theological differences demand. Above all demand. Above all we shall witness remembering with sadness those shameful events of Christian history in relation to Jews from which none of us can entirely exculpate ourselves.

NOTES

1 H Koester, *Introduction to the New Testament*, 2 vols; vol 2, *History and Literature of Early Christianity* (Philadelphia: Fortress Press, 1982), pp 274f.
2 R Jewett, *Letter to Pilgrims* (New York: Pilgrim Press, 1981), pp 5-8.
3 Op cit pp 274f.
4 Cf J C Beker, *Paul the Apostle* (Philadelphia: Fortress Press, 1980), pp 178f, 208.
5 See Paul Meyer's criticism of Käsemann's inconsistency in not keeping to his own 'dialectical' interpretation of Paul: 'Rom 10:4 and the End of the Law', in *The Divine Helmsman*, ed J L Crenshaw and S Sandmel (New York: Ktav, 1980) pp 59f.
6 Cf Käsemann, 'The Spirit and the Letter', in *Perspectives on Paul* (London: SCM, 1971), p151.
7 Georgi, *Die Gegner des Paulus im 2 Korintherbrief* (Neukirchen: Neukirchener Verlag, 1964), pp 252f.
8 *A Commentary on the Second Epistle to the Corinthians* (London: SPCK, 1973), pp 28f.
9 Cf Georgi, *Die Gegner des Paulus*, pp 268-72.
10 Op cit p146.
11 Op cit p154.
12 *Paul and Palestinian Judaism* (London: SCM, 1977); see especially pp 511-15, 543f and, more recently, *Paul, the Law, and the Jewish People* (Philadelphia: Fortress Press, 1983).
13 'Paul and Covenantal Nomism,' in *Paul and Paulinism: Essays in Honour of C K Barrett*, ed M D Hooker and S G Wilson (London: SPCK, 1982), pp 47-56.
14 W D Davies, 'Paul and the People of Israel', *New Testament Studies* 24 (1978): 11.
15 Cf 'Paul and Israel', in *New Testament Questions of Today* (London: SCM, 1969), p185.
16 Cf W D Davies, 'Paul and the Law', in *Paul and Paulinism*, ed Hooker and Wilson, pp 7f.
17 *Paul among Jews and Gentiles* (Philadelphia: Fortress Press, 1977), pp 4f, 132.
18 Martin, *Reconciliation: A Study of Paul's Theology* (Atlanta: John Knox Press, 1981), pp 26f.
19 Davies, '*Paul and the Law*', p7.
20 Op cit p5.

21 *Israel and the Apostolic Church* (Cambridge: Cambridge Univ. Press, 1969).
22 Op cit p84.
23 Cf Paul Meyer, 'Rom 10:4' pp 64f.
24 Cf Chapter 4, 'The Freedom and the Faithfulness of God in Relation to Israel'.
25 'The Jewishness of the Gospel', *Journal of Ecumenical Studies* 19 (1982): 66.
26 Op cit p4.
27 On this, see W S Campbell, 'Salvation for Jews and Gentiles: K Stendahl and Paul's Letter to the Romans', in *Studia Biblica* III (1978), *Journal for the Study of the New Testament*, Supplement Series 3 (Sheffield, 1980), pp 65-72
28 *The Witness of the Jews to God*, ed David W Torrance (Edinburgh: Handsel Press, 1982), Appendix 2a, pp 139-40.

Chapter 7

Paul's Missionary Practice and Policy in Romans

Paul was the doyen of missionary theologians in the early days of the church. Not only did he spend his life in urgent compulsive evangelisation but he also wrote and argued for a theology of Gentile mission that necessitated a revised understanding of the church's outreach and development.

Romans has traditionally and, in our opinion, wrongly been regarded as a summary of Paul's theology. This designation would have more substance were the letter regarded as a summary of Paul's theology of mission which in fact can be seen to occupy a substantial part of the letter when chapters 9-11 are included in the discussion. (1)

1 *The Contextual Nature of Paul's Statements in his Letters*

It has become increasingly clear to New Testament scholars in recent years that Paul did not set out to develop in his letters a systematic theology. We can no longer therefore legitimately use his statements as if they were abstract and timeless theology. E P Sanders concluded from his study of Paul and the law that though 'a priori' one would expect Paul to have had a clear position on the law, in fact because Paul's statements depend on the question asked or the problem posed, he does appear to have said different things on differing occasions. This may be because 'Paul did not abstract his statements about the law from the context in which they were made, nor did he consider them in their relationship to one another apart from the questions they were intended to answer'. (2) There is general agreement, however, that although Paul's statements on any topic are contingent upon the circumstances he addresses, nevertheless coherence as well as contingency is the hallmark of his thought. (3) The relevance of this for our immediate enquiry is that we must interpret Paul's statements about mission in Romans in the light of the context out of which the letter originated and to which it was addressed.

Although we cannot discuss in any detail here the reason why Paul wrote the letter to the Romans, one thing is clear. There is some factor whether in Paul's situation, or, as seems more probable in our opinion, in the situation of the Roman Christians which necessitated a consideration of the Jewish people and their response to the Gospel. This explains the unique discussion of Israel in chapters 9-11 of the letter. (4) A curious but related factor is that no one would guess from Paul's statements concerning his mission plans in chapter 1 that he is not coming immediately to Rome, but is in fact on his way to Jerusalem instead. He eventually gets round to mentioning this in chapter 15. But why the silence in chapter 1? Is this due to Paul's embarrassment about his relations with the 'Urgemeinde' in Jerusalem, or perhaps about the collection gathered from the Gentile churches for the poor saints in Jerusalem? It may even be that Paul is aware that he is suspected of being too patriotic because of his own ethnic origin in Judaism?

It seems to us that any balanced approach to the reason why Paul wrote the letter must find some basis both in the situation at Rome such as divisions within the Christian community there, and also some factor in the mission or situation of Paul himself that is somehow intimately connected with, or influenced by, the situation of the Roman Christians. Only in this way can we avoid seeing the letter as being completely determined by Paul's own needs and problems as he heads for Jerusalem, or as reflecting only the situation at Rome without any relation to the wider issues of Paul's mission policy. It will suffice at this stage simply to note that there is evidence in chapters 14-15 of divisions between 'the weak' and 'the strong' which may reflect divisions between Jewish and Gentile Christians. There is evidence also of Gentile arrogance over against Jews in chapter 11:13f and there is some indication that Paul in chapter 4 has in mind to demonstrate that Jewish, proselyte and Gentile Christians share a common ancestry in their 'father Abraham'.

Whatever the precise impetus that led to the letter being written, we are thankful for it since it has provided the fullest discussion in the New Testament of the purpose of God for both Jew and Gentile: a discussion moreover which consciously faces the realities of Jew-Gentile differences whether in cultural heritage or in relations within the churches. It is likely in view of statements by Paul, such as that he has long intended to visit the Romans and that their faith is spoken of throughout the world, that there had been Christians in Rome for a decade or more when Paul wrote his letter in 57-58 AD. According to chapter 16 which we take to be part of the original letter, there may have been at least five different house churches and there may have been a not inconsiderable number of Christians since Paul lists no less than twenty-five with whom he is acquainted. One of these references is to a couple, probably husband and wife, described as noteworthy apostles who were in Christ before Paul (16:17). [(5)] The fact that Paul addresses his letter 'to all God's beloved in Rome' (1:7) may indicate that there were different groups within the Roman Christian community who did not fully accept each other as Christians and chapters

14-15 may be further evidence for this; we note especially Paul's final admonition to 'accept one another as Christ also accepted us' (15:7). It is possible that the differences, if such there were, within Roman Christianity, arose not simply from cultural differences but from 'ecclesiastical' differences, ie the Roman Christians may have migrated to Rome from other areas where they may have been evangelised by different Christian missionaries - hence their differing interpretation of the Christian message. We must return to this in more detail later.

2. *Paul's Mission Plans in Relation to Rome*

Paul understands himself to be called in the manner of the prophets of old to be an apostle (Rom 1:1, cf also Gal 1:15). More precisely, he regards himself as 'apostle to the Gentiles' (Rom 11:13), called by God and given grace 'to be a minister of Christ Jesus to the Gentiles' (15:16-17). In liturgical terms Paul conceives of his ministry as a priestly service whereby he offers up the Gentiles to God as 'an acceptable sacrifice, sanctified by the Holy Spirit' (15:16).

Paul appears to have regarded Jerusalem as both the point of origin of his mission and also the centre of the church. However much he may be aware of the political significance of Rome, it comes behind Jerusalem in religious significance. By 57 AD, Paul has already pursued his ministry throughout the regions bordering the Mediterranean - from Jerusalem to the western shores of Greece. His pattern was to set up congregations in the main provincial centres and then move on, leaving them to evangelise their own region. But Paul would still care for them pastorally or write or visit as circumstances permitted because they are for him evidence of the validity of his own ministry and apostleship - so that effectively his own Christian achievements are bound up with theirs.

To evangelise in Paul's understanding meant not only the initial preaching of the Gospel but also the support and upbuilding of his converts who themselves would then continue the proclamation which Paul had initiated. This policy is important in helping to resolve what some regard as a clear contradiction in Paul's statements between chapters 1 and 15 of Romans. From Greece, Paul plans to move further west to Rome and then to the farthest borders of the west - to Spain. The reason why he heads for Rome and Spain at this time is because he has now no more room for evangelising in the East (15:23). This announcement is preceded in 15:19-20 by Paul's statement that he has 'fully preached the Gospel of Christ... not where Christ was already named' - lest he build on another man's foundation. The policy Paul follows here is supported by a scriptural citation from Isaiah 52:15, a passage which refers to 'many nations'.

As further explanation for his plans to visit Rome, Paul claims that for many years 'he has had a great desire to visit them' (15:23). He immediately hastens to add that his main purpose is to make his journey into Spain and it would appear that what he really wants from the Romans is missionary support for his evangelistic work in Spain. He hopes to be 'sent on his way' by them. He uses the term 'propemphthēnai', probably a technical term for providing such necessary missionary support as offering a place to stay, assistance with travel and also possibly acting as a link between the new mission station and the sending churches. (6)

So much for chapter 15, but already in chapter 1, Paul had spoken of being ready 'to evangelise' in Rome also (1:15). In v 11 he had spoken of imparting some spiritual gift to the Romans and then, as if he were afraid of sounding too presumptuous, goes on to talk of a mutual strengthening of faith between them (v 12). Again in v 13 he speaks of 'gaining some fruit among the Romans, as amongst other Gentiles'. The latter statement implies what we already know to be true - that Paul has not as yet visited or preached in Rome. But how are we to reconcile the use of the same verb 'to evangelise' in 1:15 and 15:20, coming as the latter does, immediately after Paul's stated intention of avoiding duplication or conflict by building on another man's foundation? The explanation must be, as we have suggested, that Paul understands evangelisation to apply also to the upbuilding of Christians in the Gospel. Moreover the explanation for moving to Rome is that Paul has no more room in the East - therefore he cannot now be faithful to his former policy - only in Spain can he continue his pioneer work. To get there he needs the help of the Roman Christians and to ensure that help he needs an undivided Christian community. His evangelising there has this limited sense of ensuring proper support for future mission in Spain. (7)

It is probable for various reasons that no particular apostle had been instrumental in founding the Christian congregations at Rome. Paul seems to have had many friends there and probably the best explanation is that he did not feel entirely responsible for the Roman Christians because he had not founded that church, and also because there were Christians there from other branches of the Christian mission - possibly converted through the Jerusalem church. But Paul, as God's agent in winning some of these Christians to Christ and as apostle to the Gentiles generally, has the right and obligation, not only to pray for them (1:9) but also to visit Rome to encourage and strengthen his own Gentile converts. Hence Paul's summing up of the content of his letter in 15:15 as reminding them of that which he expects them already to know.

He formally states, however, that the Gospel obligates him to all men, all races and all cultures. He is indebted to the Greek and the barbarian not only because he has learnt from both Judaism and Hellenism, but because in the Gospel he is obligated to witness to all men since the Gospel itself concerns *all*, whether Jew or Greek, barbarian, bond or free etc.

In concluding this section we note the possibility that there may have been differing groups of Christians in Rome who originated from differing branches of the Christian mission. We have already drawn attention to Paul's caution in addressing the Romans. If some of these Christians were Jewish converts of the Jerusalem church which, according to Gaston, did not believe in evangelising Gentiles, [(8)] then perhaps the origin of the phrase 'to the Jew first' might be attributed to this group. It would be important for Paul as he heads for Jerusalem with the collection not to cause misunderstanding there by interfering in a Christian community which had its earliest roots in Jerusalem. If the phrase 'There is no distinction' - attributable possibly also to Paul himself, did originate from the Christians in Antioch, then it could be that Paul in Romans is addressing a situation where competing Christian groups antagonise each other with slogans of their respective places of origin or allegiance, emphasising their differences rather than their common belonging to Christ. Whatever their situation, Paul's concern is that their quarrels or divisions should not become a hindrance to the success of the Gospel - either in his forthcoming visit to Jerusalem or in his intended evangelisation of Spain. Hence his serious concern expressed in his call for them to join together in prayer for him in both these projects (15:30f).

3. *Paul's Gospel*

(a) *God's Act in Christ as the Foundation of Paul's Missionary Proclamation.*

In important statements in the first chapter of Romans Paul declares he is not ashamed of the Gospel for it is the power of God into salvation to everyone who believes, to the Jew first and also to the Greek. According to Paul, in the Gospel the righteousness of God is revealed through faith. For Paul righteousness describes a relationship - the covenant relationship between God and his people. To be 'just' or 'righteous' is to uphold the covenant, to act in accordance with it; to be 'unrighteous' is to act in such a way that the covenant is broken. The fact that God can always be relied upon to keep His part of the covenant means that He can also be described as faithful (Rom 3:5) and the good news of the Gospel for Paul consists in the fact that God has acted in Christ to uphold His covenant with humanity despite the faithlessness of His people Israel in refusing his gospel. In 3:21-30 Paul demonstrates that God's act in Christ is both the sign of God's righteousness and the means of righteousness for those who have faith (3:25-26). (9)

Although God's act in Christ is consistent with what is already known of God's faithfulness in the Old Testament, it is nevertheless so qualitatively new in its effects and what it offers that Paul can contrast this new aeon with all that has gone before. In Rom 7 in particular, Paul shows how prior to Christ the law was weakened through the power of sin and that only through His deliverance and with the aid of the power of the Spirit (Rom 8) may men be restored to fellowship with God. So Paul emphasises the newness of the Gospel. He begins in 3:21 '*But now the righteousness of God is manifested...*' and in 8:1 he says 'There is therefore *now* no condemnation to those who are in Christ Jesus.'

In the Christ event God offers as a gift to humanity a restored relationship with Himself. With the gift goes also the demand to accept the Lordship of the Creator who is now in this way acting to restore His control over His rebellious creation. (10) It is God's purpose not only to save human beings, but the whole creation looks for its eventual redemption when the full adoption of God's sons is realised in the full redemption of their bodies (8:19f).

Along with the cosmic aspects of Paul's gospel goes his stress on the Gospel as universal. All men both Jew and Greek are frequently referred to in Romans and Paul is at pains to emphasise that what God has done in Christ applies equally to everyone. Since God is One, there can be only one way of salvation and the centrality of faith in the new aeon means that anyone is able to enter the kingdom. Since in this respect there is no distinction (3:22) then Jews and Gentiles are equally able to enter the kingdom and conversely neither are exempt from this challenge. The reason for Paul's heavy stress upon faith is precisely to emphasise the universality of the Gospel which the entrance requirement of faith ensures. The possession of the law, though itself a privilege for God's people, had placed racial limits on entry to the covenant people (3:30). But what the law does not do - 'apply equally to all' - righteousness by faith does. (11) Yet this righteousness by faith is not to be seen in total discontinuity from the law or from Judaism. The presupposition of faith in Paul is the grace of God and it is under this theme that we will study another aspect of his gospel.

(b) *Paul's Gospel as the Fulfilment of the Hope of Israel*

Paul's ministry to the Gentiles is itself the result of God's grace (15:15,12:3). His gospel presupposes the elective purpose of God for Israel which he strikingly describes (with reference to the remnant) as 'the election of grace'. The theme of grace denotes continuity and consistency between God's revelation of Himself in the past and in the present. Grace is probably what Abraham found when, according to the Genesis narrative, God called him and made him the first of the faithful. As such he is the prototype of all men of faith, including Christians. He is 'the father of us all' (Rom 4:16). In his choice of Abraham, Paul is not simply making an arbitary selection to obtain a representative believer. Abraham stands at the beginning of God's ways with Israel and demonstrates, at the outset of the giving of God's promise to bless the world in and through him (Abraham) and his descendants, that the promise originated in grace. (12) Its fulfilment to be firm (bebaian) must needs also be based on grace (4:16). The blessing promised to Abraham who was to be 'the father of many nations' (4:17), Paul believes to have arrived in Christ, whom he describes as having become 'a servant to the circumcision so as to confirm (eis to bebaiōsai) the promise of the fathers and that the Gentiles might glorify God for His mercy' (15:8-9).

In chapters 5-6 Paul sees the Christ event in terms of God's grace. By him - the Lord Jesus Christ - we have access by faith into this grace wherein we stand (5:2). Paul contrasts the reign of grace with the reign of sin. The grace of God and the gift of grace through Jesus Christ far exceed the reign of sin in Adam. 'Where sin abounded, grace superabounded' (5:20), so that those who are united with Christ cannot possibly continue in sin (6:1). Thus Romans, more than any other letter of Paul, demonstrates continuity in the divine initiative in grace. (13) The gifts and the call of God are irrevocable (11:29) and therefore Paul can speak of the privileges of Israel as a present, and not as a past, reality (9:4-5).

But this does not mean that Israel may presume and interpret the experience of divine election as a state of 'electedness'. Paul sees the failure of Jews to respond to the Gospel partly in terms of their having an exclusive understanding of election. Gaston and Sanders correctly interpret 9:30f as indicating that the Jews have sought a righteousness of their own, ie a righteousness available to Jews *alone*. (14) The result is that they have failed to see in Christ the goal of the law and Paul is full of sorrow as he realises how few of his fellow Jews have responded to the Gospel.

But he does not, because of this, deny them a future in God's purposes. He does not think in terms of their displacement by Gentiles, but rather of

Gentiles being brought in to *share* the richness of the olive tree (11:17). Here, as 11:16 indicates, Paul is thinking in terms of corporate wholes rather than individuals 'If the first fruit is holy, so is the whole lump...'.

It is through his understanding of the term 'Israel' that Paul is able to hold together what many of his interpreters have found contradictory, ie the *actual* state of Israel, by and large not responding favourably to the Gospel - and the possession of the name Israel, indicating participation in the divine purpose of election. Israel for Paul is a fluid rather than a fixed entity.(15)

In his overview of Israel's history in chapter 9, he illustrates how God throughout this history has exercised His freedom *amongst* the Israelites, to choose people for His overall purposes of mercy. The conclusion of Paul's argument in Rom 9 and Rom 11 is that God remains free to retain the Jews within His purposes, even if they are now disobedient to the Gospel, and that He is also free to bring in the Gentiles to share in their inheritance.

Thus Paul knows nothing of any doctrine which suggests that since the coming of Christ, the people of Israel have been reduced to the same level as other Gentiles as if election were a thing of the past. Rather what Paul offers is the opportunity for Gentiles to share in the inheritance of Israel. (16) He does not suggest a diminishing of Israel's privileges but rather an increase in the privileges of Gentiles. This is why at the end of his letter to Rome, he can write of 'the root of Jesse in whom the Gentiles shall hope' (15:12). The same emphasis is found in Eph 2:18-20 'Now therefore you are no longer strangers and foreigners, but fellow citizens with the saints, and of the household of God: and are built upon the foundation of the apostles and prophets.'

Paul sees it as his task to proclaim the Gospel in the period between the resurrection and the parousia seeking by means of his mission to bridge the great gap between Israel's actual state and her divine destiny.

4. *Paul's Revision of Priorities in the Christian Mission in View of the Contemporary Outcome of the Gospel Proclamation*

Whatever the precise origin of the phrase 'to the Jew first', its inclusion in Rom 1:16 in association with its corollary 'and also to the Greek' indicates that there was still some discussion as to whether it was right to concentrate the Christian mission primarily on Jews, whether it should now extend to Gentiles also, or perhaps - in the short term - should aim at Gentiles only. Lloyd Gaston has recently highlighted the great theological differences between Paul and Jerusalem despite the fact of their mutual recognition. 'The Jerusalem church is characterised by circumcision, by

Torah, and by a mission restricted to Israel.' (17) Raymond Brown has similarly outlined the diversity that existed within the early Christian mission, identifying four main types of Jewish-Gentile Christianity each of which conducted their own mission work and made their own converts. (18) One main function of Roms 9-11 is to present an 'apologia' on behalf of Paul's own understanding of the relation between his mission work and the eventual salvation of Israel. (19) It is quite clear that though Paul differs from earlier missionaries in no longer holding that Israel must be restored *prior* to the coming in of the Gentiles, this revision of priorities does not signify complete and utter despair over Israel. What we wish to consider briefly is the possible factors that led Paul to this particular missionary outlook and strategy.

It would appear that throughout his career as apostle Paul held, in common with the Jerusalem church, a fundamental belief that God would save Israel. Where they differed was on the interpretation of the means by which this end would be achieved. It follows from this that Paul must have been responsible for introducing a different view involving a different strategy from the original disciples. How did Paul arrive at this view? Did Paul's new understanding coincide with his conversion-call? Alternatively did he only gradually come to realise that God had called him to be apostle to the Gentiles? This would account for the fact that we know rather little about Paul's earlier missionary work and also why the admission of Gentiles to the church became a problem only at a later date. Did Paul first of all concentrate his efforts on winning Jews and only as a result of his failure to win Jews did he then turn to the Gentiles? (20) Rom 11 suggests a very close connection between the failure of the Jews to respond to the Christian message and the origin of a mission to the Gentiles. 'Through their failure salvation has come to the Gentiles.' 'If their trespass means riches for the world (11:11-12); if their rejection means the reconciliation of the world (11:11-15); you have received mercy because of their disobedience.' (11:30)

Paul seems to be indicating a clear causal connection between the failure of the mission to Jews and the inception of a mission to Gentiles. This might, of course, be only a general reference, referring to the rejection of Jesus by the leaders of the Jewish people. But in Romans it appears more immediate than this. There we get the impression that God almost *had* to remove some (Jewish) branches of the tree in order to make room for the unnatural inclusion of Gentile branches. (21) This would suggest that it was Paul's own reflection upon the fact of the failure of the Jews to respond that has led him to preach to the Gentiles. He concludes that God has hardened the hearts of the Jews temporarily with the explicit intention of saving the Gentiles first. It was doubtless the fact that some Gentiles demonstrated the charismatic effects of the Spirit in their lives, taken along with the negative response of the Jews, that led Paul in a secondary theological reflection on this primary historical and social reality to conclude that it was through the Gentiles God would save Israel. (22) What is not clear is the length of time that may have elapsed between Paul's conversion-call and his full realisation of the required sequence of events as described in Rom 11. At the height of his career did he regard himself as a missionary only to the Gentiles or does he now evangelise also the Jews of the Diaspora as Luke in Acts suggests?

According to Gal 2:7-9 the division of labour agreed at the Council of Jerusalem was ethnographic rather than geographic - Paul is to go to the uncircumcised, Peter to the circumcised. E P Sanders therefore finds it unlikely that 1 Cor 9:19-23 can be taken literally. When Paul's statement in Rom 15:19, where he depicts himself as working in a circle from Jerusalem to Illyricum, is put alongside 1 Cor 9:19-23, it implies that Paul is apostle to *everyone* in the Mediterranean area, whether they are Jews or Gentiles. Sanders does not deny that Paul sometimes lived as a Jew but he cannot conceive of Paul establishing two different churches in one area - observing the law in one and not in the other. Sander's solution to what he regards as a difficult question is that Peter, Paul and the others in their urgent desire to carry out their respective missions, made no special provision for Diaspora Jews. (23)

The evidence of Acts and of Rom 11:14 is that Paul did hope to win some Jews. Munck cites Jülicher's criticism of Paul's claim to have fully preached the Gospel in the east as 'gross exaggeration'; Munck himself has a better understanding of Paul. He equates 'the offering (hē prosphora) of the Gentiles' by Paul as their priest in Rom 15:16 with the 'fulness (to pleroma) of the Gentiles' of 11:25 and the obedience of the Gentiles of 15:18. It is obvious that Paul has not preached the Gospel to every individual in these areas mentioned. But Paul is able to claim he has finished his work because, as already noted, he thinks representatively, ie in terms of nations - Galatians, Achaians, Macedonians etc. (24) Munck also believes that according to Rom 10:14-21, the Gospel has already been preached to the Jews. Paul cites Ps 19:4 'Their voice has gone out to all the earth, and their words to the end of the earth'. Although the apostles to the Jews have finished their task, like Paul in the East, 'they have not been everywhere or preached the Gospel to every individual Jew, yet their task in respect of the whole of Israel has been completed. Those parts of Israel to which they have preached stand for the whole, for the Jewish people; and Paul can therefore go on to assert (10:21, and ch 11) that Israel is unbelieving and hardened'. [25] The logic of Paul's policy is further spelt out in Rom 11:16, 'For if the first fruit is holy, the lump is holy; and if the root is holy so are the branches'. Even though the immediate reference here is to Israel (to which we must return), Munck is correct to see that this view of Paul applied also to the nations.

Sanders may therefore be correct in his view that no particular agreement had been reached concerning the Jews in the Diaspora. The reason however is not just the urgency of the early Christian mission but the fact that Paul sees himself as apostle to the nations which may mean that whilst he *is* apostle to the Gentiles, his work is not *exclusively limited* to Gentiles, but like Jesus before him, he is willing and able to spend time with individuals who ethnically are outside the main focus of his mission. [26]

Thus far Paul has emerged as a practical missionary who was willing to adjust and revise his mission policies in the light of the Spirit's guidance in the face of the changing circumstances of his ministry. But Paul's awareness of the divine purpose was not simply gleaned from day to day situations in the midst of his churches. Munck has rightly stressed Paul's strong eschatological interest and the apostle's conviction that he is specially called to be the apostle to the (Gentile) nations. Paul was also a serious student of scripture; thus his authorisation for turning to the Gentiles and conducting a mission among them - instead of waiting for the conversion of Israel first - has a basis in scripture as well as in intense reflection upon the significance of success or failure in the proclamation of the Gospel. Hence the wealth of scriptural citation in Rom 9-11. [27]

In the traditional imagery of the end times, the Gentiles were to be blessed as a result of God's blessing upon Israel. Indirectly and derivatively they would share in salvation. As Paul writes Romans, however, two things are crystal clear - Israel as a whole is unbelieving and Paul's mission to the Gentiles is eminently successful. In reflection upon the scriptures Paul has come to realise that it can no longer depend on Israel whether the Gentiles may partake in the blessedness of the kingdom of God, as Jewish apocalyptic doctrine taught. The source of Paul's thought here is his perception of how God throughout Israel's history has used the nations both for Israel's salvation and Israel's correction. In Rom 9 Paul notes how God used Pharaoh no less than Israel to reveal his power and proclaim his mercy because 'he has mercy upon whomever he wills, and he hardens the heart of whomever he wills' (9:18) for 'it depends not upon man's will or exertion but upon God's mercy' (9:20). Thus according to Paul, scripture shows that God can use nations and their leaders both positively and negatively in His purpose of mercy. (28) At times Israel may experience the chastening hand of God's judgment by means of Gentile nations but her ultimate destiny is still the object of His providential purpose.

This is one source of Paul's thinking on the pattern of events in the early Christian mission. The success of the Gentile mission and the relative failure of the Jewish mission caused him to look to scripture for a new understanding of the divine activity. Just as God used the nations or their leaders for the ultimate good of Israel in times past, so now in the present, He will use the nations or Gentiles once again to bring Israel back to Himself. Thus Paul sees himself as indirectly enabling the salvation of Israel while focusing his main attention upon the Gentiles.

There seems to be general agreement that Paul believed that the final restoration of Israel would be the work of God himself. (29) The 'no' of Israel to the Gospel - her partial hardening (11:25) - would persist until the Parousia. All Israel will then be saved (11:26-32) when the fullness (plērōma) of the Gentiles has come in. This has normally been taken to represent 'the full number of the elect from among the Gentiles', but Paul thinks representatively and collectively rather than in terms of elect individuals. As Munck has shown, behind this is the tradition which we find in Mk 13:10 'that the Gospel must first be preached to all nations before the Parousia'. (30) Paul has in mind the conversion of representatives from all the nations, the first fruits of the harvest of redeemed humanity. It is this offering which Paul as apostle to the Gentiles seeks to provide and thus to fulfil the expected pilgrimage of the nations to worship the God of Zion.

One other aspect of Israel's final redemption probably originated from Paul's study of scripture. The final 'yes' of Israel will come after 'the fullness of the nations' but Paul envisages it as happening through jealousy. In the words of Deut 32:21, 'I will provoke them to jealousy with them that are no nation, I will anger them with a nation void of understanding', Paul found a clue as to the means which he believed would be effective in finally turning the Jews to God. (31) When they perceived the blessings enjoyed by Gentiles, they themselves would be jealous when they realised what they were missing. The importance for us of this perception of Paul is not so much in whether history has shown it to be justified, but rather in the fact that he studied the scriptures for guidance in seeking solutions to missionary problems which from a human point of view seemed insurmountable, ie 'the hardening of the Jews'. One question still remains unanswered - what is the relationship between the jealousy resulting from the fullness of the nations and the final conversion of Israel? As we noted, this outcome is generally taken to be by the direct action of God Himself - but the jealousy motif suggests that it is in fact the winning of the representatives from the nations which causes Israel's restoration. The latter fits in better with Paul's own statements and policy which suggest that he sees himself as indirectly contributing to the salvation of Israel.

5. *Unity and Diversity: Paul's Mission in a Pluralist Situation*

Although it appears that Paul's normal practice would be to establish one church for both Jews and Gentiles in each area where he worked, it is possible that there was greater diversity in Rome than was normal because it was a Christian community lacking any one apostolic founder. What is distinctive in this letter is that Paul in chapters 14-15 accepts the right of both 'the weak' and 'the strong' Christians to follow their own consciences.

He calls for tolerance and mutual acceptance, not in the short term only until differences are overcome, but they are to accept one another openly and without reservation as Christ has accepted them. (32) Thus it would appear that although Paul can be somewhat authoritarian and uncompromising when the truth of the Gospel is at stake, as in Galatians, when it is a matter of differing Christians following different lifestyles, he is in fact very tolerant. As far as is humanly possible, he seeks for explicit evidence of Christian oneness in Christ. He is not afraid to indicate that he sides with 'the strong' (15:1), but nevertheless he insists on the freedom of 'the weak' to live differently. This corresponds well with his statements in 1 Cor 7:17, where he outlines his policy that Christians should continue in the calling in which they were called. (33) Thus it seems that in discerning the will of God, Paul was careful to accept as given the situation which originated in Rome either prior to, or independently of, his own mission (rather than trying to undo it). He accepts the diversity as given and as an abiding reality.

His collection project which he has organised over a long period of time is now, as he writes to the Romans, well-nigh complete and he heads for Jerusalem with the collection and representatives of the Gentile churches. This collection is an expression of Paul's concern with unity between the Jewish and Gentile wings of the church. He accepts the Jewish Christians in Jerusalem as brethren, but there is some doubt about whether they will feel free to accept a collection from Gentiles that might compromise them with their Jewish neighbours.

It would appear then that Paul recognised the autonomy of the Christian conscience and was particularly willing to accommodate to the practices of others in a context where his pattern of Christian living differed from that to which these Christians had been originally introduced. Diversity in unity rather than a monochrome uniformity is the model of the church which emerges from Paul's letter to Rome.

6. *Conclusion*

Romans is written after the earlier period of Paul's mission work in which the concordat about respecting separate mission areas and spheres of work had been operative. After Paul lost the battle over table-fellowship between Jews and Gentiles at Antioch, he was forced to branch out as an independent missionary doing pioneer work and concentrating on setting up mixed churches mainly of Gentiles with some Jews who no longer followed a Jewish life-style. [34] But he has now finished all such work in the East and needs the help of the Romans for a mission in the West. [35] The peculiar origin and development of the house churches in Rome meant that there was the possibility that Paul could have been accused of building on another apostle's foundation. But Paul as apostle to the Gentile nations feels called and obligated to come to Rome. In so doing he is forced to consider his own and the Roman Christian's attitude to Christians (and Jews) who differ radically from them.

Paul's theology of mission is thus constructed to meet the demands inherent in this diverse context. The picture of the apostle that emerges here is far from being that of a thoughtless activist rushing around the world under the duress of an overwhelming but unenlightened zeal. We discover instead an apostle pursuing a definite policy which has both an apocalyptic and a scriptural basis. Although Paul may sometimes give the appearance of being somewhat in a strait-jacket, this is certainly not true. He is neither unaware of, nor unwilling to adjust to, changing circumstances in his mission work. Romans shows how seriously and positively he took these into account. Paul looks for divine guidance as to the detailed policy and strategy required to put into practice the divine will in each given situation.

Paul sees himself as called to co-operate with God's universal and cosmic purpose revealed in the Christ-event. His call is thus similar to the prophets of old, and the pattern of divine activity is to be discerned from a study of the scriptures. The final events of salvation will turn out to be a modified version of the hopes expressed by the prophets, especially Second Isaiah. Paul is like the prophets who called Israel to covenant faithfulness, in the context of the nations - whom Yahweh could use to discipline her when unfaithful. But in Romans it is not a question of Israel over against the nations. Nor is it a question of Jew *or* Gentile, but Jew *and* Gentile within the overarching plan of God. The mission of Jesus, like that of Paul according to Romans concerns both Jew and Gentile (15:8-12). Gentile inclusion does not signify the revoking of Israel's heritage (11:29) but rather the way in which Israel will be restored in a renewed covenant which includes Gentiles also. In the renewed covenant there is no need for Gentiles to become Jews and, correspondingly, there is no need for Jews to give up their Jewishness on accepting the Gospel.

In the diversity of the Roman house churches, some of which were possibly loosely attached to synagogues, the renewed covenant demands mutual acceptance in Christ, despite cultural or racial differences. On the one hand this meant that a mainly Gentile house church must be willing to accept a Christian Jew who wanted to worship with them. But it would also mean that if there were Jewish house-churches still in contact with synagogue life and discipline, the churches of the Gentiles must likewise acknowledge such as fellow-members in Christ, despite their differing life-style (and vice-versa). Only thus will all God's beloved in Rome be able to assist in preventing the rejection of Paul and the collection in Jerusalem, and likewise provide the proper missionary support for the new outreach in Spain. Only as the Gentiles are brought to faith will Israel be provoked to emulation and Israel's recovery of faith usher in the eschaton, the resurrection of the dead. (36)

We see thus that in respect of Israel, the covenant, the law and the scriptures, Paul's mission theology is not simply the inbreaking of a new order with the subsequent destruction of the old - it is rather the transformation of the old by Him who makes all things new. (37)

NOTES

The original draft of this paper was prepared in 1985-6 at the request of Professor John Ferguson, then President of the Selly Oak Colleges. It is published here in grateful appreciation and memory of his life and work, particularly at Selly Oak.

1 Cf N A Dahl 'The Missionary Theology in the Epistle to the Romans' *Studies in Paul* Augsburg 1977 p70f. Dahl is one of a small number of scholars who have considered Romans in this light. He stresses that Paul's theology and his missionary activity were inseparable from each other; he characterises Paul's theology as a 'christocentric theology of mission with biblical history and eschatology as its framework' (pp 70-1).

2 In *Paul, the Law and the Jewish People*, Fortress 1983, pp 145f.

3 Cf J C Beker *Paul the Apostle: The Triumph of God in Thought and Life*, Fortress 1980, espec. p92.

4 Cf 'Why did Paul write Romans', Chapter 2 in this volume. Dahl has a different view, 'It is not the problems of a local church but the universal gospel and Paul's own mission which in this letter provide the point of departure for theological discussion' (op cit 78). For other viewpoints see *The Romans Debate* ed by K P Donfried (Augsburg 1977) and Dieter Zeller, *Der Brief an die Römer*, Regensberg 1985, pp 11f.

5 Cf C E B Cranfield *The International Critical Commentary: Romans*, Vol 2, T & T Clark 1979, pp780f.

6 Cf E Käsemann *Commentary on Romans*, SCM 1979, pp 398-404; cf also Robert Jewett, 'Paul, Phoebe and the Spanish Mission' in *The Social World of Early Christianity and Judaism: Essays in Tribute to K C Kee,* ed J Neusner et al, Fortress Press 1988, pp 142-61.

7 Cf Käsemann's comment, 'If Paul is speaking emphatically of "evangelising", all the reservations in vv 10-12 seem to be pointless', op cit p20. Cf Also M Kettunen's comment, 'Rome therefore has its importance for Paul primarily in reference to the journey to Spain', *Der Abfassungszweck des Römersbriefes* (Helsinki, 1979) p161. W Schmithals, because of the apparent conflict between 1:13f and 15:14f, concludes that Paul wrote two letters to Rome, *Der Römerbrief als historisches Problem*, Gütersloh 1975. However, there is little manuscript evidence for his thesis, cf H Gamble *The Textual History of the Letter to the Romans*, Eerdmans 1977.

8 L Gaston 'Paul and Jerusalem' in *From Jesus to Paul* eds P Richardson and J C Hurd, Wilfred Laurier University Press, Waterloo, Ontario 1984, pp 61-73.

9 Cf P Achtemeier *Romans: Interpretation Commentary*, John Knox Press 1985, pp 67f.

10 Cf E Käsemann, op cit p29.

11 Cf Achtemeier, op cit p69.

12 Cf Chapter 3, 'Romans III is a Key to the Structure and Thought of the Letter' p32f.

13 This is not to deny a strong element of discontinuity; see 'Christianity and Judaism: Continuity and Discontinuity', Chapter 6 in this volume pp70f.

14 Cf L Gaston 'Paul and the Torah' in *Antisemitism and the Foundations of Christianity*, ed A T Davies, New York 1979, p66, and Sanders op cit p38.

15 Cf 'The Freedom and Faithfulness of God in Relation to Israel' Chapter 4 in this volume, pp43f.

16 Ibid p33, cf also Achtemeier op cit p165.

17 'Paul and Jerusalem' op cit pp 65-6.

18 R E Brown and J P Meier *Antioch and Rome: New Testament Cradles of Catholic Christianity*, Paulist Press 1983, pp 1- 8.

19 Contra Beker who speaks of a dialogue with Jews op cit p91. Beker does recognise the apologetic element in Romans but puts too much emphasis upon polemic op cit pp 78-83.

7. *Paul's Missionary Practice and Policy in Romans*

20 Cf Sanders op cit pp 185-90. On Paul's conversion cf 'Some Notes on Paul's Conversion' by J Gager, New Testament Studies, 27 (1981), pp 697f.

21 Cf Achtemeier op cit pp 177f.

22 Cf 'The Freedom and Faithfulness of God in Relation to Israel', Chapter 4 in this volume, pp51f.

23 Op cit p189.

24 Cf J Munck *Paul and the Salvation of Mankind* SCM 1959 p52; see also A Hultgren *Paul's Gospel and Mission*, Fortress 1985.

25 Op cit p53f.

26 Ibid.

27 Cf Chapter 4 above. Much research is now being devoted to this aspect of Paul. Cf H Hübner, *Law in Paul's Thought*, T T Clark, Edinburgh 1984 and H Räisänen, *Paul and the Law*, Mohr, Tübingen 1983.

28 Paul's theology derives from the premise that God has consigned (sunekleisen) all to disobedience 'so that He might have mercy upon all (11:32). Cf my article in n15 above (p31).

29 Cf Sanders op cit pp 194-5.

30 Op cit pp 134f, Cranfield op cit p575.

31 Cf Cranfield op cit p 556.

32 Cf R Jewett *Christian Tolerance*, Westminster 1982, p134.

33 Contrary to some recent scholarship, Paul did not force all Jewish Christians to make a complete break with Jewish law, customs etc, cf my article in n15 above, p44, n60; also Cranfield op cit pp 845f and E Larsson 'Paul: Law and Salvation' *New Testament Studies* 31 (1985) pp 425-36; contra F Watson, *Paul, Judaism and the Gentiles*, Cambridge 1986, p100.

34 Cf J D G Dunn, 'The Incident at Antioch', Journal for the Study of the New Testament, 18 (1983) 3-57.

35 Cf R D Aus, 'Paul's Travel Plans to Spain and the "Full Number of the Gentiles" of Rom 11:25', Novum Testamentum 21, (1979) 232-62.

36 R P Martin takes Rom 11:12 (a), Israel's fall into unbelief and riches resulting for the Gentiles (the reconciliation of the world) as the first event leading to the eschaton; the second will be Israel's recovery of faith leading to the resurrection of the dead (Rom 11:15) *Reconciliation: A Study of Paul's Theology*, Marshall, Morgan and Scott (1981) p134.

37 Cf my article 'Salvation for Jews and Gentiles: Krister Stendahl and Paul's Letter to the Romans' *Studia Biblica* 1978 Vol III, Sheffield University Press (1981) pp 65-72.

Chapter 8

Religious Identity and Ethnic Origin in the Earliest Christian Communities

1. *Introduction*

The famous church historian Adolf Harnack writing in the early part of this century raised a question which has re-emerged in the recent discussion of Paul and his relation to Judaism. Harnack questioned whether Paul may not have been forced to tolerate for a time the existence of separate Jewish Christian congregations. Harnack could find no evidence to prove that Paul did not in fact do so. This was for the apostle, however, a temporary measure permitted in the face of weakness, and determined by expediency rather than principle. (1)

In a similar vein, Wilhelm Zoellner, in 1930 opposed a too individualistic interpretation of Ephesians 2:14f and maintained that the issue in this passage is not so much a problem of the individual (Christian), but the problem of whether or not to have separate churches for Jewish Christians and for Gentile Christians. (2)

In its study report 'The Church and the Jewish People' the Faith and Order Commission of the World Council of Churches also discussed the question of separate Jewish Christian congregations. On the basis of Eph 2 the report decided against separation: 'We are not advocating separate congregations for them. History has shown the twofold danger which lies in this: the danger of discriminating despite all intention to the contrary, and the danger that such separate congregations tend to evolve sectarian traits. But more important than these considerations is that in Christ the dividing wall has been broken down and Jew and Gentile are to form one new man; thus any separation in the church has been made impossible'. (3)

The report nevertheless acknowledged the importance of diversity in unity: 'However, without detracting in any way from what has just been said, there is room for all kinds of peoples and cultures in the church. This implies that Jews who become Christians are not simply required to abandon their Jewish traditions and ways of thinking; in certain circumstances it may therefore be right to form special groups which are composed mainly of Jewish Christians'. (4) The hesitation on this issue in the church in the modern period is similarly reflected in the writings of New Testament scholars. W D Davies in his 1976 presidential lecture to the Society for New Testament Studies claimed that 'In Christ Jews remain

Jews and Greeks remain Greeks. Ethnic peculiarities are honoured'. (5) But E P Sanders in his recent book *'Paul, the Law and the Jewish People'* says that this recognition was true 'only so long as ethnic peculiarities did not come into conflict and that when they did, the factors which separated Jews from Greeks had to be given up by the Jews'. (6) Sanders asserts that 'Paul's view of the church, supported by his practice, against his own conscious intention, was substantially that it was a third entity, not because it was composed of both Jew and Greek, but also because it was in important ways neither Jewish nor Greek'. (7) In practice as well as theory the church was separate from Israel. Sanders elaborates: 'If conceptually Paul, despite himself, had to make the church a third entity, it is all the more the case that it was a third entity in concrete social reality... the meetings of the church were not meetings of the synagogue... the Corinthian correspondence shows that the church and synagogue were socially distinct'....(8)

Contemporary multicultural and multifaith issues demand that Christians clarify their thinking and their attitudes on this issue. We need to be clear on the extent of diversity in New Testament times in order to understand and to respond adequately to the pluralism of our own society. But clarity is demanded for another reason.

This is best expressed by Jakob Meuzelaar in his assertion that 'an abolition of all differences in the body of Christ has in the past... again and again led to the Christian view that the Jew as Jew no longer has a right to existence!' (9)

2. *What Paul Would not Tolerate: the Making of Ethnic Distinctions Absolute*

If any one viewpoint may be cited as being most characteristic of Paul many would agree that it is his principle 'there is no distinction' (Rom 3:22 and 10:22). It is the second of these references which is the more precise - 'there is no distinction between Jew and Greek'. Whilst we may generalise on the basis of biblical texts we must be careful to distinguish between what Paul actually said and what we legitimately consider are the implications of his statements. Paul maintains that since the coming of Christ there is no distinction as regards membership of the people of God between Jew and Greek. A third text in Romans, ie ch 2:11 helps to clarify Paul's meaning. Despite his references 'to the Jew first' in this letter, Paul is anxious to maintain the absolute impartiality of God - hence 2:11 'for God shows no partiality'. (10) Thus Jews and Greeks are equally acceptable as members of the eschatological people of God and for both there should be genuine equality regarding membership qualifications. Faith in Christ is the only criterion as regards entry and other requirements such as circumcision for Gentiles must not be added to it.

Essentially Paul's stance as regards 'no distinction' or, to be more precise, 'divine impartiality to Jew and Greek' constitutes an assertion concerning God - it is theology rather than anthropology. It denies ultimate significance to ethnic distinctions rather than their continuing existence. In practice the impartiality of God rules out the possibility of Gentiles being regarded as second class citizens within the church. They are freely accepted in the Gospel as Gentiles and not merely as potential Jews.

Therefore it is a 'sine qua non' of Paul in his relationship with Jewish Christians that they recognise the right of Gentile Christians to continue to live as Gentiles after they have trusted in Christ. Paul could not negotiate on this point - it was a matter of sheer principle. [(11)] To retract on this would be tantamount to acting as if Christ had not come, as if the new age of the Gospel had not arrived.

E P Sanders is doubtless correct in his exegesis of Rom 9:30f. He understands the reason for the Jews' rejection of the Gospel as being not because they sought a *wrong* goal, ie righteousness by works, nor that they sought a *right* goal by the wrong means, ie in a legalistic way. Rather they failed to believe in the Gospel because they sought their own righteousness, ie a righteousness available to Jews *alone*, only to those who possess the law. [(12)] For Paul it is of the essence of the Gospel that it is available to Gentiles on the same terms as Jews. Anyone who denies this cannot be a Christian or if he should think he is, Paul would designate him a 'false brother' because he does not truly recognise Gentile Christians as brothers in Christ (cf Gal 2:4).

Because Paul cannot yield on this point does not mean that he opposed all things Jewish or that he would discourage Jewish Christians from following a Jewish lifestyle after they had become Christians. [(13)] This stipulation that Jewish Christians recognise the right of Gentile Christians to be accepted into the people of God and continue to live a Gentile (Christian) lifestyle, does not mean that such Jewish Christians as recognised this, should not also have the freedom to continue to live in a Jewish life style. New Testament scholars have in the past tended to presume that all Jewish Christians who wished to continue to follow a Jewish life style must necessarily deny the right of Gentile Christians to follow a Gentile lifestyle. But logic does not demand this conclusion. The two positions, ie Jewish Christians continuing to follow a Jewish pattern of life, and Gentile Christians continuing to follow a Gentile pattern of life, are not mutually exclusive.

In the opinion of many Jews and possibly of some Christian Jews, they probably were seen in this light, but in Paul's theology this was definitely not the case. Paul differed from these in that he did not seek a Jewish form of unity within the church, ie one national people, and one law under one God of Israel. (14) It was not Judaism or Jewish Christianity that provided the theology that legitimated a Jewish life style for Jewish Christians. (15) It was in fact Paul's own theology that validated equally the right of Gentiles to live as Gentiles and Jews to live as Jews in Christ. It is to this theology we must now turn.

3. *The Basis of Paul's Ethic of Tolerance: A Concrete Orientation to the Lordship of Christ*

Paul's theology of mission was not an abstract construct dangling from a universal principle. (16) It was in essence both concrete and contextual. In Paul's theology the basis for toleration of diversity within the Christian family is his understanding of faith. Ernest Käsemann describes this as 'a concrete orientation to the Lordship of Christ which grasps it, in which its breadth leaves room for the peculiarities of the members, which does not impose uniformity... No one must make his faith a norm for others as they seek to serve Christ'. Paul's understanding of faith by definition presupposes variety and diversity among Christians. At the same time we must note that Käsemann also interprets Paul in opposition to what he regards as a too individualistic emphasis in Bultmann's existentialist approach. (17)

Robert Jewett has further developed this understanding of faith by paying particular attention to the phrase 'metron pisteōs', measure of faith or measuring rod of faith in Rom 12:3. For him the 'measuring rod of faith' consists in the norm that each person is provided with in the appropriation of the grace of God. Thus faith includes a measuring rod that allows for differentiation. What Paul warns against in Rom 12:3, is either imposing that norm on others or failing to live up to it oneself.

Jewett's contention is that faith for Paul is not a single dogmatic standard as has traditionally been supposed. Faith in Christ has pluralistic possibilities. Each person has a unique norm of faith that should be maintained in integrity. Faith still consists in 'the individual appropriation of grace, but there are political, ideological, racial and temperamental components that are legitimately connected with faith thus comprising the peculiar 'measuring rod' that each person in the church has been given'. (18) To fail to respect the integrity of one's fellow Christian's 'measuring rod of faith' is to absolutise faith by imposing it on others and is in effect to make oneself into God. Tolerance in this understanding of Rom 12-15 rests on the pillar of the autonomous conscience, and it is only when Paul's argument about the individuation of faith is understood that genuinely tolerant unity among Christians is possible. (19) Some would question, however, whether Paul himself was genuinely tolerant in matters of faith.

That Paul's understanding of authority and power has frequently been misunderstood is evident from the conflicting opinions concerning him. Dogmatic and intolerant have been common epithets to describe his personality. Recently the studies by J H Schütz and Bengt Holmberg have enabled a distinction to be drawn between official legitimacy and charismatic authority, and demonstrate that Paul possessed the latter but not the former. (20) This explains why Paul would put his view so strongly to one of his congregations and yet accept that they themselves must make the final decision on local matters. They too were charismatics like Paul himself, (21) even though as their spiritual father, he normally expected from them both loyalty and obedience in the Gospel.

The new sociological understanding of authority and power in the early church, enables us better to appreciate both the diversity and the consequent difficulties within the early Christian communities. (22) Paul despite his critics did not aspire to be God. Freedom was of the essence of his gospel. (23) So Jewish Christians and Gentile Christians would decide for themselves the life style which in conscience they felt called to follow. Their adherence to one group or another would not be determined either by Peter or by Paul or entirely by their ethnic origin; ultimately it would be a matter of personal conviction and of voluntary adherence to one group or another. Even Paul must respect 'the measuring rod of faith' of those who disagreed with him. In this way it can be seen that it is in fact Paul's own theology which legitimates a Jewish Christian life style which he himself may not in fact have actually advocated.

4. *Pluralism in the Early Christian Mission*

In recent scholarship the diversity of the New Testament theologies as well as their unity has been emphasised. (24) A major problem of research is how to enter imaginatively into the missionary situation of Paul's day when most of the New Testament as we now have it had not yet been written.

We have stressed that Paul operated contextually in determining the concrete will of God in any situation. (25) We need now to ask what was the situation prior to Paul's Gentile mission and what was his policy in relating to other apostles and their work. Paul was not the first to proclaim the Gospel to Gentiles nor even the first to allow a Gentile life style for

Christians. (26) The situation in the early days was probably a very fluid one. According to Rom 15:20, Paul made it his ambition to preach the Gospel where Christ had not yet been preached lest he build on another man's foundation. (27) It has too readily been assumed that this 'foundation' refers to a Gentile mission similar in kind to that of Paul, but led by other apostles or evangelists. It would now appear that there may have been much more diversity within the Christian mission than we have previously realised. Evidence in the New Testament of differing policies and practice is found particularly in Gal 2 and the parallel account in Acts 15 of the meeting of the council at Jerusalem.

Bengt Holmberg maintains that the result of Paul's unsuccessful opposition to Peter in the Antioch incident was that 'the church in Antioch was divided into a Jewish and a Gentile section, each observing its own eucharist.' (28) A significant feature in this incident was that Peter's behaviour, even if it did not go against the letter of the Jerusalem Council agreement, was undoubtedly a departure from the custom of the church at Antioch. A mixed church reverts to two separate eucharists. Our question is, would Paul have sought to force a single eucharist upon such a church if this had not been the policy prior to his arrival? It seems that the outcome of the division at Antioch was that Paul separated from Barnabas and launched his own independent mission; in the future he would avoid the repetition of such incidents by going to areas where the Gospel had not yet been preached. (29)

Wherever Paul and his associates conducted their mission work, from the very beginning the church would be a mixed church of Jews and Gentiles. It would appear that once this pattern was established, Paul would not allow any subsequent division to interfere with the oneness in Christ which he regarded as the norm in his churches. But Paul's influence would extend only to his own communities, and in cities such as Antioch and Rome in the churches which were not founded by Paul there would be other kinds of Christian groups. Thus we would expect to find very different situations in these cities from those where the Pauline mission had determined the pattern of Christian living. Raymond E Brown warns against the facile assumption that wherever Paul writes to a church, the Pauline type of Christianity is dominant in that city, thereby depicting the Mediterranean area monochromatically as Pauline in its Christianity. (30)

This brings us to the question of what exactly was agreed at the Council of Jerusalem. In Gals 2, Paul claims that James and Cephas and John gave to Paul and Barnabas the right hand of fellowship, 'that he should go to the Gentiles, and they to the circumcision'. This suggests an ethnographic division of missionary labour, rather than a geographic one. (31) This interpretation does not rule out Paul's preaching to some Jews, nor does it limit Peter to Palestine. But it does open the door to complicated situations for future mission work, (32) especially in areas where there may have been a large population of Jews in a Gentile area as was the case at Antioch and Rome. Problems were also likely to arise from the movement of Christians from one place and one congregation to another. This would enhance the opportunity to change for Christians with a developing theology.

Holmberg in his recent study investigates several possible interpretations of the division of missionary labour which we have noted above. He is sympathetic to the view that 'the mission to the circumcision' could signify 'the mission field belonging to Jerusalem or the Holy Land'. The Jerusalem church would evangelise the Jews of the Holy Land, while the church of Antioch would be entrusted with the Christian mission outside this area, including the Jews of the Diaspora. Other scholars believe that no special consideration was given to the Jews of the Diaspora. Nevertheless Nickle and Holmberg are doubtless correct in describing the division of missionary labour as 'primarily a compromise aimed at making possible the simultaneous co-existence of two missionary enterprises relatively independent of each other'. (33)

According to Holmberg, the Jerusalem Council conceded the Antiochene practice of not circumcising Gentiles who became Christians, and Paul interpreted this as 'an irreversible approval of his own law-free gospel, including his missionary methods and their consequences'. (34) But there were at least three differing interpretations possible (a) Paul's interpretation, as outlined above, as the liberal extreme, (b) the rigorist interpretation of Paul's Judaistic opponents who insisted on circumcision and who, unlike Cephas and James, were unwilling to concede anything to Paul and (c) the interpretation of Cephas, James and Barnabas and the Jerusalem and Antioch churches (or part of them whom they represented). (35)

Raymond Brown has recently maintained that to think only in terms of a two fold division among early Christians is too simplistic and to Holmberg's three fold positions he adds another possible stance. (36) Brown argues that 'during most of the First Century a theological distinction signalled by 'Jewish Christianity' and 'Gentile Christianity' is imprecise and poorly designated'. (37) He believes that one can discern from the New Testament at least four different types of Jewish/Gentile Christianity, stemming from the fact that Jewish Christians of different persuasions converted Gentiles who shared the respective theology of their missionaries. [38]

Type One, consisting of Jewish Christians and their Gentile converts, who insisted on full observance of the Mosaic Law, including circumcision, for those who believed in Jesus. This movement, which originated in Jerusualem, had some success in Galatia and Philippi and perhaps elsewhere. Both Gal 2 and Acts 15 indicate the presence of such people, whom Paul bitterly opposed.

Type Two, consisting of Jewish Christians and their Gentile converts, who did not insist on circumcision but did require Gentiles to keep some purity laws. This movement, which also originated in Jerusalem, was associated with James and Peter. It became the dominant Christianity of Antioch, probably of Rome, and Pontus, Cappadocia and sections of the province of Asia.

Type Three, consisting of Jewish Christians and their Gentile converts who did not insist on circumcision for Gentile Christians and did not require their observing purity laws in regard to food. It is likely that both Group Two and Group Three insisted on Jewish purity laws forbidding marriage among kin since 1 Cor 5:1 and Acts 15:20, 29 are probably rejecting the same form of 'porneia'. Antioch was the original departure point of their mission, and Paul was its most famous representative. According to Acts 20:16, 21:26 and 24:11, this type of Christianity did not entail a break with the cultic practices of Judaism (feasts, temple), nor did it impel Jewish Christians to abandon circumcision and the Law.

Type Four, consisting of Jewish Christians and their Gentile converts who did not insist on circumcision and Jewish food laws and saw no abiding significance in the cult of the Jerusalem Temple. Only this type is properly Hellenist in contrast to the three preceding varieties of 'Hebrew Christianity' and only this type may be considered fully non-law-observant. It began at Jerusalem, spread to Samaria with Philip and eventually to Phoenicia, Cyprus and Antioch. A later more radicalised variety of this type is encountered in the Fourth Gospel and the Epistle to the Hebrews where levitical sacrifice and priesthood are considered abrogated and the feasts have become alien 'feasts of the Jews', so that Judaism has become another religion belonging to the Old Covenant.

Brown has rightly drawn attention to the diversity of the early Christian mission. It may even be possible that a fifth type of Christianity emerged in Rome since Rom 11 seems to indicate the existence of a Hellenist Type Christianity that was self-consciously Gentile. [39] Brown also has rightly alerted scholars to the fact that ethnic affiliation taken on its own is a poor designation of theological stance. We are convinced however that ethnic differences are still very basic to the theological divisions and therefore to identity within the early church.

A crucial text indicating Paul's policy in relation to pluralism is 1 Cor 7:17f 'Only let everyone lead the life which the Lord has assigned to him, and in which God has called him. This is my rule in all the churches. Was anyone at the time of his call already circumcised? Let him not seek to remove the marks of circumcision. Was anyone at the time of his call uncircumcised? Let him not seek circumcision. For neither circumcision counts for anything nor uncircumcision, but keeping the commandments of God'. The only concession Paul makes is that if a slave can gain his freedom, he ought to avail himself of the opportunity. The references here are specifically to circumcision but the general thesis is that each one should continue in the type of Christian vocation into which he was first called. This would appear not only to acknowledge different forms of Christian life but also to confirm their validity as an on-going pattern and not merely as a way of life soon to be outgrown. Robert Jewett sees a development between Corinthians and Romans in connection with the eating of meat. 'The difference between Corinthians and Romans at this point is really quite substantial. Whereas Paul developed a plan in Corinthians to gradually overcome elements of pluralism, his programme in Rome is to allow that pluralism to stand on a permanent basis'. (40)

We do not wish to pursue the question of the difference between the two letters but simply to use Jewett's insight in relation to Romans. This indicates that by the time of writing his last major letter Paul had developed a policy which both allows and affirms the continued existence of pluralism within the church. That pluralism, we wish to maintain, included groups of Jewish Christians who wished to, and who were permitted to, continue to live a Jewish life style after they became Christians.

5. *Two New Testament Texts which apparently Indicate the Obliteration of Distinction between Jew and Gentile in Christ*

(a) *Gals 3:26-29*

In this passage it has been argued, we have evidence that Paul and probably even his predecessors sought to obliterate the distinctions between Jew and Gentile within the Christian community. There is substantial agreement that Gal 3:28 emerges from a pre-Pauline baptismal tradition. (41) 'Form-critical analyses converge in the delineation of Gal 3:26-28 and its classification as a baptismal confession quoted by Paul' says Elizabeth Schüssler Fiorenza in her recent study on this passage. (42)

Wayne Meeks interprets Gal 3:28 in the light of the myth of androgyny that was widespread in Hellenism, Judaism and especially in gnosticism. Basic to his view is the image of the new man renewed in the image of his creator (Gal 3:10 and certain gnostic texts). Meeks takes Paul to mean by 'neither male nor female', 'the eschatological restoration of man's original, divine androgynous image'. (43)

Brinsmead in his study of Gal 3:28 discusses it in relation to 1 Cor 12:13 and Gal 3:10-11 where similar statements occur. (44) He believes that the same formula is behind Paul's statements in 1 Cor 12:13 and that in fact it may have been Paul's enthusiastic baptism statement in Gals 3:28 which contributed to the Corinthian excesses. But on account of the particular self-understanding on the part of the Corinthian Christians who claim to have attained the androgynous state, Paul deliberately omits the male female reference in Cor 12. (45) It seems, therefore, we have evidence here of a belief widespread in early Christianity which probably was related to the dominical saying in Matt 22:30 'For in the resurrection they neither marry nor give in marriage, but are like angels in heaven'. (46)

The fact that Paul cites an earlier formula may mean that he explicitly agrees with it, or that the Galatians used it, or that his opponents were making capital out of it. It is likely that if the latter were the main reason for Paul's reference, then this formula would not be as characteristic of Paul's theology as we might expect, and that we ought to examine the context carefully to discern what Paul means by it and how he makes use of it, particularly in the light of several recent studies on Galatians.

Fiorenza sets out the baptismal announcement which Paul uses in Gal 3:26-28 as follows. (47)

i)	3:26	(a)	For you are all children of God
ii)	3:27	(a)	For as many as were baptised into Christ
		(b)	Have put on Christ
iii)	3:28	(a)	There is neither Jew nor Greek
		(b)	There is neither slave nor free
		(c)	There is no male and female
iv)	3:28	(d)	For you are all one

It is important to note that the third and final pair of the baptismal pronounciation differs in formulation from the preceding two, in so far as it does not speak of opposites but of male *and* female.

H D Betz in his recent major commentary on Galatians considers Gal 3:26-29 to be 'the goal towards which Paul has been driving all along'. (48) In his study of Galatians R B Hays rightly notes that the central section of the letter 3:1-4:11, in which our formula occurs, should be read as a coherent whole on its own terms. Verses 26-29 are not only the goal towards which, but also the premise on which, Paul argues throughout 3:6-25. The argument essentially is that Christians are one with Christ and share his destiny. (49) N A Dahl outlines the development of the thesis in the chapter as follows. In Gal 3:6-9 Paul begins with the image of Abraham as the father and model for believers. But in 3:13-19 he proceeds to use an exegetical tradition in which Jesus alone is the promised messianic offspring of Abraham - the heir to the inheritance. Then in 3:26-29 Paul weaves together these two strands of thought and interprets baptism with reference to Gen 1:27 to conclude that Christ, as the image of God, is the prototype of redeemed mankind, the new creation. Gentiles who in baptism have put on Christ are therefore Abraham's offspring and heirs of the promise. (50)

It is our conclusion therefore that in the Galatian context, the unification-saying in 3:28 is being used polemically against 'a competing interpretation in which the angelic state was purported to be actualised in some other way - that is, by a sacramental system based on Jewish calendrical laws, climaxed and epitomised by circuncision'. (51)

In opposition to this, Paul argues that in baptism, believers put on Christ - they are initiated into the climax of the Christian faith, baptism is both beginning and ending. Ch 3:27-29 functions within this debate; Paul here claims a sacramental realisation of eschatological deliverance without reservation.

(52) Thus in Christ, the divisions of the fallen human order and even of the original creation are overcome and healed. That is why neither circumcision nor uncircumcision means anything, but new creation (Gal 6:15). (53)

It would appear, therefore, that it is the specific context Paul addresses in Galatians that causes him to introduce an apparently over-realised eschatology, such as he later has to oppose in Corinthians. In practice, despite what Gals 3:28 may appear to claim, all distinctions between Jew and Gentile, male and female were not disregarded entirely within the Christian communities. This is not to suggest that baptismal proclamations had *no* social consequences. As Fiorenza notes, 'a slave woman who became a Christian in the First Century heard this baptismal pronunciation as a ritual 'performative utterance' which not only had the power to shape 'the symbolic universe' of the Christian community but also determined the social inter-relationships and structures of the church'. (54) Fiorenza continues, 'that such an expectation of free status on the grounds of baptism was not merely excessive enthusiasm is apparent if we look at the first opposite of the baptismal-formula, Jew-Greek'. (55) That such 'religious equality' had social-ecclesial consequences for the inter-relationship of Jewish and Gentile Christians is apparent from the Antioch incident. Moreover since it was no longer circumcision but baptism which was the primary rite of initiation, this meant that women could become full members of the people of God and this generated a fundamental change. 'While one was *born* into Judaism... in baptism Christians entered into a kinship relationship with people of very different racial, cultural and national backgrounds... and therefore both Jewish and Gentile women's status and role were drastically changed'. (56) Despite Meek's interpretation, Fiorenza interprets 'no longer male and female' in terms of the first couple (cf Mark 10:6) and not in terms of an androgynous being. 'As such, Gal 3:28c does not assert that there are no longer men and women in Christ, but that patriarchal marriage - and sexual relationships between male and female - is no longer constitutive of the new community in Christ. Irrespective of their procreative capacities and of the social roles connected with them, persons will be full members of the Christian movement in and through baptism'. (57)

Fiorenza also considers Paul's interpretation and adaption of the baptismal declaration of Gal 3:28 in his letters to the community of Corinth. Here he unequivocally affirms the equality and charismatic giftedness of women and men in the Christian community. Women as well as men are prophets and leaders of worship in the community. Women as well as men have mutual rights and obligations within the sexual relationships of marriage. (58) But 'Paul's impact on women's leadership in the Christian movement is double-edged. On the one hand he affirms equality and freedom. He opens up a new independent life style for women by encouraging them to remain free of the bondage of marriage, and restricts their rights not only as 'pneumatics' but also as 'women', for we do not find such explicit restrictions on the behaviour of men *qua* men in the worship assembly'. (59) The unfortunate outcome of this was that the post-Pauline and pseudo-Pauline tradition drew out these restrictions in order to change the equality in Christ between women and men, slaves and free, into a relationship of subordination in the household. (60)

What is clear, however, is that even if there is debate concerning Galatians 3:28, certainly in Corinthians Paul retains the distinction between male and female for the sake of missionary success and for the unity and well-being of the church. We believe that in a different context the same would also apply to Christian Jews and Gentiles. Paul was not indifferent to, or unaware of, the differences between Jewish and Gentile Christians. We conclude therefore that Robin Scroggs puts Paul's position correctly when he declares 'Paul wanted to eliminate the inequality between the sexes, while the gnostics wanted to eliminate the distinction between the sexes'. [(61)] Robert Jewett takes a similar view when he states 'the authentic Pauline letters move on to a progression that leads to a full acknowledgement of equality, while maintaining an insistence on the divinely given quality of sexual difference'. [(62)] Thus, despite what our baptismal formula seemed to suggest, sexual differences are not eliminated within the Christian community, even if for a time in the earliest days some Christians attempted to make it their ideal. There is no need to argue that the social relationships of slave and master were abolished even though they must have been modified between Christians. It would seem obvious therefore that although the inequality between Jew and Gentile was absolutely negated and abolished within the Christian communities, nevertheless distinctions between Jewish and Gentile Christians did remain, [(63)] were permitted, and most likely resulted in certain areas in distinctive Jewish-Christian congregations.

Although we do not mean to suggest there is anything like an exact parallel, we have already argued that Paul's theology is based on the concrete situation and, in this instance, being born a Jew is similar at least to being born a woman. [(64)] In both cases Paul refuses to allow any claims to superiority but this does not necessitate a complete disregard for, nor any reluctance towards accommodation to, sexual and ethnic differences.

(b)*Ephesians 2:11-22*

We are not concerned here to give an exegesis or interpretation of this entire passage but only with one theme which is at the centre of it - that is 'the one new man' of v 15 'hena kainon anthrōpon'. Although Ephesians is probably not by Paul, it is certainly Pauline in thought and its theology certainly merits consideration on this point. We are really asking one main question: does Ephesians, in other respects a very Pauline letter, suggest that the differences between Jews and Gentiles are abolished in one new humanity which is the church? In our discussion here we are very grateful for the very thorough studies of Ephesians by Markus Barth and, more recently, by William Rader of Ephesians 2:11-22. [(65)]

We noted in the introduction to this essay that E P Sanders claimed that Paul, against his better intention, had to make the church 'a third entity'. Clement of Alexandria was probably the first Christian to use the phrase 'new man' to refer to the people formed out of Jews and Gentiles, [(66)]

although he does not simply equate the 'new man' with the church. Clement's successor, Origen interpreted the dividing wall of Eph 2:14 in two ways - as that between men and angels as well as that which divided Jews and Gentiles. The early church fathers who used Eph 2:11-22 in combating Gnostic views emphasised two themes - the flesh and blood manhood of Jesus Christ, and the continuity of the church with Israel, the latter being the more important theme. (67) In opposing Gnostic views the fathers tended simply to accept their opponent's identification of the new man with Jesus, overlooking the context which indicates that the new man is the unity of Jews and Gentiles. But Origen also developed the concept of Christ as Cornerstone, uniting Jews and Gentiles. (68)

It would appear that for the fathers of the first three centuries, Ephesians 2:11-22 witnessed primarily to the continuity of the church with Israel; but thereafter commentators began to put more weight on discontinuity with Israel, and the church tended to understand itself as 'the church of the Gentiles' rather than as 'the church out of Jews and Gentiles'.(69)

It was John Chrysostum in his commentary, who more than any other, stressed the discontinuity between the church and Israel. (70) Although in the West, Augustine emphasised the continuity of the church with Israel more than the discontinuity, in the East Chrysostum's interpretation dominated. The latter had a certain antipathy against Jews which was expressed much more harshly and forcibly in his sermons against them. He therefore assumes that 'the commonwealth of Israel' (Eph 2:12) is not the empirical Jewish community but a 'heavenly commonwealth'. He could not avoid admitting that the promise was made specifically to Jews, but he adds immediately 'they were unworthy'. More significantly, Chrysostum repeatedly emphasises that in Christ the Gentile is not joined to the Jew but both are lifted to a new status. The uniting of the two is accomplished by completely removing the differences between them. For Chrysostum both Jew and Gentile become a third entity - the Christian. His interest was not in the relationship between Jews and Gentiles, but chiefly in the relationship of the individual with God. Unfortunately the main outlines of this approach have dominated interpretation over the centuries. (71)

In the nineteenth century many writers used the term 'higher unity' to describe the situation in which the hostility between Jew and Gentile was overcome. Behind this probably lies F C Baur's Hegelian view that Ephesians presents Christianity as 'a unity standing above the antitheses of Jew and Gentile'. According to Baur, 'as the distinction between Jews and

Gentiles was cancelled in the unity of the new man, so Christianity stands above Gentilism and Judaism as the absolute religion'. (72) This higher unity was probably conceived by Baur as implying the rejection of membership in a particular racial or national community - the universalism of Christianity was considered at odds with the particularism of Judaism and for some at least, the higher unity simply meant that Christians were superior to Jews. In later periods, a certain evolutionary hypothesis of human development was sometimes associated with this theme. (73) But the most serious legacy of Baur was the view that since Christianity is the absolute religion, then Judaism (and Gentilism) must be negatively related to it.

In the twentieth century the question of the unity of the church in relation to race and nation arose acutely with the so-called 'Aryan paragraph', a regulation introduced in 1933 according to which Jewish Christians were denied the right to serve as pastors in the church in Germany. This was part of the new National-Socialist Government's programme to keep non-Aryans from public office. Dietrich Bonhoeffer spoke out against this regulation, maintaining that the exclusion of Jewish Christians from fellowship in congregations of Gentile Christians, violates the nature of the church. (74)

The Margburg Theological Faculty also opposed the Aryan paragraph, claiming that any Christian who does not recognise full unity between Jewish and non-Jewish Christians in the church and who does not want to actualise this unity in the constitution of the church, deceives himself both with regard to Christ and to the scriptures. Rudolf Bultmann declared that no classifications of people whether based on modern or ancient concepts can be used to separate members of the church. (75)

In answer to the argument that there were separate congregations of Jewish Christians in New Testament times, the Marburg faculty replied that the separation was on doctrinal, not racial grounds. The separated congregations were those of Jewish Christians who required as a basis of entrance the observance of the law. Also they were not forced by the Gentile Christians to be separate, but stayed separate by their own conviction, the practice of which excluded other Christians. (76)

In contrast to the Marburg faculty, the Erlangen faculty supported the Aryan paragraph on the grounds that one's membership in a particular people is a divine command for loyalty to that people - the biological tie is to be acknowledged by Christians in attitude and deed. They pointed out that the Reformers not only recognised national characteristics but actually promoted them. (77) The reason for the position taken above is that some Christians sincerely believed that a general emphasis upon the universality of the church actually made it irrelevant to life, where the diversity of nation, culture, race and sex is significant. Bonhoeffer opposed this view whilst acknowledging its sincere concerns. The church needs human differences and therefore different kinds of people must not be kept apart from one another. The nature of the church requires diversity and therefore in the church 'Jew remains Jew, Gentile Gentile... the church is not the fellowship of people of the same kind, but rather precisely of strangers, who are called by the word'. (78) For Bonhoeffer 'the contrasts remain, they even become sharper' in Christ. (79)

This overview of the history of interpretation has highlighted some of the issues involved in the understanding of the 'new man' of Ephesians 2. The most substantial treatment of the theme in recent times is that by Markus Barth and it is to this that we must now turn. Barth specifically stresses the social dimension of Ephesians. By virtue of the fact that the letter is addressed to Gentile Christians and yet the author refers to himself and others as 'we', indicates that a continuing difference between Jewish and Gentile Christians was recognised. Like the very early fathers, Barth interprets Ephesians 2 primarily in terms of the church's continuity with Israel. (80) Like Bonhoeffer, he maintains that 'the new man' is not constituted by the abolition or denial of differences between Jews and Gentiles, but the 'new man' is constituted by the ending of the hostility between Jew and Gentile and by their common worship of the father. Barth opposes translations of the 'one new man' such as 'new humanity', new nature, or 'new personality' because they give the impression that out of two (old) *things*, a new *thing* was made. But the text speaks only of the creation of a new person, 'a single new man' and he relates this to Gal 3:28 arguing that the translation there also should be 'you are all one *person*, not one *thing*, since the Greek uses the masculine gender. Barth concludes that no other person can be meant here except the 'bride of Christ'. (81)

Thus for Barth it is precisely in the joint worship of the Father by Jews and Gentiles that reconciliation consists. 'Among the NT books, Ephesians alone calls God's covenant partner 'one new man' and emphasises that this man consists of two, that is of Jews and Gentiles'. (82) Although Barth holds that Gentiles are incorporated into Israel - they are not absorbed so as to lose their identity, and Jews likewise. 'Their historic distinction remains true and recognised even within their communion...' (83) Eph 2:15 proclaims that the people of God is different from a syncretistic mixture of Jewish and Gentile elements. 'The members of the church are not so equalised, levelled down, or straightjacketed in a uniform, as to become a 'genus tertium' that would be different from both Jews and Gentiles'. (84)

The social dimension of Barth's interpretation originates from this view of continuing diversity within the church. To enjoy unity in diversity means not imposing the privileges or preferences of the one group upon the other and hence creates genuine tolerance. 'Above all, the joining of "the two" into the "one new" whole reveals that neither of the two can possess salvation, peace, life, without the other'. " In the Messiah" and under His rule, there is no resurrection and ascension except together with one's neighbour. Thus the "one new man" is created to be a social being. New existence is social existence'. (85)

Barth goes on to argue that the unity of Eph 2:11-22 refers not only to the uniting of Jewish Christians with Gentile Christians but rather to the unity of the church out of Jews and Gentiles with Israel. We will not explore this further dimension here as it adds nothing to the argument we are proposing, although it is perfectly in accord with it. (86)

Our survey of the various understandings of the 'one new man' is I believe adequate to substantiate our view that Eph 2:15, as we have similarly argued in respect of Gal 3:28, does not deny that Jews can remain Jews even within the church.

6. *Conclusion*

Christian identity must clearly and unequivocally be determined by Christ. But that allegiance is neither static, nor does it exist in a theological, cultural or ethnic vacuum. The very fact that it is commitment to Christ means that the identity of any Christian group must always be subject to change, to the guidance of the Holy Spirit. In this commitment nothing is absolutely sacred, not even one's identity. (87)

A study of the New Testament plainly indicates that there was a major dispute in the early church about whether or not Christians should, or even could, lead a Jewish life style. Our study has shown that in the earliest days a division of labour was recognised by the Christian leaders that was most likely ethnographic in basis. Paul was to go to the Gentiles, Peter to the Jews. Thus ethnic distinctions were acknowledged but only within the 'umbrella' of the one Christian mission which was very diverse in its operation. The concern about unity and its maintenance is evident from the fact that Jerusalem got itself involved in the conflict at Antioch. But it is also evident in Paul, who despite his pains to stress independence from Jerusalem, is also concerned to demonstrate the recognition and acceptance of his work among Gentiles by the 'pillars' of the church. Moreover he himself spent a lot of time and energy organising the collection from his Gentile congregations for the poor saints in Jerusalem.

For Paul the church in Jerusalem is still the source and centre not only of the churches in Palestine, but of *all* the churches.

We have concluded that Jewish Christian congregations probably did exist given the relative pluralism of the early Christian mission. These were not merely tolerated by Paul but actually justified by his particular understanding of the charismatic endowment of the Spirit. This meant that Paul and his co-workers regarded such congregations (and in fact all Christian congregations) not as the outcome of compulsory ethnic segregation but as voluntary associations based upon theological conviction.

Paul was absolutely opposed to the view that Gentile Christians should be forced to become Jewish proselytes. Eph 2 shows how Gentile Christians acquire through Christ all that proselyte status purported to offer. The existence of Jewish Christian congregations was not in conflict with Paul's stand on this principle. Jewish exclusivism and superiority are entirely ruled out by Paul. Ethnic distinctions are not disregarded, but neither are they ultimate nor to be regarded as absolute. The only ultimate is the new creation.

In practice, there was probably great fluidity and diversity concerning the relationship between those Christians and Jewish and those of Gentile origin in the earliest period of the church. Christians of Jewish origin would certainly be welcome, provided their convictions allowed them to join congregations whose members followed a Gentile-Christian life style. Alternatively, given the limited geographical distribution of large concentrations of Jews in the ancient world, and the rapid spread of Gentile Christianity, there would be few places where Jewish Christian congregations (following a Jewish life style) were the only Christian assembly available. (88) In most cases Christians of Gentile origin would neither wish to, nor be forced to, join a congregation following a Jewish-Christian life style. In general, individual convictions would be respected, but the diversity and the fluidity would demonstrate that although ethnic distinctions were acknowledged, they were neither ultimate, nor absolutely binding for all Christians.

Thus pluralism existed within Christianity from the very beginning and pluralism without pressure to conform was the ideal, even if it was not always or everywhere the actual practice. Faith in Christ was not without differentiation and mutual tolerance was encouraged by Paul. The longing for eschatological unity and cosmic reconciliation of all things did not negate the continuing existence of Christians as Jew or Gentile, male or female. So too the goal of a new humanity was not, in the early centuries, perceived as inaugurating a third race that is neither Jewish nor Gentile.

Then as now, it is precisely in the reconciliation of differing peoples, of Jews and Gentiles - that the grace of God is made visible. Reconciliation consists not in the elimination but rather in the overcoming of differences in Christ. Its goal is the eradication of the hostility that springs from differences.

Our conclusions are relevant for the church in contemporary society. Is the ideal or goal of the church a monochrome humanity that has no identifiable regional or national character? Are Christians naively hoping for an ecumenism that is culture-free, an international Christian culture that transcends the weaknesses and limitations of local cultures and national characteristics? Christian unity does demand that all Christians recognise each other as brothers in Christ, but does it demand that all the brothers look alike, behave alike or perhaps even think alike? Unity and uniformity must be clearly differentiated. (89)

This essay also leads us to consider the attitude of Christians to the diversity of faith in a pluralist society and especially to the Jews. In recent times Christians have proved more open to the possibility of those Jews who have become Christians continuing to live as Jews after they have acknowledged Christ, (although these are not my concerns in this essay). This same willingness must be extended back to earliest Christianity also. It is now necessary to acknowledge that in theory at least, it was possible then for Christians to continue to live as Jews as well as Christians. This is necessary because our response to this issue is indicative of our understanding of the element of continuity between Christianity and Judaism. There has always been debate concerning the measure of appropriation or rejection of Judaism within Christianity and one's attitude to the question of separate Jewish Christian congregations in the earliest period is a key indicator of one's response on the wider issue. (90) For Christians it is a major test of their tolerance and maturity to acknowledge positively the continuing existence of Judaism within and without the Christian tradition. Hence the point of this chapter.

NOTES

This chapter originated from a seminar paper read at the International Association for the History of Religions 15th Congress held at the University of Sydney, August 1985.

1 *Die Mission und Ausbreitung des Christentums, Leipzig 1924, p69.*

2 'Die Kirche nach dem Epheserbrief', in *Die Kirche im Neuen Testament in ihrer Bedeutung für die Gegenwart*, ed F Siegmund-Schultze, Berlin, 1930, pp13 ff.

3 *Faith and Order Studies, 1964-1967*, Geneva 1968, p73.

4 Ibid.

5 'Paul and the People of Israel', New Testament Studies 24, (1977), p23, now included in W D Davies, *Jewish and Pauline Studies*, Fortress 1984, pp 123-152 (139).

6 *Paul, the Law and the Jewish People*, Fortress 1983, p178.

7 Op cit p178-9.

8 Op cit p176-8.

9 *Der Leib des Messias*, Assen 1961, p86.

10 Cf J M Bassler, *Divine Impartiality: Paul and a Theological Axiom* SBL Dissertation Series 59, Scholars Press 1982.

11 Cf E Käsemann, *Commentary on Romans*, ET, SCM 1980, pp 91f especially p104, 123 and 254.

12 Op cit pp 36-41. For a full discussion of Rom 9:30f see C E B Cranfield, *Romans: International Critical Commentary*, Vol 2, Edinburgh 1979, pp 503f.

13 Cf Paul Meyer, 'Romans 10:4 and the End of the Law', in *The Divine Helmsman*, Ktav, New York, 1980, p66; W D Davies, 'Paul and the People of Israel', op cit pp 140f and C E B Cranfield op cit pp 340, 519 and 852f.

14 Cf Peder Borgen, 'Thoughts on Christian Unity in the New Testament', in *Paul Preaches Circumcision and Pleases Men*, Tapir Publishers, Trondheim 1983, pp 131-54.

15 Cf C K Barrett's, 'If Paul believed that any obligation lies upon Christians, it will not be a legal obligation; its foundation and sanction will have to be found elsewhere, '*Freedom and Obligation* SPCK London, 1985, p16; Cf also E Käsemann op cit p379 and his essay, 'Worship and Everyday Life', *New Testament Questions of To-Day*, SCM, 1969, pp189- 95.

16 Cf D Senior and C Stuhlmueller, *The Biblical Foundations for Mission*, SCM, 1983, p171.

17 *Commentary on Romans*, op cit p379, and *New Testament Questions of To-Day*, op cit pp 1-22 and 168-82. See also J Koenig, *Charismata: God's Gifts for God's People*, Westminster Press 1978, pp 108f and J Schütz, *Paul and the Anatomy of Apostolic Authority*, Cambridge 1975, p237 n1.

18 Cf *Christian Tolerance: Paul's Message to the Modern Church*, Westminster Press, Philadelphia 1982, pp 62f. Markus Barth has consistently stressed the social function of doctrine in Paul, cf 'Jews and Gentiles: The Social Character of Justification in Paul', Journal of Ecumenical Studies, V, (1968) 241-67. N A Dahl claims that 'Paul does not present the doctrine of justification as a dogmatic abstraction', 'The Doctrine of Justification: Its Social Function and Implications', *Studies in Paul*, Augsburg 1977, p115.

19 Cf R Jewett, op cit pp 65-67.

20 For Schütz see n. 16 above. B Holmberg, *Paul and Power: The Structure of Authority in the Primitive Church as Reflected in the Pauline Epistles*, Lund and Fortress 1980. Cf also E Best, *Paul and his Converts,* Clark, Edinburgh, 1988; although he does not deal specifically with Romans, Best

rightly emphasises the element of reciprocity between Paul and his converts.

21 Cf J Schütz op cit p258 and J Koenig op cit pp 48f and 108ff.

22 In addition to Schütz and Holmberg see also G Theissen, *The Social Setting of Pauline Christianity*, T T Clark 1982; Wayne Meeks, *The First Urban Christians*, Yale, 1983; H C Kee, *Social Aspects of Early Christianity*, SCM 1980; E Schüssler-Fiorenza, *In Memory of Her*, SCM 1983 and J H Elliott, *A Home for the Homeless: A Sociological Exegesis of 1 Peter*, Fortress 1981.

23 Cf E Käsemann, *Romans* Section IV, pp 131-252.

24 Eg E Käsemann, 'Unity and Diversity in New Testament Ecclesiology', Novum Testamentum VI (1963), pp 290-97, and J D G Dunn, *Unity and Diversity in the New Testament*, SCM 1977.

25 Cf J C Beker's emphasis upon contingency and coherence in Paul the Apostle: The Triumph of God in *Life and Thought*, Fortress 1980.

26 Cf Sanders op cit pp 179-191, Holmberg op cit p69.

27 Cf Borgen op cit pp 49-54, Holmberg op cit p46.

28 Op cit pp 32-34.

29 Cf Holmberg op cit p31.

30 *Antioch and Rome: New Testament Cradles of Catholic Christianity* by R E Brown and J P Meier, Paulist Press 1983, p8.

31 On this see Holmberg op cit pp 30f and E P Sanders op cit pp 186-7.

32 Op cit pp 151-154.

33 K F Nickle, *The Collection: A Study in Paul's Strategy*, London 1966, p45, Holmberg op cit pp 30-33.

34 Op cit p20.

35 Op cit p21. Holmberg rightly notes that the presence of Jewish Christian missionaries in Pauline church areas in not necessarily evidence of *intentional* meddling by the Jerusalem church, whose agents may have abused their authority op cit pp 44-47.

36 'Not Jewish Christianity and Gentile Christianity, but Types of Jewish/Gentile Christianity', Catholic Biblical Quarterly 45, 1983, pp 74-79. This article is similar to the introduction to *Antioch and Rome* (cf n. 30 above).

37 Op cit p75.

38 In the above article, Brown refers to these as 'Types' but in his section of the book, also referred to above, he speaks of 'Groups'. This may reflect a certain ambiguity on his part. He recognises that there may be many more 'diversities' in NT Christianity, but he claims that at least these are solidly verifiable. (*Antioch and Rome p8*).

39 C K Barrett speaks of 'five lines of preaching', op cit pp 16 and 99-102. I have developed my views on this theme in an unpublished paper, 'The Roman Christian Community: The Spectrum of Jewish-Gentile Christianity at Rome', presented at the SBL annual meeting, Dallas 1983.

Cf also W D Davies essay, 'Paul and the Gentiles: A Suggestion concerning Romans 11:13-24', in *Jewish and Pauline Studies*, Fortress 1984, pp 153-63.

40 Op cit p134. We do not interpret the 'welcoming one another' and 'praising God with one voice' of Rom 15 as necessarily demanding only one identical type of Christian congregation. Modern Christians tend too readily to think anachronistically of one large congregation of people worshipping together in one church building.

41 Fiorenza and Betz note Pauline additions but there is a general agreement that the core of the traditional formula is 3:28 a/b/c; cf Fiorenza op cit pp 208f; cf also H D Betz, *Galatians: A Commentary on Paul's Letter to the Churches in Galatia*, Hermeneia, Fortress 1979, pp181-201; Bernard H Brinsmead, *Galatians: Dialogical Response to Opponents*, SBL Dissertation Series 65, Scholars Press 1982, pp 146f, and Richard B Hays, *The Faith of Jesus Christ*, SBL Dissertation Series 56, Scholars Press 1983, p29.

42 Op cit p208.

43 'The Image of the Androgyne: Some Uses of a Symbol in Earliest Christianity', History of Religions, 13, 1974, pp 165ff (197).

44 Op cit p157.

45 Op cit pp 146-161; cf also Fiorenza, op cit p211.

46 Cf Brinsmead op cit p155, Fiorenza op cit pp 208f.

47 Op cit p208.

48 Op cit p181.

49 Op cit p 232-5.

50 Cf N A Dahl, 'Promise and Fulfilment', *Studies in Paul*, p133.

51 Cf Brinsmead op cit p156.

52 'He (Paul) appears to border on enthusiasm', Brinsmead op cit pp 141f.

53 It is striking that when Paul in 1 Cor 7:19 repeats this statement the phrase 'a new creation' is replaced by 'keeping the commandments of God'. It is also significant that in 1 Cor Paul is at pains to reassert the distinction between male and female in 11:2-16 and 14:33 (b) - 36. Cf Meeks op cit pp 200-202.

54 Op cit p210. P Perkins disagrees and states '...evidence suggests that the equality of all "in Christ", which is a sign of the new creation, was not understood to be a project that was to be translated into the social sphere of the old creation', *Ministering in the Pauline Churches*, Paulist Press 1982, p60.

55 Op cit p210.

56 Op cit pp 210-211.

57 Ibid.

58 Op cit p235.

59 Op cit p236.

60 Ibid.

61 'Paul and the Eschatological Woman', Journal of the American Academy of Religion Supplements 40, 1972, pp283f.

62 'The Sexual Liberation of the Apostle Paul', Journal of the American Academy of Religion Supplements 47, (i), 1979, p74f.

63 We find a parallel here with Jewett's summary of the male-female debate... 'It seems that Paul was struggling to maintain two seemingly contradictory points: differentiation of sexual identity on the one hand and equality of honour and role on the other', (op cit pp 74f). There is debate amongst scholars as to whether household codes had to be introduced to deal with the excesses of women and slaves which threatened the stability of the Pauline churches, cf J Crouch, *The Origin and Intention of the Colossian Haustafel*, Göttingen 1972, p144; more recently see David Verner, *The Household of God: The Social World of the Pastoral Epistles*, SBL Dissertation Series 71, Scholars Press 1983.

64 Cf Wayne Meeks comments, 'The social implications of continuing or abandoning Jewish ritual practices must have been at least as important, both for the various opponents of Paul and for Paul himself, as theological and Christological beliefs. For Paul, of course, the pragmatic factors were inseparable from the theology and Christology', *The First Urban Christians*, p223 n41.

65 M Barth, *Ephesians*, Anchor Bible 34, New York 1974, and W Rader, *The Church and Racial Hostility: A History of the Interpretation of Ephesians 2:11-22*, Mohr 1978.

66 Cf Rader op cit p16.

67 Cf Rader op cit pp 20f.

68 Ibid.

69 Cf Rader op cit p51.

70 Cf Rader op cit p52.

71 Cf Rader op cit pp 32-35.

72 Cf Rader op cit pp 171f.

73 Rader says that such commentators 'since they believe that after becoming a Christian, a Jew remains a Jew and a Gentile remains a Gentile, are inclined to consider Jew and Gentile as representing positive aspects of human life', op cit p172.

74 Cf Rader op cit p214.

75 Cf Rader op cit p214-5.

76 Cf Rader op cit p217.

77 Cf Rader op cit pp218-9.

78 Cf Rader op cit p220.

79 Ibid.

80 Op cit pp 292 and 310f. On the meaning of 'new' in the NT cf Chapter 6 in this volume, pp72f.

81 Op cit p309 and 295f.

82 Op cit p310. For an alternative interpretation of Eph 2, cf A Lincoln,"The Church and Israel in Ephesians 2," CBQ, 49 (1987), pp601-27: but see also NA Dahl, "Gentiles, Christians, Israelites in the Epistle to the Ephesians,"

in *Christians among Jews and Greeks: Festschrift for Krister Stendahl,* ed GWE Nicklesburg et al, Fortress, Philadelphia, 1986, pp31-39.

83 Op cit p310.

84 Ibid. The uniqueness of Eph 2 is that it contains both the concepts of the people of God and the body of Christ. The former forces us to consider the church in historical perspective. If this is not done, an exclusive concentration on the idea of the body of Christ may lend support to antisemitism. Cf Rader op cit p247.

85 Op cit pp 34 and 311.

86 Op cit pp 34 and 270. Cf also Rader op cit pp 225f. It could of course be argued that Barth's view ensures the continuance of Jews as Jews. This we acknowledge but our discussion here has to be limited to the issue of Jewish Christians.

87 According to D Senior and C Stuhlmueller 'The biblical witness alerts us to a continual and inevitable dialectic between the call to mission and the pastoral needs of the already gathered community... The bible does more than take note of this inevitable balancing act between identity and mission. From the Christian perspective, at least, God's scale tilts in favour of outreach over identity'. Op cit pp 340-41.

88 Sanders states 'when ethnic peculiarities came into conflict... the factors which separated Jews from Greeks must be given up by the Jews' op cit p178. We question whether this would happen if only one Gentile Christian arrived in the area - would the whole congregation have to change its life style immediately in this instance? We cannot rewrite church history on the basis of a supposed inflexibility of principle on the part of Paul, particularly in situations where he himself was not directly involved.

89 See A B Ulanov's comment 'Any personal value - a concern for racial equality, for peace, for the end of sexual discrimination - if elevated to absoluteness can become a tyranny that only forces us into new kinds of divisive hostility. Against the tyranny of human standards stands the person of Christ. The bond of peace is a person, not a doctrine'. 'The Two Strangers', Union Seminary Quarterly Review, 28, 1975, pp 273-83, as quoted by Rader op cit p210.

90 Although it would be wrong to claim that the Holocaust resulted only from anti-Judaism within Christianity, it *is* legitimate to stress that a Christianity that negates Judaism theologically by depicting the phenomenon of its continuing existence within or without the church - whether in the past or in the present - merely as a result of human sin, has no resources to resist any regime that seeks to annihilate Jews. It may in fact implicitly conspire with such a regime in its antisemitic policies.

Chapter 9

Did Paul Advocate Separation from the Synagogue?

1. *Introduction*

A major watershed in the interpretation of Paul is generally acknowledged as having emerged with the publication of E P Sanders *Paul and Palestinian Judaism* (SCM 1977). His attack on the misrepresentation of Judaism contained in much of this century's scholarship (particularly the Lutheran) has received widespread support. (1) Scholars are now beginning to produce Pauline studies in the post-Sanders mould. H Räisänen is one such and the present study by Francis Watson, *Paul, Judaism and the Gentiles: A Sociological Approach*, (CUP 1986) follows in like vein. (2) Sanders' thesis is essentially that Paul opposes Judaism not because of any inherent errors such as 'self-righteousness' or 'legalism', but simply because it is not Christianity. (3) Watson's study attempts to give a historical and sociological grounding for this viewpoint. (4)

Watson diagnoses in the Lutheran approach to Paul a basic flaw, which is apparent even in historically conscious scholars such as Bultmann or Käsemann. This concerns the relationship between Paul's historical situation and his theology. The Lutheran approach has assumed that in Paul's teaching on justification and the law, we have the permanent essence of the Christian gospel, which though issuing from a concrete historical situation, is now to be interpreted existentially, in comparative isolation from its origins.

In opposition to what he perceives to be an unwarranted isolation of theology from history, Watson adopts a sociological perspective in order to examine how Paul's theorising is related to the concrete problems he faced - particularly the legitimacy of the law-free gospel for the Gentiles and the status of the Jewish people. Unlike some scholars' approach to the sociological study of the New Testament, this author refuses to regard sociology simply as an exotic newcomer but rather as 'a natural and inevitable concomitant of the historical-critical method'. New Testament scholars have always been interested in the 'Sitz im Leben' of a tradition or text, ie the social reality underlying them. Watson's thesis is that 'the social reality which underlies Paul's discussions of Judaism and the law is his creation of Gentile Christian communities in sharp separation from the Jewish community' (5). Paul's theological reflection thus legitimates the separation of church from synagogue. A sociological analysis of how sectarian groups work may enable one to reconstruct a 'Sitz im Leben' with much greater clarity and precision, but as a natural extension of accepted historical method rather than as a radically new departure.

Watson's sociological analysis operates on the hypothesis that a text presupposes an existing social situation and is intended to function within the situation in ways not necessarily apparent from the text itself. He is clear, however, that sociological analysis is not a satisfactory way of filling in gaps in our historical knowledge - it is not a substitute for historical evidence, but 'a way of interpreting the evidence'.

Watson employs two sociological models: the first is 'the transformation of a reform-movement into a sect' and the second follows from this - if a sectarian group is to establish and maintain separation from the religious body from which it originated, it will require 'an ideology legitimating its state of separation, ie a theoretical justification for its separate existence'. This may involve firstly, a denunciation of the group's opponents; secondly, the use of antitheses, of which the positive members (eg light, truth) defines the group's members, and of which the negative members (eg darkness, error) defines the community from which the group is trying to distance itself and thirdly, a reinterpretation of the religious traditions of the community as a whole in the light of the belief that the sectarian group is the sole legitimate heir to those traditions. (6).

Watson is aware of the danger of 'ideal types' but believes that despite the uniqueness of each individual historical phenomenon, common underlying sociological patterns may be observed. He then proceeds to apply the patterns (denunciation, antitheses and reinterpretation) to the Qumran community, to the Johannine community and finally to the Pauline communities. These patterns appear to be supported by what evidence we have; Watson is aware however that 'Paul and his congregation seem to have been the only early Christians to have adopted an attitude of sectarian separation from the Jewish community prior to AD 70' (7).

The above view is arrived at by a rejection of the evidence of Acts in favour of the Pauline epistles. Contrary to the former, Paul is not to be seen as in any sense a law-abiding Jew. He and his colleagues at Antioch abandoned their mission to the Jews because they became convinced that their failure to make converts was due to their hearers' divinely ordained hardness of heart. So they turned to Gentiles instead and ensured success (which Watson assumes to have been of some significance for Paul) by setting aside certain offensive commandments of the law. This involved a complete break between the church and the synagogue. Thus we find in Paul's letters a deliberate attempt to transform the movement which had begun as a reform-movement into a sect, in response to rejection. Paul's attitude towards Judaism, we learn, exactly fits 'the structure of an ideology legitimating separation, derived initially from other sources' (8). The author then devotes a chapter to the Galatian crisis and another to Philipppi, Corinth and the Judaisers. It will be evident to readers that the thesis proposed in this book fits better the Paul of Galatians than that of Romans. Since the whole of the second half of the book is devoted to the latter, I intend to concentrate my discussion on this section in which the significance of the methodology already outlined begins to become apparent.

In order to clarify the issues, I will consider Watson's contribution from three perspectives: (1) the merits and limitations of the sociological approach (2) the author's success in achieving his objective to de-Lutheranise Paul and (3) Paul as a sectarian - did he advocate separation from the synagogue for *all* Christians?

2. *The Merits and Limitations of the Sociological Approach*

In this study the concentration is upon the historical and sociological rather than the theological. Watson sees a (common) social reality behind Paul's discussion of Jerusalem and the law, ie Paul's creation of Gentile Christian communities in sharp separation from the Jewish community. This social reality would then link letters such as Galatians and Romans under one heading; their commonality would be basic rather than their differences. However, much recent scholarship has tended in the opposite direction. Historically the search for a 'Sitz im Leben' of a text has tended to involve more stress on the differences and less on the common ground shared in the 'Sitz im Leben' of different texts. Does the sociological approach here not tend to minimise the differences in approach between Galatians and Romans on the theme of Judaism and the law?

Again one might well question whether the social reality which underlies Paul's thought is entirely different from that of the Jesus movement in Palestine. But if the Jesus movement was essentially a renewal movement and Paul is sectarian in attitude, it would appear that the social reality behind their thought must be different. By including the phrase 'in sharp separation from the Jewish community', Watson concentrates not just on the new reality of the Pauline communities, but also on their separateness. This may suggest that Paul is also thus separated from the earliest manifestations of the Christian movement in a somewhat arbitary fashion. Sociology is not history, but sociology of religion needs to develop adequate ways of describing the pre-history of a group that may later develop into a separate sect. [9]

A strength of Watson's sociological approach is that he sees the cohesiveness of Paul's statements about the law not primarily at the theoretical level, but at the level of practical strategy. In principle this insight should enable scholars to transcend some of the debates about Paul's apparently contradictory statements about the law, which Räisänen stresses. The merit of this approach is that one can observe Paul making use of various types of theoretical legitimation which are not always compatible with one another as pure theory but which can all contribute to the same practical goal. It is important, as Watson stresses, to ask not simply about what Paul is *saying*, but also what he is *doing*. Yet this distinction between statement and strategy is not without its own problems. One ought to distinguish between Paul's thought-world, his thought and the communication of his thought. It is in the application of these insights to particular chapters of Romans that some of the inherent complexities emerge.

To describe Rom 2 as Watson and Räisänen do, as denunciation is somewhat questionable. [10] Paul does denounce all inconsistency (including Jewish) in this chapter. But what account is to be taken of the fact that 2:17f is couched in the diatribe style, as Stowers recent research has demonstrated? Are we to read this section literally as if it represents Paul's considered opinion about Judaism? Again, in describing it as denunciation, is there not included the implication that Romans is a polemical letter and that the diatribe style in particular contributes to this polemic? Due regard, however, to the rhetorical style of this chapter indicates that Paul is here not conducting a debate with opponents, but in keeping with the character of the diatribe, [11] is seeking through dialogue with an imaginary interlocutor, to draw out the implications of shared experience as a good teacher would do with his students. Thus the process depicted in such dialogical passages is not so much *polemical* as *pedagogical*. When we note that the entire discussion deals with the question of 'the true Jew' (2:28), then it is clear that whatever denunciation there is, cannot be a denunciation of Judaism as such, but an inner-Jewish discussion of God's impartiality in respect of both Jews and Gentiles.

On another level, it may also be questioned whether in viewing Paul's statements as legitimation of an (already) existing reality (ie his Gentile-Christian communites), one necessarily fails to take fully into account that other significant dimension of Paul's thought - the coming apocalyptic triumph of God already inaugurated in Christ, which because of its prospective nature, becomes formative of the reality. (12) However useful it may be for scholarly purposes to treat the theological purely as rationalisation, one cannot ignore the fact that theology, in Paul's own view of things, provided the basis for his mission. (13) His use of scripture in Rom 9-11 clearly manifests that for the apostle, theology was as much a *cause* as a *consequence* of the existing social reality. On the basis of this it will be necessary to question Sanders' view that all that Paul found wrong with Judaism was that it was not Christianity.

3. *How well does Watson succeed in his Attempt to de-Lutheranise Paul?*

Lloyd Gaston maintains that the law-gospel antithesis is the most fundamental root of theological anti-Judaism. Gaston claims that the God of the Old Testament was rescued from Marcion at the cost of making him both anti-Torah and anti-Israel. Thus Marcion's notion of an *inferior God* was replaced by the notion of an *inferior and disobedient people*. The outcome of this inner-Christian conflict was that the anti-Judaic themes were thereby placed in a new apologetic context, appended to ideas of God and of Christ in ways which came perilously close to permanence. (14) Shades of Marcionism have not been absent from some Lutheran scholarship. Adolf von Harnack saw fit to regard Marcion as guilty only of an exaggerated form of Paulinism. (15) If this is at least partially true, how may we achieve a more balanced and less exaggerated form of Paulinism than that of Marcion? It is clear that the antithesis of faith and works, seen by many as fundamental to Paul, must be reconsidered. Sanders has opened up the way to do this. Watson seeks to continue the process. He rightly notes that Paul does not present Judaism as a religion of pure achievement any more than he presents his gospel as a religion of pure passivity. So for Watson the antithesis of faith and works merely *asserts* the separation of the church from the Jewish community; it does not provide a theoretical rationale for that separation. (16)

The problem with this approach is that the author here retains the hermeneutic of antithesis between Paul and Judaism but presents it now in a new form. We may well ask how much this actually differs from the traditional Lutheran approach. To take the term 'works of the law' as referring not to morality in general, but to the practice of the law within the Jewish community means that Paul is not depicted as opposing a particular attitude to the law such as legalism, but the actual practice of the law within Judaism. Thus Watson has apparently not sufficiently considered Dunn's criticisms of Sanders for mistaking Paul's opposition to 'works of the law' for opposition to the law 'per se'. (17)

Dunn's solution is preferable in that he takes 'works of the law' to refer not to the practice of the law itself, but to the use of certain stipulations of the law such as circumcision, food laws etc, as the accepted badge of covenant membership which were used by both Jews and their neighbours as determinants of Jewish identity. For the typical first century Jew, it would have been virtually impossible to conceive of participation in God's covenant and so in God's covenant righteousness, apart from these 'works of law'. For Paul faith in Jesus Christ became the primary identity marker relativising all others. In Dunn's case, therefore, Paul attacks not the law itself but this particular Jewish self-understanding.

The problem with the traditional Lutheran approach is that because of the law-gospel debate, Paul's statements to Gentile Christians (ie in Galatians) concerning their (possible) proselytism to Judaism have been frequently interpreted as a blanket criticism of Judaism as such and not merely of the view that required all Gentile Christians to Judaize.

Sanders' reappraisal of first century rabbinic Judaism has diminished the attraction of this particular approach. But by interpreting 'works of the law' and all Paul's statements as a rationale for the separation of the new communities from Judaism, Watson has renewed the 'Paul versus Judaism' antithesis, somewhat in the manner of the Lutheran pattern, which he himself is attempting to transcend.

Sociologically speaking, it is comparatively easy to envisage Paul striving for the separation of his Gentile Christian communities over against Judaism. But to stress this too strongly is to minimise the significance of Paul's greater struggle - not against Judaism but against sin and the powers of this age. Thus the real opposition to Paul is not Judaism as such but the world of sin - the powers of evil. The new creation is bursting in to overcome these but Judaism as such ought not to be viewed as always, or inevitably part of the old aeon, as Käsemann tends to regard it. [18] Such a tendency leads inexorably to a one-sided interpretation of Rom 10:4 ie that Christ ends the law, rather than being its goal or fulfilment.

The thesis I have been arguing for in this section is that Sanders' approach now offers a genuine opportunity for Christian scholars to reassess the Gospel and to remove anti-Judaic assertions that are not of its original essence. However Watson's presentation of Paul as arguing ideologically for separation between the new and old communities, renews the previous antithesis in a most exaggerated form as when, for example, he states that Paul wished 'to inculcate in his converts a horror of life under the law, ie life in the Jewish community'. [19]

4. *Did Paul seek to Transform a Reform Movement into a Sect?*
There seems to be very little firm evidence that this was Paul's intention. [20] Sanders perceptively suggests that Paul did not deliberately set out to separate the church from Judaism despite the fact that his congregations were socially distinct from the synagogue. His solution is that Paul implicitly and perhaps even unintentionally paved the way for the historical outcome of the church emerging as a 'third entity'. [21]

Sanders sees the course of Early Christianity as involving 'the simultaneous appropriation and rejection of Judaism'. [22] Watson goes further and depicts Paul as advocating the separation from the parent body.

He only succeeds in sustaining this argument by dismissing the whole of Rom 11 which he sees as Paul's attempt to make his own view more attractive and persuasive by presenting it as far as possible in the context of Jewish Christian beliefs and hopes. [23] Watson sees Rom 4 and Rom 9 as requiring the abandonment of the old notion of election as applying to the Jewish community as a whole, and therefore Paul is apparently contradicting himself in his statements in ch 11. What we are faced with here is the question of whether Paul revises Jewish doctrines such as election or repudiates them entirely. W D Davies has criticised Sanders' view of Paul's conception of Christ as Lord as being 'antithetically related to Judaism'. [24] Scholars divide on these points and Watson has taken up one option but only at the cost of dismissing ch 11 which is essentially the quintessence of Paul's argument in chs 1-11.

A better solution to the apparent inconsistency would have been to maintain, as Watson does, that Paul in chapter 11 presents a one-sided (pro-Jewish) view of election but that he is forced into this in order to counter-balance the one-sided Gentile Christian view outlined in 11:17f.

We come back finally to our own scholarly presuppositions. With Käsemann and many others, we would wish to stress Paul's Jewish background and his close interaction with this. But the tendency to see a polemic against Judaism as fundamental to Paul is difficult to transcend. In the history of interpretation, there are relatively few scholars who regard Romans as being written primarily to address a Jewish Christian minority. [25] Watson however attaches himself to this group, arguing that Paul writes to persuade the Jewish Christians to accept his viewpoint - involving the social reorientation of separation from the synagogue and living in future the life style of Paul's Gentile Christian communities.

Holmberg has recently stressed Paul's concept of authority as being different from the authoritarian attitude with which he has often been credited. (26) But there is little evidence of this liberal approach here - instead the Jewish Christian minority in Rome have no option but to concede. This is contrary to the tendency in recent research by scholars such as Robert Jewett. The latter maintains that what is distinctive about Paul's teaching in Rom 14-15 is that only in this letter does Paul fully accept diversity of life-style within the church and moreover envisages it here as an abiding reality, rather than a passing aberration. Thus Romans on this view would represent Paul's mature reflection upon, and response to, differing creeds (1:3f) and differing life styles (15:7f). (27) The apostle's zeal is for harmony and mutual acceptance - not for the radical separation of the Jewish and non-Jewish elements, or a denial of the legitimacy of alternative life styles as Watson suggests. (28)

The discussion in Romans probably indicates that Paul did foresee the possibility of divorce between his communities and the Jewish community. But his clear statements in the letter against sectarian attitudes - 'do not boast over the branches that have been broken off' etc - and his actions in the collection project, prove that he opposed this divorce and dies in the hope that the marriage would continue. (29)

It is no accident that Paul refuses to give the term 'Israel' a wholly Gentile Christian or even a Gentile Christian and a Jewish Christian content. For him it still refers to all God's people and God determines in his election who these shall be! Likewise he refuses to allow the word Jew to be equated with unbelief. One might say that the Jew for him is still a potential Christian; more significantly, however, we note that Paul still speaks in terms of the true Jew. Is he, in fact, defining Christianity in terms of Judaism? Some might even claim that Paul is asserting that the true Christian is the true Jew (2:28). (30) But that would imply that Judaism as such is a 'given', a static entity that cannot be changed. (31) Moreover, we must bear in mind as noted above that in Romans even the term Israel is somewhat fluid; ultimately even Israel is defined by the freedom of the God of Israel. On the other hand, we must also keep in mind that when Paul writes Romans, Christianity as a separate entity has not yet fully emerged. The only possible candidate for a specifically Christian title is the word 'saint', but this has an element of ambivalence and certainly is not intended to exclude Jews.

Watson starts from the premise that the Pauline communities and the synagogue were socially distinct. From this he argues that Paul's letters provide the rationale for separation. But a major problem for Watson's interesting and challenging approach is that he has not given sufficient attention to Israel's dual status in Paul's theology. Israel is beloved of God and yet stands in opposition to Paul's gospel. Paul's *theology* does not provide a rationale for separation but on the contrary seeks a resolution of the separation in the coming eschatological triumph of God. The latter is the key to how Paul deals with the problem of division between Jew and Gentile in Rome. One might argue that Watson's conclusions are the price one necessarily pays when seeking a specifically sociological approach. I am of the opinion, however, that the same end could have been equally well served had the author concluded that Paul's strategy in Romans is to seek the social reorientation of both Jewish *and* Gentile Christians through the Gospel rather than the separation of church and synagogue. And, of course, this implies a *theological* as well as a *sociological* reorientation of both groups.

NOTES

This chapter originated from a short lecture delivered at the British New Testament Society Conference at St Johns College, Durham, September 1987.

1 See J D G Dunn, 'The New Perspective on Paul', BJRL, 35 (1983), pp 95-122.
2 H Räisänen, *Paul and the Law* (WUNT 29, Mohr, Tübingen, 1983). It is not suggested that there is a consensus on these issues; for an alternative approach see H Hübner, *Law in Paul's Thought*, Clark, Edinburgh 1984.
3 Op cit p552.
4 Op cit p67.
5 Op cit p19.
6 Op cit p20.
7 Op cit p45.
8 Op cit p48.
9 Cf Richard L Rohrbaugh, '"Social Location of Thought" as a Heuristic Construct in New Testament Study', JSNT 30 (1987) pp 103-119. Cf also M Hooker, *Continuity and Discontinuity: Early Christianity in its Jewish Setting*, Epworth, London 1986 esp 11, 54, 74-5. Contra Meeks, 'Breaking Away: Three New Testament Pictures of Christianity's Separation from the Jewish Communities', in *To See Ourselves as Others See Us: Christians, Jews, 'Others' in Late Antiquity,* Ed J Neusner and ES Frerichs, Scholars Press, Chico, 1985, pp 93-115 (106).
10 Cf Watson op cit pp 109f and Räisänen op cit p101.
11 Watson has failed to take account of S Stower's study *The Diatribe and Paul's Letter to the Romans* (SBLDS 57, Chicago, 1981. Cf also by the same author, 'Paul's dialogue with a Fellow Jew in Romans 3:1-9', the Catholic Biblical Quarterly, 46, 1984, pp 714f.

12 Cf J C Beker, *Paul the Apostle: The Triumph of God in Life and Thought*, Philadelphia, 1980, especially ch 8, 'Paul's Apocalytic Theology (pp 135f).

13 Cf J Hultgren, Paul's Gospel and Mission, *Fortress, Philadelphia*, 1985.

14 Cf Gaston's summary conclusion 'Retrospect' in the volume of essays, *Anti-Judaism in Early Christianity*, Vol 2 *Separation and Polemic*, ed by S G Wilson, Wilfred Laurier Univ Press, Waterloo, 1986, pp 163f.

15 Cf S G Wilson, 'Marcion and the Jews' op cit pp 45-47.

16 Watson gives an excellent critique of the view that salvation occurs solely through God's grace which he holds to be 'a deep misunderstanding of Paul', op cit pp 120f.

17 Cf Dunn as in n1 above and also 'Works of the Law and the Curse of the Law', New Testament Studies 31, 1985, pp 523- 542 and H Räisänen's response in the same issue', 'Galatians 2:16 and Paul's Break with Judaism', (pp 543-553).

18 Cf Käsemann, *Commentary on Romans* SCM 1980 pp 282f. For a more recent and more positive view of the law in Paul see Robert Badenas, *Christ the End of the Law* JSNTS 10, Sheffield University, 1985.

19 Op cit p47; cf also pp 61 and 70.

20 Wayne Meeks significant study, *The First Urban Christians: The Social World of the Apostle Paul*, Yale Univ Press, New Haven, 1983, does not provide a clear answer to this issue. Meeks addressed the question whether sectarian analysis would fit a Pauline church at the SNTS meeting in Paris 1978, but concluded that the evidence is ambiguous.

21 Cf Sanders, *Paul, the Law and the Jewish People*, Philadelphia, 1983, pp 171f.

22 Op cit p210.

23 Op cit pp 172f.

24 Cf the preface to the fourth edition of *Paul and Rabbinic Judaism*, Fortress 1980, pp xxxiii.

25 Cf 'Romans III as a Key to the Structure and Thought of the Letter', Chapter 3 in this volume.

26 B Holmberg, *Paul and Power*, Coniectanea Biblica NT Ser 11, Lund 1978.

27 Cf *Christian Tolerance: God's Message to the Modern Church*, Westminster 1978, pp 62f; also 'The Redaction and Use of an Early Christian Confession in Rom 1:3-4', in *The Living Text: Essays in Honour of E W Sanders*, ed D E Groh, R Jewett, Univ Press of America, 1985, pp 99f.

28 Cf Chapter 9 esp pp114f.

29 Cf D Fraikin, 'The Rhetorical Function of the Jews in Romans', in *Anti-Judaism in Early Christianity*, Vol I - *Paul and the Gospels* ed P Richardson (see n14 above) pp 103-4.

30 Cf Fraikin, op cit pp 105-6.

31 I am grateful to Professor Leander Keck of Yale Divinity School for some helpful comments incorporated here which he kindly offered in response to the original draft of this essay.

Chapter 10

Paul's Strategy in Writing Romans: His Understanding and Use of Israel's Role in Eschatological Salvation

1. *Introduction*

In almost every discussion concerning the historical relationship between Christianity and Judaism, the apostle Paul and the evaluation of his life and work play a decisive role. However, the recovery of the historical Paul is no easy task. His image tends to be refracted through the theological spectacles which the interpreter happens to be wearing. It was Krister Stendahl who some years ago warned us of the danger of viewing Paul through Reformation spectacles. (1) E P Sander's research has further clarified the issue by distinguishing the Reformation view of faith and works from Paul's controversy with first century Palestinian Judaism. (2)

Recently F Watson has sought to continue the process of 'de-Lutheranising' Paul, using a historical and sociological approach rather than a theological one. (3) This author sets out to demonstrate that the theology which the Lutheran Reformation and its modern counterparts find in Paul - rather than being shown to spring from a particular sociological context - is not present in Paul at all. (4) Watson approves Sanders' thesis that Paul opposes Judaism not because of any inherent errors such as self-righteousness or legalism, but simply because it is not Christianity. He attempts to give a historical and sociological grounding for this viewpoint. (5) New Testament scholars have always been interested in the 'Sitz im Leben' of a tradition or text. Watson's thesis is that 'the social reality which underlies Paul's discussions of Judaism and the Law is his creation of Gentile Christian communities in sharp separation from the Jewish community'. For Watson therefore, 'Paul's theological reflection legitimates the separation of church from synagogue'. (6)

What we wish to investigate here is not just the assertion discussed in the last chapter that the break between Judaism and Christianity had already occurred. More significant is the hypothesis proposed - that Paul encouraged both by word and deed this lasting divorce. Stendahl and Sanders' proposals were tending to lead scholarship to a more realistic and less subjective assessment of first century Judaism. Watson, however, whilst generally continuing this trend, by positing that Paul is intent on the separation of his communities from the Jewish community for sociological, if not for theological reasons, ultimately, in my opinion, works against the present tendency. (7) It is one thing to argue that Paul was deeply implicated and certainly not guiltless in the outcome of the series of events that culminated in the divorce between the Christian movement and Judaism. But it is quite another to insist that Paul consciously and deliberately advocated separation. (8)

The purpose of this chapter is to consider Paul's strategy in Romans and to argue that Paul seeks to bring about a change of attitude in all Christians in Rome - not just in those of Jewish origin; that he will oppose all boasting and all misrepresentation from whatever source, and present contrary arguments to bring about harmony among the house churches in Rome. At some points it is clear that Paul is being critical of some aspects of Jewish (Christian) behaviour. At others it will be evident that he is attacking Gentile presumption. Paul, in fact, tries to be even handed, not to obviously take sides. (9) However, a good case can be argued for the view that in Romans Paul attempts to give a positive view of Judaism; the image of the Jew is far from being a consistently negative one - Paul's gospel is not formulated in antithesis to Judaism; he even appears to argue from the Jewish perspective and he is severely critical of Gentile Christian presumption. This strategy would seem to suggest that although the Christians in Rome who followed a Jewish life-style were not without need of correction, nevertheless the fact that Paul, in Romans II especially, is distinctly pro-Jewish and criticises the Gentile Christians, means that a positive understanding of the nature of the Jewish heritage was demanded.(10)

2. *Paul's Gospel in Romans is not formulated in Antithesis to Judaism*

The nature and content of Paul's gospel is fundamental to our understanding of his relationship to Judaism. If it had been formulated in such a manner that its substance stood in complete opposition to the faith of Israel, then it would be difficult not to blame Paul for the separation between the Church and Judaism. Recent developments indicate a fresh understanding of the historical Paul and his message, and offer the opportunity for reassessment of this issue.

Sanders in his studies of Paul acknowledges his concurrence in much scholarly opinion which stresses Paul's christological criticisms of the law. Where Sanders parts company with much traditional Pauline interpretation is that he will not accept the criticism of Jewish legalism which often goes hand in hand with this as, for example, in Käsemann's commentary on Romans. Over against faith in Christ, Käsemann sees a human tendency to self-achievement and the Jew even in his law keeping is guilty of this. (11) By generalising legalism so that it becomes the human tendency to self-achievement, and making a direct connection between christology and the renunciation of all self-striving, 'the prime point of accepting Christ becomes the renunciation of achievement'. (12) It follows that those who deny Christ are therefore necessarily guilty of self-assertion. Thus Paul's christological objections to Judaism are regarded as directed against that self-righteousness which is typical of Judaism - an unsupported assumption. (13) Sanders in his earlier work *Paul and Palestinian Judaism*, compared Paul's pattern of religion with that of Palestinian Judaism in order to demonstrate that Rabbinic Judaism was not a religion of good works. He found the picture of Rabbinic Judaism as a legalistic religion of works-righteousness to be one-sided and mistaken. The supposedly legalistic Judaism described by scholars such as Schürer, Bousset, Billerbeck and Bultmann has often served a very obvious function - it acts as a foil against which superior forms of religion are described. (14)

But for Sanders, despite the paucity of references to it, the covenant is presupposed as the basis for the Rabbinic pattern of religion. Palestinian Judaism is essentially a religion of covenantal nomism - obedience and grace go hand in hand. (15) The twin pillars on which the Rabbi's understanding of salvation rested were election and atonement. God chose Israel by his grace 'for his own sake'. As a consequence of the election and in his role as king, God gave the Israelites commandments to obey - not as a means of salvation but as man's proper response to the covenant. (16)

According to Sanders, Paul's basic critique of Judaism springs from his conviction that salvation is to be found only in Christ. Thus Paul, in his theology, does not proceed from an analysis of a problem to a solution but from solution to problem. It is only as a Christian that Paul sees what is wrong with Judaism - it is not Christianity and therefore cannot be right. He is in fact judging Judaism not on its own terms but by Christian presuppositions. The heart of Paul's theology rests on an equation between 'righteousness by faith' and 'life in Christ'. It is only as Paul is 'in Christ' that he has real righteousness and this transforms entirely his perspective.(17)

Sanders has successfully demonstrated the fallacy of seeing Paul's christological objections to Judaism as being directed against typical Jewish self-righteousness. Rather their fault was that they sought a righteousness exclusive to Jews alone. (18) Sanders concludes that 'the supposed objection to Jewish self-righteousness is as absent from Paul's letters as self-righteousness itself is from Jewish literature'. (19) The Judaism attacked by

Paul is not the Judaism of the Lutheran caricature but Judaism as it really was. It was Paul's christological exclusivism which was his weapon in excluding Judaism - since God's way of salvation is through faith in Christ, Judaism is automatically disqualified. [20]

Watson seeks to develop Sanders' findings in a sociological direction. He pays particular attention to the phrase 'works of the law', one of the most contentious phrases in the debate about Paul's attitude to Judaism. For Watson this phrase refers not to morality in general but to the practice of the law within the Jewish community. In correlation with this, 'faith in Jesus Christ' refers not to 'a willingness to receive God's grace as a free gift, and to renounce reliance on one's own achievements, but to the Christian confession of Jesus as the Messiah and the social reorientation which this entails'. [21] Thus for Watson 'the antithesis between faith and works does not express a general theoretical opposition between two imcompatible views of the divine-human relationship. It merely expresses Paul's conviction that the church should be separate from the Jewish community'. [22] Moreover the antithesis itself does not provide a reason for this separation but simply asserts its necessity.

This revised view of 'works of the law' enables Watson to affirm that faith in Christ for Paul is neither passive nor opposed to all moral endeavour. Also there is now no theoretical reason why the practice of the Jewish law and confession of Jesus as the Messiah should be incompatible. [23]

The virtue of Sanders' interpretation of Paul is that his view does not force us to argue that Paul opposes Judaism because of some inherent failing in Judaism as a religion. Watson's sociological approach has similar merit. But his view shares with that of Sanders the related problem that it then appears rather arbitary that Paul should oppose the law or Judaism.[24] Watson's explanation is that 'Christ is incompatible with circumcision not because Christ involves a theological principle (receiving salvation as a pure gift) which is incompatible with an alleged principle underlying circumcision (earning salvation) but because Paul has already decided that the church is only the church, when the church is separate from the Jewish community.' [25]

This explanation is not convincing to us but our main argument in this section is that Sanders' interpretation of Paul releases scholars from necessarily having to interpret Paul's gospel as having been formulated in direct antithesis to Judaism. This is further supported by Watson's demonstration that there is no inherent incompatibility between the practice of the Jewish Law and the confession of Jesus as Messiah. Both

Sanders and Watson also maintain that Paul does oppose, among other things, the Jewish understanding of election, but we will return to that in a later section. We note in conclusion that according to Paul's gospel it was not seeking one's own righteousness through self-assertion that was wrong, but putting one's confidence in anything other than God in Christ.

3. *The Diatribe Style in Romans does not signify a Consistently Negative Image of the Jew*

A major factor in the emergence of divergent interpretations of Romans is the diatribe style which Paul frequently uses, particularly with reference to the Jews. (26) Confusion concerning the significance of Paul's rhetoric has, I am convinced, often resulted in caricatures of Jews and Jewish Christians as always objecting to Paul's teaching. (27) The resultant distortion has readily harmonised with the incipient anti-Judaism pervasive in much Pauline scholarship until relatively recently. Little research on the diatribe style of Romans had been carried out since Bultmann did his doctoral study. Stowers has recently remedied this and the significance of the rhetoric of the letter must now be allowed to influence contemporary discussion of its purpose and content. (28) The view taken here is that even if Stowers' conclusions meet with modification and qualification in future research, nevertheless the rhetoric of the letter is such that it cannot be regarded as mainly polemical.

The problems surrounding Paul's statements about Judaism begin with the traditional interpretation of Rom 1:18-2:29. On this we find statements claiming that Paul sets up a trap for the Jew by allowing him to concur with Paul's condemnation of Gentile sinners (1:18-32), and then accusing Jews of doing the very same thing (though the form of sinning may be different). (29) The best reading of 2:1 does not in fact support this particular interpretation. (30)

However it is not just the actual interpretation of a particular verse that is at issue but, more seriously, Paul's attitude to the Jew and to Judaism in Romans. Obviously a writer who sets a trap for the self-righteous, judging Jew, cannot with any consistency be viewed as anything but the enemy of Judaism in the remainder of the letter. Thus right at the beginning of the letter the scene is set for treating Paul's statements about Judaism as distinctly hostile and consistently polemical in tone. It is no surprise therefore in view of such assumptions that later when Paul speaks of the advantage of the Jew this is very quickly shown to be no advantage at all! There is and there is not an advantage a Jew!

What is more alarming is a secondary aspect of stressing the Jew as

Paul's target for condemnation i.e. that the Gentile escapes censure, because attention is focused elsewhere. It is most surprising that so many commentators have failed to ask themselves why Paul should so readily condemn Jewish failings in writing to a mainly Gentile audience, especially one that already demonstrates this same tendency. From a paraenetic perspective, it is incredible that Paul should so openly appeal to, and therefore reinforce, the bias of his intended audience.

J C Beker, aware of the apparently conflicting elements in Romans in regard to Judaism interprets it accordingly - as a 'dialogue with Jews': 'The main body of the letter confronts Judaism'. (31) 'In Romans Paul does not attack Christians for adopting Jewish ways or circumcision but demonstrates instead the way in which Judaism is accounted for in the Gospel. The dialogue with the Jews is at the same time an apology for the Gospel'. (32) 'Romans exhibits a basic apology for Israel but until 11:11 (except for the interruption at 3:1-4) the apology has the character of a radical polemic': but 'the sharpness, the polemic against Israel's election self-consciousness, is for the sake of the apologetic'. (33)

Beker's lively use of language reveals a certain ambiguity on the issue of Paul's attitude to the Jew in Romans. In particular there are one or two casual generalisations that need to be clarified - eg Paul wants to destroy 'the pre-eminently Jewish sin of boasting'. (34) This is shorthand for the Jewish boast in election but he does not indicate this. Similarly phrases like 'the Jewish target', 'the weight of the indictment falls on the Jew', by repetition have a cumulative effect. Thus despite Beker's efforts to demonstrate that Romans presents a more balanced picture of the place of Israel in salvation history than Galatians does, (35) sentences such as 'the Jew highlights sin in its more demonic aspect' strike a certain note of dissonance. (36)

What ought to be asked is why should Paul wish or need to 'set a trap for the Jewish auditor'? (37) Only a clarification of the rhetorical style of the letter can help to overcome this problem. Just as we stress the overall tone of what Beker has written, so the tenor of Paul's statements in Romans needs to be investigated. If the letter is both polemical and apologetic as Beker suggests and if the apologetic is more dominant than the polemic, what significance does this have for the traditional interpretation of Paul's attitude to the Jew and Judaism in Romans? It would certainly militate against the tendency to describe Rom 2 under the heading of 'denunciation' as Räisänen and Watson have recently done despite Stower's work on the diatribe. (38)

A proper acknowledgement of Rom 2:17-29 as being in the diatribe style means that we view Paul as conducting a debate with an imaginary interlocutor who may be either a certain type corresponding to a specific vice or perhaps a representative of a school of thought. Ch 2:17-29 is an apostrophe to an imaginary Jewish interlocutor in the style of the diatribe. (39) It follows that Paul's conversation partner in 3:1-9 may also be the same imaginary Jewish person. (40)

Thus the entire section may be an inner-Jewish discussion in which Paul talks to an imaginary interlocutor about God's righteousness and impartiality. The type of discussion is probably designed to show the integration and correlation, rather than opposition, between God's measure of justice and measure of mercy. (41) Paul aims to demonstrate that it is absurd to conclude that because God is faithful to the Jews, he is a judge who shows partiality and as such is no longer fit to judge the world.

So this is not intended as an anti-Jewish debate. It is in fact a debate that probably often took place among Jews at this period - even apart from the problem of Gentile Christianity. (42) Granted that 2:17 is very direct and censorious in tone, it must be remembered nevertheless that such dialogues are in the diatribe almost always directed towards students or potential students. The Jew should not be seen as Paul's enemy or even necessarily as Paul's opponent. 'He' represents a position that Paul discusses, caricatures or even demolishes - not Judaism as such. The process depicted in such dialogical exchanges is not *polemical*, but rather *pedagogical* and *protreptic*. (43)

The rhetorical style suggests a reasoned discussion with an interlocutor who is a student or partner in the discussion. Probably the situation indicates that Paul is seeking to develop or draw out the implications of some of the beliefs which he and the Christians in Rome hold in common. Stowers suggests that 'Paul's dialogue is a subtle lesson for Gentile Christians on how to keep open the discussion with those who belong to the tree on which they have been grafted. Rom 3:1-9 portrays two Jews discussing the fate of Israel now that the Messiah has arrived in an unexpected way. Paul's Gentile readers are allowed to overhear what is said'. (44)

But can we infer from considerations of style the nature of Paul's audience? Does the fact that Paul chooses an imaginary Jewish interlocutor give any indication as to which kind of audience he is addressing in Romans? We have noted that it is wrong to see the censorious statements as indicating a polemic against Judaism. The issue is whether Paul is talking to and with Gentile Christians about Judaism or whether he is talking to and with Jewish Christians about their common heritage. The dialogue is *about* Judaism - it is couched in Jewish terminology - but is it with Jewish Christians or Gentile? This question is very difficult to answer. I do not believe that Beker is technically correct to claim that Romans is a dialogue with Jews. (45) The Jew as the imaginary interlocutor is purely a rhetorical fiction and the issue could equally well be the priority of Israel in salvation history, and Gentile Christianity's attitude to this, just as much as issues specifically relating to Jewish Christians.

We cannot agree therefore with Watson's view which sees the 'single purpose' pervading the various themes of Rom 1-8 as being 'to persuade Jewish Christian readers to accept the legitimacy of Pauline Gentile Christianity and to deny legitimacy to the claims of the synagogue'. (46) As far as we can judge, there is no evidence that the synagogue was a temptation to the Christians in Rome. Beker, in support of his view of the letter as a dialogue with Judaism, rather fancifully suggests that there were some among the Gentiles (who in his view had recently abandoned the synagogue as 'God fearers' and or proselytes) who may have needed a warning 'against a possible backsliding to the synagogue.' Beker bases this statement on Rom 11:20 but there is little basis for his comment at a point in the letter where Paul warns Gentile Christians in the most explicit manner, not to be anti-Jewish in their attitudes or theology, (rather than to be too pro-Jewish). (47)

It could be argued that since in the diatribe there is normally little distance between the fictional and real audiences, (48) then this would support the interpretation which sees the censorious language in Romans 2 as addressed to Jews or Jewish leaders. But even if this be granted, Romans 2 is only one chapter in a long letter, and must not determine the interpretation of the whole.

It is significant that every instance of the terms for boasting where the words are used negatively occurs in a dialogical text either in apostophes (2:17, 23, 11:18), or in objections or questions (3:27, 4:2). (49) The theological significance of boasting has played an important part in the Lutheran understanding of faith and works. Usually, as we have stressed, it is the Jew who is accused of boasting of his achievements or privileges. What must be noted, however, is that the same style permeates the condemnation of (Jewish) arrogance in Romans 2 as that of Gentiles in Romans 11. Stowers calls for further investigation of the complex of ideas and stylistic patterns in Romans. (50)

What is striking in scholarly studies is the relatively minor significance given to the condemnation of Gentile boasting alongside that of Jewish, especially since Paul in Rom 11 explicitly names the Gentiles as worthy of indictment. Although it is a feature of the diatribe that the objector need not always represent the same position, (51) there has been a tendency in Pauline studies to believe that the objector is always a Jew. (52) Again we must not regard every fictional opponent as necessarily representing a typification of false theological positions against which Paul is polemicising, as Käsemann tends to do. (53) Stowers argues that the apostrophes of 2:1-5 and 2:17-24 should not be understood as part of a supposed Pauline polemic against Judaism or Judaisers. The picture of the pretentious Jew Paul adopts here is a necessary component in his positive sketch of what it means to be a true Jew. (54) Certainly it is clear that Paul opposes all inconsistency between profession and practice, between self-understanding and actual life-style whether it be on the part of Jews or of Gentiles.

We are arguing here only the point that the image of the Jew in Romans has tended to be unduly negative, and that the diatribe style has been partly instrumental in sustaining this bias. The relevance of this can be seen when contrasted with Watson's view. What is significant in his case is that although he (rightly) stresses the call to mutual acceptance in ch 15:7 of the (two) differing groups in Rome, he nevertheless sees the primary addressees, and the burden of correction in a large part of the letter as directed towards, the Jewish Christian group. (55) Is it not the case that the more negative one's picture of Judaism, the more likely it is that the Jewish element should be regarded as most in need of correction?

It is hard to find sufficient evidence in the letter for the view that the primary audience is the Jewish Christians. 'Weak' like the term 'wet' in recent British political debate, is not likely to have been a self-selected designation. It is the chosen and value-laden description of those who distance themselves from the attitudes and life-style of 'the weak'. Paul includes himself among the strong (15:1), but this does not imply that they are blameless. It is most unlikely that the deficiencies were primarily those of 'the weak'. Whilst we agree with Watson that it would be difficult for Jews to accept Gentile Christians who did not keep the law, it is also clear that many Gentiles despised certain aspects of the Jewish faith. (56) The content of Rom 14-15 does not support the view that 'the weak' are the primary addressees. It would support the view that Paul's strategy in writing Romans is the social reorientation of both the Jewish and Gentile Christians. This accords better with Jewett's claim that the peculiar stance of Romans over against Paul's other letters is that only in Romans are differing Christian life-styles accepted as an abiding feature of the Christian communities. (57) If only 'the weak' were to be reorientated, it would appear that the diversity would soon be overcome. (58)

Whilst we have noted above that in the diatribe there is normally not much distance between the fictional and real audiences, there is necessarily some distance. Jewett illustrates this well when he notes how Paul develops general principles applicable to all from what seems to be one concrete instance of the man who is 'weak in faith' (14:1). Also Paul deliberately selected the extreme positions at opposite ends of the 'liberal-conservative' spectrum in Rome 'in order to make the general principle of tolerance inclusive of all the positions inside this range. ' (59) What is significant here is that Jewett rightly emphasises Paul's strategy of being inclusive, rather than directing his paraenesis to only one section of his potential audience.

The fact that Romans is about the relationship between two peoples - Jews and Gentiles - and their mutual relation through the Gospel (and Paul's mission) as well as the fact that the opening chapters stress divine impartiality in grace and judgement to both, implies a duality of application. It could be argued that the 'groups' were more numerous than two and that both 'sides' may have been predominantly Gentile in origin, some having adopted proselyte status. (60) If this were the case, then the issue in Romans would be the significance of Jewishness among (mainly) Gentile Christians. But the diatribe style makes it difficult to distinguish between questions which might have been asked by Jews, from those which might have been asked by others about the status of Jews or a Jewish life-style. The latter was of some interest to Gentile Christians and impinged closely on Paul's Gentile mission. It could be argued that much of the discussion in Romans is not Paul's polemic against Judaism, but rather his reinterpretation of Judaism for a mainly Gentile Christian audience. The diatribe style would support this apologetic rather than the (traditional) polemical interpretation.

However our main contention is that only if the diatribe style is ignored or misinterpreted, can the image of the Jew in Romans be seen as consistently negative. The fact that Paul concludes chapter 2 with a description of "the true Jew" is further proof that he neither views Judaism from a sectarian stance, nor is his image of the Jew consistently negative. (61) Stowers admirably sums up our findings in this section - "It is anachronistic and completely unwarranted to think that Paul has only the Jew in mind in 2: 1-5 or that he characterises the typical Jew." (62)

4. *Paul in Romans resists the Gentile Christians' Sectarian Tendencies*

The mark of a sect is that it regards itself as the sole legitimate possessor of the religious traditions of the whole community. It denies the claim made to them by the rest of society. (63) Our question is - does Paul write as a sectarian in Romans? It could be argued that there is sufficient evidence to support such a claim in the case of Galatians. (64) The most suitable passage in Romans to refute this claim is ch 11:16f.

In this passage Paul does not argue that there is a new olive tree - there is only one olive tree with one root. Even though it is clear that he speaks of Jews who do not believe in Jesus as Messiah who, according to his analogy 'were broken off', he nevertheless speaks of the Gentiles being 'grafted in among them'. It is not a displacement of Jews by Gentiles. There is in fact a faithful remnant of Jews still part of the original tree as Paul has already pointed out in 11:5, 'Even so at the present time, there is a remnant according to the election of grace'. (65) Paul's prophetic warning to Gentile Christians is that presumptuous arrogance may mean that they will have no permanent place in the 'olive tree', and likewise if the unbelieving Jews, 'the broken off branches', do not continue in unbelief, they will not be permanently excluded.

Paul drives home the point by the very analogy he uses. W D Davies has pointed out that there are few trees less productive than the wild olive. (66) Thus the Gentile Christians are reminded that in and of themselves, they have nothing to boast of. They do not bear the root, but are dependent on it (11:18). Beker has rightly stressed the historical priority of Jewish Christianity and the 'heilsgeschichtlich' role of Israel in Paul's theology in Romans. (67) In addition Paul reminds the Gentiles that they are wild olive branches grafted contrary to their original nature into a good olive tree. His thesis is that the God who can do this unnatural feat will surely be able to graft back again 'the natural branches' into *their own* olive tree (11:24). (68) But he puts this in the form of a question because as yet it is only something that can be devoutly hoped for. The point however is very clear - the Gentiles have not taken over the tree and the Jews have not been finally rejected. The wild olive shoot is grafted in, only to *share* the richness of the olive tree (11:17).

A related and similar point is made in Roman 15:27. Here the argument is that is the Gentiles have been made partakers of the spiritual blessings of the Jews, they are in debt to them and ought therefore at least to share their material blessings with them as the collection for the saints in Jerusalem symbolised. But once again, it is not a takeover of Jewish privileges by Gentiles, but a sharing of them that Paul describes here.

It is in his use of the term 'Israel' that Paul leaves absolutely no doubt as to his stance on this issue. Although he comes very close to speaking of an Israel within Israel in 9:6f, he checks himself and simply maintains that 'not all who are descended from Israel are Israel'. He distinguishes seed of promise from children of natural descent, but he never suggests that God does not keep his promise to Israel. Paul's thesis is that Israel's identity is determined by God alone. On the other hand, he does not suggest that the term Israel might refer only to Gentile Christians. These do not enter the discussion until 9:22f and even then it is quite plain that Paul intends to signify an extension of the covenant to them rather than a new covenant with them that replaces the old entirely. (69) (Gentile) Christians as the 'new Israel' is not a Pauline conception and Peter Richardson's thesis that this description represents a post New Testament development still stands. (70)

When Paul speaks of Jews who at present do not believe in Jesus, he nevertheless calls them 'Israelites' and he acknowledges that as such they can still be described as possessing election privileges (even though at the moment he believes that they are refusing to enjoy the greatest privilege of all - Jesus, the Messiah).

The same is true with regard to the scriptures. Paul does not simply assert that the Christians alone know the true meaning of scripture. (71) He argues as a Jew of his own time from the scriptures he shares with his own people and he still acknowledges that the Jews were entrusted with the oracles of God (ta logia 3:2).

It must be admitted that there were elements in Paul's gospel that certainly could be misinterpreted in an exaggerated fashion to signify an anti-Jewish attitude. Doubtless Paul did need to defend himself against such opinions and probably he was not entirely guiltless in respect of their origin. He himself may have used the careless phrase or failed to see the wider significance of a particular statement. But in Romans he faces fairly and squarely the issue as to whether or not there is any advantage in being a Jew. His answer is, in the end, an extremely positive one, and the fact that he felt able to face this issue and to treat it in the way he did should leave no doubts as to his attitude to separation from the synagogue. Not only did he himself not have a sectarian attitude towards his ancestral faith but he specifically repudiates such a tendency among his Gentile converts.

5. *Paul in Romans writes from the Jewish Perspective as a Reformer who seeks the Renewal of his own People*

In contrast to Paul's negative attitude to sectarian Gentile Christians is his positive attitude to his Jewish heritage. Scholars have noted the Jewish form of argument and the presentation of ideas in Romans from a Jewish perspective: (72) 'Not from the Jews only'; 'to the Jew first and also to the Greek'; 'our father Abraham'. In these and numerous other statements, particularly in Rom 9-11, Paul writes as a believing Jew. What is distinctive about Paul's approach in Romans is that he does not merely argue for his own understanding of the Gospel, but he does so in this instance by relating it in a positive way to his Jewish heritage, as we see from the following:

The Gospel was 'promised beforehand through his prophets in the holy scriptures;' the Gospel concerning his Son, who was descended from David (1:3-4); (73) in the Gospel the righteousness of God is revealed through faith and for faith (1:17). The Jew has an advantage because the Jews are 'entrusted with the oracles of God' (3:2). 'Now the righteousness of God has been manifested apart from law, although the law and the prophets bear witness to it' (3:21); the 'redemption which is in Christ Jesus, whom God put forward as an expiation (mercy seat or means of atonement) by his blood' (3:25). (74) The promise to Abraham and his descendants that they should inherit the world ... 'depends on faith in order that the promise may rest on grace and be guaranteed to all his descendants ' (4:16).

This is one way that Paul relates his message to Jewish life and hopes. Another is more problematic but also significant. W D Davies claims that Paul's use of 'the law of Christ' even in Galatians 'is a stumbling block to those who set Paul in total opposition to the Law and even all law'. (75) In several places in Romans Paul relates law and gospel in positive or at least partially positive ways. This is demonstrated in the phrases, law of faith (3:27); the law of the Spirit (8:3); the just requirement (dikaiōma) of the law (to be fulfilled in us) (8:4); God's law (8:7); Christ, the goal (telos) or end of the law (10:4); love is the fulfilling of the law (13:10). These taken together with Paul's concluding argument that 'Christ became a servant to the circumcised to show God's truthfulness in order to confirm the promises given to the patriarchs...' (15:8), reveal a concern unique in Paul's letters to demonstrate positive continuity between the new way and the parent faith in Judaism.

The problem here is not to deny or affirm this concern but to evaluate its significance. Thus Sanders is able to maintain that Paul writes from the Jewish perspective but nevertheless sees the course of early Christianity as involving 'the simultaneous appropriation and rejection of Judaism'. (76) More precision is required in order for us to assess Paul's role in the emergence of Christianity as a separate entity.

Sanders and others have stressed the fact that Paul radically revises or even rejects the Jewish doctrine of election. Watson holds that 'Romans 4 and 9 in particular require of Jewish Christians a complete abandonment of the old notion of election as applying to the Jewish community as a whole'. (77) But in apparent self-contradiction, Paul argues in Rom 11 that 'the Jewish doctrine of election is to a large extent compatible with his own view of the failure of Israel and the salvation of the Gentiles'. Watson sees this as Paul's attempt 'to make his own view more attractive and persuasive by presenting it as far as possible in the context of Jewish-Christian beliefs and hopes'. (78) I take the view that what Watson notes concerning Rom 11 is the characteristic of the letter as a whole. His problem is that he misinterprets Paul's discussion in Rom 9:6f as attacking Judaism's 'emphatic theology of grace', (79) and then is unable to reconcile Paul's clear and coherent argument in this chapter with Paul's other clear and coherent argument in Rom 11. It is not good exegetical procedure to deal with chapters as separate sections when chapters 9-11 are so obviously one continuous argument. (80)

Watson fails to distinguish between Paul's revision of the doctrine of election and a complete rejection of its teaching. Only by involving Paul in the most blatant and immediate self-contradiction can one maintain that he completely rejects the doctrine of election. Even if Paul's teaching here had the social function of making the Jewish Christians 'realise that their future lies not with their fellow Jews but with the Gentiles whom God has called', (81) it is quite clear that he himself does not *self-consciously* reject the doctrine of election - 'the gifts and the call of God are irrevocable', (11:29) is still his position. Therefore the most that we can claim here is that Paul reinterprets or revises the doctrine of election from his own messianic viewpoint.

What has emerged in Paul's discussion is typical of the wider debate about Paul's relation to Judaism. Is Paul to be viewed as offering a revised form of Judaism, 'a covenantal nomism in Christ', which also incorporates Gentile believers, or is he introducing a radical new religion? (82) Here Davies and Sanders have parted ways and the discussion has really only just got under way. We believe that Davies correctly questions Sanders' claim that the category of the Lordship of Christ in Paul supersedes that of Messiahship, thus reducing the significance of apocalyptic for the apostle. Thus, despite Sanders' general agreement with Davies' stress on Paul's Jewish background, Davies nevertheless regards his view of Paul's conception of Christ as Lord as being 'antithetically related to Judaism'. (83) We believe that Davies is correct in this criticism and in his thesis that Sanders' view on this issue has the effect of 'consigning Paul to a vacuum' - 'the outcome is to underestimate the messianic discussion of his thinking which was not submerged by Paul's use of the term 'Lord' for Christ. (84)

The same ambivalence in the scholarly discussion emerges also in relation to Paul's understanding of righteousness. We would wish to stress that 'righteousness carries with it covenantal overtones in Paul'. (85) J Dunn has also recently drawn attention to this. He notes that in Galatians 2, Paul appeals to Jewish sensibilities: 'this understanding of "being justified" is thus evidently something Jewish, something which belongs to Jews "by nature", something which distinguishes them from "Gentile sinners" '. Dunn emphasises the 'covenant language which stems from Israel's consciousness of election. . Paul deliberately appeals to the standard Jewish belief, shared also by his fellow Jewish-Christians, that the Jews as a race are God's covenant people'. (86)

Dunn disagrees with Sanders and maintains that 'to be justified in Paul cannot be treated simply as an entry or initiation formula. God's justification is his acknowledgement that one is in the covenant whether this is an initial, repeated or final acknowledgement (or vindication) by God.' Thus Dunn believes that justification by faith is not a distinctively Christian teaching. (87)

The outcome of this is that when Paul uses the phrase 'works of law', he cannot be referring to 'covenant works' ie works related to or done in obedience to the law of the covenant. Instead Paul is referring to 'particular observances of the law like circumcision and the food laws - possibly also the observance of special days and feasts'.

The reason why Paul opposed these 'works of the law' was because they were regarded by both the Jews and their Gentile neighbours as 'badges of covenant membership'. They were identity markers for the Jews themselves and the outside world regarded them as distinctly Jewish. Thus for the typical first century Palestinian Jew, it would be virtually impossible to conceive of participation in God's covenant, and so in God's covenant righteousness, apart from these 'works of law'. (88)

Thus Dunn maintains that when Paul denied the possibility of 'being justified by works of the law', it is precisely this Jewish self-understanding which he is attacking. Jewish Christians may have felt their belief in Jesus as Messiah did not require them to abandon their Jewishness, to give up the accepted badge of identity markers of their religion. The only restriction to covenantal nomism is faith in Christ, but Paul pushed what began as a qualification on covenantal nomism into an outright antithesis. For him faith in Jesus Messiah is not simply a *narrower* definition of the elect of God, but an *alternative* definition. 'From being one identity marker for the Jewish Christian alongside the other identity markers (circumcision, food laws, sabbath) faith in Jesus as Messiah becomes the primary identity marker which renders the others superfluous'. (89) Thus for Paul now that

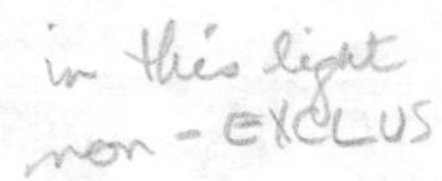

the time of fulfilment has come, the covenant should no longer be conceived in nationalistic or racial terms. No longer is it an exclusively Jewish qua Jewish privilege. The covenant is not thereby abandoned. Rather it is broadened out as God has originally intended. (90) With Christ's coming God's covenant purpose had reached its intended final stage in which the more fundamental identity marker (Abraham's faith) reasserts its primacy over narrowly nationalistic identity markers of circumcision, food laws and sabbath. (91)

Dunn's interpretation of 'works of the law' makes for a more consistent understanding of Paul than that of Sanders or Watson. It enables us to see Paul more of a revisionist of Jewish doctrines than someone who formulated his views in antithesis to them. This view enables us to make sense of Paul's positive statements about the law and also to understand why he was always in dispute on this same theme. Dunn is quite clear that Paul has not broken with Judaism. (92) His approach contrasts sharply with Watson's thesis that Paul wishes 'to inculcate in his converts a horror of life under the law, ie life in the Jewish community'. (93)

Sanders is perceptive on this issue. He is aware that Paul did not deliberately set out to separate the church from Judaism despite the fact that his congregations and the synagogue were socially distinct. His solution is not that Paul intended but that Paul implicitly and perhaps even unintentionally paved the way for the historical outcome of the church emerging as a 'third entity'. (94) Dunn acknowledges that Paul's revision did involve something of an artitrary hermeneutical procedure whereby the example of Abraham was treated not only as typical and normative, but also as relativising those subsequent scriptures which emphasise the prerogative of Israel. (95) In his own defence, Paul, I am sure, would argue that the advent of Jesus as Messiah necessitated the revised perspective.

Dunn describes Paul's new view of justification by faith as the transition from a basically Jewish self-understanding of Christ's significance to a distinctly different understanding - the transfer from a form of Jewish Messianism to a faith that sooner or later *must* break away from Judaism to exist in its own terms. (96)

I am not sure that Dunn is correct to argue this. Paul did not view his theology thus. I do not believe that this was part of his strategy, at least certainly not in Romans. We must be careful not to speak retrospectively of historical necessity. We are in danger of confusing what we now know to have been the *actual* outcome with either the *logically* or *historically necessary* outcome. Perhaps we should say that despite Paul's intention, his own conception of his theology and action, his position was such that

Christianity was *likely* in the end to separate from Judaism; but that *also* implies the triumph of Pauline theology and of Gentile Christianity. We, as Gentiles are, perhaps, too inclined to see this as historically inevitable. (97)

6. *Paul's Eschatology as the Key to his Strategy in Romans*

In one respect at least modern scholars are at a disadvantage in studying Paul. Along with the usual problem of lack of data, we have another - we know too much! This is because we know that after 1900 years, Paul's hopes for Israel have not yet been realised. So some scholars review Paul's theology in Romans 11 and come up with the solution that Paul envisaged two covenants, one for Jews and another for Gentiles. (98) The alternative to this is for many historically conscious and religiously sensitive scholars too drastic to contemplate. That is to presume that Christianity has simply displaced Judaism in the divine favour. Abhorring such a theology, the two covenant theory is seen as a viable alternative. Faced with an apparent choice between criticising some element in Judaism, or of removing the "raison d'etre" of Christianity (if there is nothing in Judaism to condemn), a theory that appears to explain Paul's attitude to Judaism, his theology of the Gentile mission and his anguish over Israel in Rom 9-11 (99), seems admirable in every respect. After all, theological doctrines have both a positive and a negative function - they tell us what their authors wish to negate as well as what they wish to affirm.

Nevertheless I am not persuaded that such a doctrine can justifiably be based on Paul's writings. (100) The problem is that we now know that what Paul hoped for - the winning to the Christian view of Jesus as Messiah of all Israel - has in fact not yet happened. We find it difficult therefore to hold together elements which to us today appear much more disparate then they did to Paul in his time. Paul was engaged in an inter-family dispute. (101) Christianity had not yet emerged as a separate entity. How we interpret the situation at the time Paul wrote to the Romans will vary according to our individual presuppositions. Some may see Paul as becoming impatient with Jerusalem, frustrated by Judaisers etc and therefore on the point of advocating complete separation for his mainly Gentile Christian communities. But another view is also feasible - ie that Paul is doing his very best to hold together what was already in danger of breaking asunder. The collection project, his concern about his reception in Jerusalem and request for prayer for his visit along with his pro-Jewish statements in Romans, are indicative of how seriously Paul regarded the question of unity between the two wings of the church. (102) I opt for the latter view of Paul.

There is a danger in viewing Paul only within the limited context of his own mainly Gentile Christian communities. This approach tends to view Paul as a unique and solitary apostle in what I would describe as 'the Melchizidek style' ie without parallel or predecessor! It tends to ignore Paul's continuing efforts to retain some meaningful links with the 'pillar apostles' in Jerusalem. The sociological study of the Pauline communities may even reinforce this one-sided approach. W Meeks notes that the Pauline churches were 'socially distinct' from the synagogue. (103) Though in this we agree, we are inclined to stress that 'socially distinct' must not be equated with 'mutually exclusive'. Sociology of sects can help us to some extent in looking at the early Christian communities. But its emphasis upon boundaries, exclusiveness, and upon the social world of the Christian group may distract us from the plain historical fact that real continuities and dual membership must, temporarily at least, have existed. Here again sociological approaches, whilst illuminating many important areas, are in the end no substitute for a properly historical approach. (104) In the study of the relation of church and synagogue in the earliest period, an assessment of continuities as well as of discontinuities is necessary; we must neither let ourselves be misled by, nor lay the blame for our conclusions upon, the sociological or other tools we may employ.

To put Paul properly in context requires a sociology of Jewish Christianity as well as of the Pauline churches. Simply to state that the Pauline groups were socially distinct by no means tells the whole story. We need to be able to demonstrate the continuities between the Pauline groups and their leaders with the Jewish Christian communities and their leaders. (105) We also need to know how both of these regarded themselves in relation to that part of Judaism still opposing the Christian view of Jesus as Messiah.

It appears to me to be an incontrovertible fact that Paul and Peter (and probably the other apostles also) agreed that different life-styles were perfectly permissible for Jewish Christian and Gentile Christian communities, *provided* they gave mutual recognition to each other as brothers in the faith. (106) I am arguing therefore for the necessity for some such agreement as Paul reports in Gals 1-2, whereby a distribution of areas of work including differing forms of Christian life style was mutually agreed. (107) The complications this may have led to in practice were probably legion, but the alternative is no less daunting. This would force us to argue that Paul opposed the right of Jewish Christians to continue to live as Jews after they became Christians and that therefore there must have been a division within early Christianity as deep as F C Baur envisaged.

10. *Paul's Strategy in writing Romans*

The evidence for regarding Paul as advocating a sectarian separation from the synagogue is not to be found in his epistles. Some scholars may see it as a virtue that Paul should wish to separate from Judaism. It is interesting that Watson, having argued that Paul both advocated and sought to actualise the separation of Christian communities from Judaism, goes on to ask whether Paul is indeed a theologian worthy of the Christian's emulation. (108) He correctly infers that such a person cannot be a fitting model. Had Paul in fact actually advocated separation I would agree with him, but I consider his hypothesis unproven.

What we are faced with here is the very serious question whether Christianity is fundamentally sectarian in its roots. Rosemary Ruether has suggested that it may indeed be inherently and inevitably anti-Jewish in its very essence. (109) I would regard both of these suggestions as being exceedingly serious. If Jesus sought to renew his own people as a reformer from within but Paul advocated separation, then we do need to ask the question whether Paul's form of Christianity may not be both an historical accident and a regrettable error. On the other hand if Paul, like his Lord, seeks to reform his people from within, then the sometimes sectarian face of the Johannine community in John's gospel may be capable of reasonable historical explanation *after* the separation of Christians from the synagogues had already taken place. John then becomes the aberration that requires explanation rather than Paul. (110) This is the image of Paul which most of his writings, and particularly Romans, supports.

But the missing element in Paul which modern scholarship needs always to remember is his eschatology. J C Beker ably describes Paul's confidence in the ultimate triumph of God. For a sect to separate from the parent body is in fact to despair of them and of their society as a whole. But Paul in Romans is an apostle of hope, of confidence in the power of God now revealed in the Gospel. Paul does not go to Jerusalem with the collection merely to prove the validity of his own Gentile mission. His visit must have had some significance for the Jerusalem Christians as well. We need to stress both what Paul hopes *for* them as well as what he hopes *from* them - ie recognition etc. (111)

In maintaining that Paul did not advocate separation from Judaism we must give some indication of the actual state of the relationship between the new faith and its parent body when Paul wrote Romans. If Paul did not advocate 'divorce', perhaps 'the marriage' was already in trouble! Even the fact that Paul in Romans denies the possibility of separation between the two may in fact be proof of strains that were already actually apparent, as Daniel Fraikin has recently noted. (112)

Thus Paul's affirmation of the faith from the Jewish perspective may indicate that *another* view or form of Christian faith was becoming a possible option. Paul refuses to allow the tensions to escalate to the point of complete separation. Moreover he also will not allow that view of Israel which sees no present or future 'heilsgeschichtlich' role for Israel - despite his own acknowledgement of her present refusal of his understanding of Jesus as Messiah. Thus Paul's definition of the new faith from the Jewish perspective is his way both of affirming that God has not finished with the Jews and that the new faith is not self-supporting (however self-sufficient the Roman Gentiles may feel).

Fraikin's essay deals with some of the issues which I have raised. Fraiken sees Paul's situation as being that of 'a reform movement which fails to win the majority'.

'As the new movement meets with the resistance of the old, there comes a point when it has to conclude that the mother body will not follow. In as much as its identity and credibility is still attached to the latter, the reform group has to reinforce its claims to the truth in that original tradition, protest its fidelity, and explain in its own terms the failure of the others to join. At a later stage, which probably requires more social visibility and success, the new group will claim to itself the name and all the values of the other.' (113)

I am in full agreement with Fraiken that Romans reflects the intermediate stage of such a process, and that the Gentile Christians though they are rejected by Israel are asked by Paul not to reject Israel in return.

Watson rightly argues that however contradictory Paul's statements may appear on the theological level, they do cohere and that most admirably at the practical level. (114) This is a useful insight rightly stressing the social function of Paul's statements rather than merely their theological validity. But to stress the practical here may in fact prove to be too practical! The 'practical level' for Paul included both the human possibilities, needs, aspirations etc, but also the divine purpose and power in which both Jews and Gentiles were called to participate. God's new act of righteousness in the sending of His son to renew the covenant with Israel and to fulfil its original intention for the Gentiles also, meant that in the future God, in His own way and time, must intervene in power to complete His new creation.

Romans gives the impression that this hope was weak and in need of revival, at least among the Gentile Christians. But if the Jewish Christians were somewhat alienated by their messianic faith from their fellow Jews and if the Gentile Christians despised them, it is likely that they too may have been somewhat despondent, lacking in assurance and confident hope. (115) Paul's prayer is - 'May the God of hope fill you with all joy and peace in believing, so that by the power of the Holy Spirit you may abound in hope'. (15:13) Paul's letter confirms that what now appears paradoxical and contradictory, ie Israel, 'elect for the sake of the fathers', but at enmity with Christians as far as the Gospel is concerned - will one day be resolved and 'all Israel' will be saved (11:26). This is Paul's scenario of the future as he looks at disobedient Israel and imperfect Christians in the light of God's new act in Christ. Thus he looks for a social reorientation of both Jewish and Gentile Christians in Rome. (116) The letter is written to seek to bring all God's beloved in Rome to share Paul's perspective on Israel, to support his mission and collection visit, in fact to share his symbolic universe. (117)

What is probably most conclusive for the position argued here is that Romans is singularly lacking in terminology for the Christians as a separate group over against Israel. The saints (1:7, 15:25, 26, 32) is the only candidate. Taking this alongside Paul's notable care and reserve in his use of the terms 'Jew' and 'Israel' means that he must have been quite self-conscious about what he was doing. So Paul's terminology also reveals his eschatological hopes. He refuses to write off Israel. Like Abraham he is willing 'to hope against hope'.

7. *Conclusion*

We have argued several main points. We have insisted that it is now evident that there is no real justification for maintaining that Paul's gospel is formulated in antithesis to Judaism. His Damascus experience was not simply a reversal of all his previously held convictions, (118) and Sander's work has shown that new options are now possible in the interpretation of Paul's theology. With Watson we maintain that there is no inherent contradiction between belief in Christ and the practice of the Jewish law.

The diatribe style, properly understood, emphasizes the apologetic and pedagogical purpose of Paul in Romans rather than the polemical. The objector is not necessarily a pious Jew or any kind of Judaizer but someone whom Paul wishes to educate and strengthen in their faith.

Paul in Romans argues from the Jewish perspective in that he assumes the prerogatives and heritage in Israel. 'Not from the Jews only' seems to be his starting point. But he also stresses divine judgement and impartiality, so that there is a demonstrated equality of Jew and Gentile in Christ. What has been called 'a dialogue with Judaism' turns out to be Paul's reinterpretation of Israel's role in the divine purpose for Jews,

Gentiles and the world. With Dunn we see Paul revising and reintepreting covenant and election but not rejecting his Jewish heritage in such a way as to leave him isolated from his own roots. Thus Paul uses the abiding election of Israel to foil an attempted severance of Gentile Christian branches from their Jewish trunk.

Paul's strategy, faced with division in the house-churches at Rome, is to emphasize continuity between his messianic faith and the faith of Israel. He stresses the unity of all God's people and their mutual interaction in the divine purpose. God can use the nations and Israel freely to fulfil His purpose; He can use them to discipline one another; and there is certainly no prospect of 'separate development' for either. Thus the collection visit, Paul's intended visit to Rome and subsequent mission in Spain, as well as Paul's gospel itself all cohere in demonstrating both the universality of grace and of judgement. Although Paul recognizes and affirms the separate history and identity of Jew and Gentile, God for him is one; the divine purpose includes both Jew and Gentile, and together in reconciliation and harmony they point the way to a world renewed and restored according to the fulness of God's covenant purpose. It is this hope that enables Paul to have hope for Israel - at present rejecting his gospel - and at the same time to reject Gentile Christian interpretations of the contemporary mission situation in presuming that the people of Israel have been 'written-off' and that they have taken their place. Gentile ingrafting is not for their sakes alone, but to reinvigorate Israel. (119)

NOTES

1 Cf Stendahl's essay, 'The Apostle Paul and the Introspective Conscience of the West', Harvard Theological Review, 56, (1963) 199-215.

2 *Paul and Palestinian Judaism*: *A Comparison of Patterns of Religion*, London 1977.

3 *Paul, Judaism and the Gentiles: A Sociological Approach*, SNTS Monograph Series 56, Cambridge 1986. On his approach see especially pp 19-22. Watson's study led me not only to consider whether Paul advocated separation from the synagogue as discussed in the previous chapter, but also to review here the wider issues of Paul's relation to his Jewish heritage and the use he makes of this in Romans.

4 Op cit p64.

5 Op cit p67.

6 Op cit p19.

7 Watson's study offers an excellent development of the critique of the Lutheran view of Paul already initiated by Sanders. In its conclusions, however, the study still leaves Paul in a very antagonistic stance towards Judaism, similar to the former Lutheran position, though now for

sociological rather than theological reasons.

8 We do not posit a major development in Paul's theology between Galatians and Romans - the main difference is due to the differing 'Sitz im Leben' of the two letters. Sanders has argued that only in two passages in his letters, ie 2 Cor 3:4-18 and Phil 3:3-11, does Paul compare in an evaluative way, the old dispensation and the new. This is not always recognised in the interpretation of Galatians. Cf Sanders, *Paul, the Law and the Jewish People*, Philadelphia 1983, p137.

9 Op cit p19.

10 We are presuming here the conclusions arrived at in Chapter 9.

11 *Commentary on Romans*, ET London 1980, pp 272, 281-3.

12 Cf Sanders op cit p156.

13 Ibid.

14 See especially pp 37-57.

15 Ibid.

16 Op cit p180.

17 Op cit pp 442-47 and 522.

18 *Paul, the Law and the Jewish People*, pp 38f.

19 Op cit p156.

20 Op cit pp 46-48.

21 Op cit p64.

22 Ibid.

23 Op cit pp 64-69.

24 Cf J Dunn's comment - 'The Lutheran Paul has been replaced by an idiosyncratic Paul who turns his face against the glory and greatness of Israel's covenant theology and abandons Judaism simply because it is not Christianity', 'The New Perspective on Paul', Bulletin of the John Ryland's Library, 65, 1982-3, p101.

25 Op cit p69.

26 Paul's use of the diatribe does not reflect street-corner preaching. We assume that it is now permissible to speak of the diatribe not as a technical term for a genre in antiquity but as a dialogical form of literature related to the rhetorical genre of the philosophical school which had incorporated a specific pedagogical tradition with its own style and methods. Cf S Stowers, *The Diatribe and Paul's Letter to the Romans*, SBL Dissertation Series, 57, Chico, California 1981 especially pp 75f.

27 On this see Chapter 3 in this volume especially pp 29f and notes 40-48. I am also drawing on material in this section from a paper given in the Pauline seminar at the SBL meeting in 1982 entitled 'Romans: A Dialogue with Jews? The Demise of the Jewish Objector' (unpublished). W Wuellner is one of the few NT scholars who has studied the diatribe, cf *The Diatribe in Ancient Rhetorical Theory*, ed. W Wuellner, Graduate Theological Union, Berkeley, 1976 and "Paul's Rhetoric of Argumentation in Romans: An Alternative to the Donfried-Karris Debate", in *The Romans Debate*, Augsburg, Minneapolis, 1977, 152-74. Cf also K P Donfried, "False

Presuppositions in the Study of Romans" in *The Romans Debate,* pp 120-51

28 Watson has unfortunately not considered Stowers' work. The result is that insufficient attention is paid to the diatribe's influence in Watson's interpretation. Cf A J Wedderburn, 'Paul and the Law' Scottish Journal of Theology, 38, p616.

29 Eg P Minear, *The Obedience of Faith: The Purposes of Paul in the Epistle to the Romans*, London 1971, p48, and G Bornkamm, 'The Revelation of God's Wrath', now in *Early Christian Experience*, SCM 1969, pp 46f (59).

30 For a different understanding see C K Barrett, *A Commentary on the Epistle to the Romans*, London 1957, pp 42f and P Achtemeier, *Romans*, Interpretation Series, John Knox, Atlanta, 1985 pp 44f.

31 *Paul the Apostle: The Triumph of God in Life and Thought*, Philadelphia 1980, pp 24-25.

32 Op cit p77.

33 Op cit p88.

34 Op cit p81.

35 Op cit p89.

36 Op cit p82.

37 Op cit p79.

38 Cf Wedderburn op cit p616, Watson op cit pp 109f.

39 Cf Stowers, op cit p98.

40 Cf Stowers, 'Paul Dialogue with a Fellow Jew in Romans 3:1- 9', The Catholic Biblical Quarterly, 46, 1984, pp 714f.

41 Cf Stowers, op cit p719.

42 See the excellent study by Jouette Bassler, *Divine Impartiality: Paul and a Theological Axiom*, SBL Disseration Series 59, Chico, CA, 1982. By stressing divine impartiality rather than the human condition, Bassler brings fresh insight to Rom 1-3, demonstrating in particular the unity of 1:16 - 2:11, (pp 121f).

43 Cf Stowers op cit pp 117f, 152f and 174f. On some of the residual problems of Paul's indictment of the Jew in 2:17f, cf CEB Cranfield, *Romans, ICC*, Clark, Edinburgh, 1975, Vol 1, 168ff; Sanders, op cit p129 and H Räisänen, *Paul and the Law*, Fortress, Philadelphia, 1986, p99; see also JDG Dunn, *Romans, Word Bible Commentary,* Word Books, Dallas, 1988, Volume 1 pp109f

44 Op cit p722.

45 Op cit pp 86-91. See also Sanders op cit p58, 75.

46 Op cit p160.

47 Op cit p91; cf also Stowers, *Romans*, p114.

48 Cf Stowers op cit p99. W. Wuellner maintains that Romans is in the demonstrative genre, "Paul's Rhetoric" op cit pp152 ff.

49 Cf Stowers op cit p118.

50 Ibid. I am grateful to Neil Elliott for a copy of a seminar paper on "Paul against Gentile Christianity: The Rhetoric of Romans 1-4", the initial outcome of his rhetorical/critical study of the Letter at Princeton

Seminary.

51 Cf Stowers op cit p129. On the relation of Gentiles to the Jewish Law and whether Paul held to the universal validity of the Law, cf L Gaston, *Paul and the Torah*, University of British Columbia Press, 1987, 9f, 11, 15, 23-25, 35-44.

52 Eg R Bultmann, *Theology of the New Testament* (New York, 1951) Vol I, pp 108-9 and E Käsemann op cit pp 83f. It is, in this respect noteworthy, that T Schmeller in his recent study of the diatribe still concludes that the person addressed in 2:1f is the Jew, *Paulus und die Diatribe,* Aschendorff, Munster, 1987, pp274, 279ff.

53 Cf Stowers, *Romans*, p3. Contra Stowers, we take the pretentious boasting to mean that the Jew relies on the possession of the law as insulation against divine judgement, whereas for Paul Torah signifies accountability for both Jew and Gentile.

54 Op cit pp 116-7.

55 Op cit pp 96f, 160 and 171f.

56 Cf Cranfield, op cit p568. Watson draws attention to this but exaggerates somewhat in claiming that Paul 'identifies circumcision with castration', op cit p62. Paul in Rom 2:25ff neither renounces circumcision nor regards it as optional, cf Sanders, op cit p117 n24; cf also J Marcus,"The Circumcision and the Uncircumcision in Rome," New Testament Studies, Vol 35 (1989), pp67-81.

57 Cf R Jewett, *Christian Tolerance: God's Message to the Modern Church*, Westminster Press, 1978, pp 62-67.

58 Watson's view that Paul wishes to convert the Jewish Christian congregation in Rome to Paulinism (op cit pp 98- 100) implies this. But is not this 'making one's faith a norm for others' which Jewett, (n58 above) and Käsemann (op cit p379) both oppose?

59 Op cit p30

60 Beker brings out these aspects very well. See especially pp 71f.

61 Contra Watson who writes of Pauline Gentile Christians - 'they are the "true Jews" ... in contrast to those who are Jews in name ...' op cit p122.

62 Op cit p112

63 This is the working definition used by Watson op cit pp 40 and 69.

64 Watson recognises that in Galatians, denunciation is directed primarily against the Judaisers, and not the Jewish community as a whole. But he holds that the Judaisers are seen in 4:25 as the representatives of the Jewish community, so the distinction is not significant. In this way Galatians can be interpreted as advocating a sectarian stance, op cit pp 61 and 67f.

65 Watson is unable to reconcile this concept with Paul's argument in Rom 9, and thus concludes that on the theological level Paul contradicts himself; Watson holds that Romans is, however, 'a highly coherent piece of writing when considered from the standpoint of its social function', op cit pp 170-72.

66 Davies suggests that Paul turns the tables on Gentile Christians who were prone to look down on their Jewish associates, both Christian and others. Gentile Christians coming from the wild olive have nothing to contribute - to be fruitful they have to be grafted on to the cultivated tree which had Abraham, the father of Israel, at its root. 'A Suggestion concerning Romans 11:13-24' in *Jewish and Pauline Studies*, Fortress 1985, pp 153-63.

67 Beker states, 'because the priority of Jewish Christianity is indissolubly connected with the priority of Israel in salvation-history, the nature of the priority had to be delineated, lest Jewish Christianity become either sectarian and divorced from Gentile Christianity or a negligible item in an increasingly Gentile church, which in this manner would lose its salvation-historical base in Israel', op cit p90.

68 Davies surmises that in the allegory of the olive tree, Paul was engaged not only with the Gentile Christians but also with the Gentile world and its anti-Judaism, op cit p163.

69 On this see my article 'The Freedom and Faithfulness of God to Israel', Chapter 4 in this volume.

70 *Israel in the Apostolic Church*, SNTS Monograph Series 10, Cambridge 1969.

71 Cf W D Davies, 'Paul and the People of Israel' in *Jewish and Pauline Studies* op cit p132. The Old Testament is not just a support for Paul's thought but it is itself the basis from which Paul argues, cf O Michel, *Der Brief an die Römer,* KEK 14 Aufl, Göttingen, 1978, p 306.

72 Cf Sanders op cit pp 81-83, 183, 198. W D Davies op cit pp 131f; Beker op cit pp 90f. Watson op cit pp 172-3.

73 Cf R Jewett 'The Redaction and Use of an early Christian Confession in Rom 1:3-4 in *The Living Text: Essays in honour of E W Sanders, Ed D E Groh & R Jewett*. Univ. Press of America, 1985, p99f.

74 Recently A J Hultgren has demonstrated the parallels between Rom 3:21-26 and the cultic imagery of the Day of Atonement, *Paul's Gospel and Mission*, Fortress 1985, especially chapter 3, pp 47f. 99

75 Cf the preface to the fourth edition of *Paul and Rabbinic Judaism*, Fortress 1980, p33.

76 Op cit p210.

77 Op cit p172. See also Sanders op cit pp 46f and Beker op cit pp 87f.

78 Op cit pp 172-4. Watson is unable to reconcile Rom 9 and Rom 11 because he interprets the former as an argument for the election of Gentiles *rather* than Jews - instead of recognising it as an argument for the election of Gentiles as well as Jews, cf especially p170.

79 Op cit p164.

80 Cf J Piper, *The Justification of God: An Exegetical and Theological Study of Romans 9:1-23*, Grand Rapids, 1983.

81 Op cit p164.

82 Davies discusses in his preface (see note 75 above) pp 30f, what Sanders had written in a critique of Davies' views in *Paul and Palestinian Judaism*

pp 422, 478-90.
83 Op cit p31.
84 Op cit p34.
85 Cf P Achtemeier op cit p56.
86 Op cit pp 105-106.
87 Ibid.
88 Cf Dunn op cit pp 107-110.
89 Op cit pp 112-3.
90 Op cit pp 114f.
91 Ibid.
92 Op cit pp 120f.
93 Op cit pp 47f and 151.
94 Op cit pp 171f especially 178.
95 Op cit p122.
96 Op cit p115.
97 J Gager reminds us that 'Our sense of the past is created for us largely by history's winners', *The Origins of Antisemitism*, Oxford 1985, p265.
98 Eg K Stendahl, *Paul among Jews and Gentiles*, London, 1977, especially pp 4f.
99 Sanders correctly acknowledges that despite disagreements over Paul's theological statements, there can be no doubt among scholars as to his actual feelings for his fellow- Jews, op cit p193.
100 See my critique of K Stendahl's views on this, "Salvation for Jews and Gentiles: Krister Stendahl and Paul's Letter to the Romans," *Studia Biblica*, III, JSNTS 3, Sheffield, 1980, pp 65-72; contra C Plag, *Israels Wege zum Heil,* Stuttgart, 1969. Cf also J Gager, op cit pp 204, 218, 251ff and L Gaston, op cit p 67. For more recent discussion cf also JDG Dunn, *Romans*, Vol 2, pp 650f and 675f; H Hvalvik, "A 'Sonderweg' for Israel: A Critical Examination of a Current Interpretation of Romans 11: 25-27", JSNT, 38 (1990) pp87-107; H Räisänen, "Paul, God and Israel: Romans 9-11 in Recent Interpretation," *The Social World of Formative Chritianity and Judaism, Essays in Honour of HC Kee*, Fortress, Philadelphia, 1989, 178-206.
101 Cf Sander's comment in relation to Paul - 'Punishment implies inclusion', op cit p192 and W D Davies, op cit p36.
102 Paul's feelings - his anguish, and his actions - in gathering the collection and taking it with representatives of his churches, reveal with some clarity Paul's genuinely ecumenical concerns here. What he did is as important, sociologically speaking, as what he wrote. Scholars have increasingly recognised that Paul saw himself as 'engaged in a thoroughly Jewish task, bringing the Gentiles into the eschatological people of God', cf Sanders op cit p198.
103 Cf *The First Urban Christians: The Social World of the Apostle Paul*, New York, London 1983 p168. See also Sanders op cit p176. Cf also Chapter 9, p130, n9.

104 Watson rightly stresses this and sees his sociological interpretation not as an exotic newcomer, but as 'a natural and inevitable concomitant of the historical-critical method', (op cit p9); not as a substitute for historical evidence, 'but a way of interpreting the evidence' (p10).

105 Cf. B Holmberg, *Paul and Power,* Coniectanea Biblica 11, Lund, 1978

106 The nature of this recognition is difficult to define, but it must exist otherwise the alternative is to claim that Paul did not distinguish messianic Jews from the rest of the people and this is inconceivable. As Watson notes, 'the hostility of those who to a large extent share one's religious traditions, and yet deny one's legitimacy represents a particularly significant threat to hope', op cit p146.

107 Contra Watson's scepticism concerning such an accord, op cit p54.

108 Op cit pp 180-81.

109 *Faith and Fratricide: The Theological Roots of Antisemitism*, New York, 1974, p181. See also J G Gager, op cit pp 247f.

110 Cf Watson op cit pp 43f and Wayne Meeks 'The Man from Heaven in Johannine Sectarianism', Journal of Biblical Literature, 91 (1972), pp 44-72.

111 Rom 15:16 (leitourgos) and 15:27 (leitourgēsai) indicate the reciprocal nature of the relationship between the mission of Paul to the Gentiles and the collection for Jerusalem. A rejection of the latter will signify a rejection of what Paul understands God to be doing through him in the mission and the collection. Cf N R Petersen, *Rediscovering Paul*, Fortress 1985, p145.

112 "The Rhetorical Function of 'the Jews' in Romans," in *Anti-Judaism in Early Christianity*, Vol 1, Ed P Richardson and D Granskou, Wilfrid Laurier University Press, 1986, pp 91-106.

113 Op cit pp 103-4.

114 Op cit p22.

115 Watson rightly stresses that hope requires social support; in his view the union of the two separated congregations in Rome will increase hope by providing additional social support, op cit pp 145-6.

116 Contra Watson, op cit p173, who stresses only the reorientation of the Jewish Christians.

117 Cf Petersen, op cit pp 144f.

118 On this see most recently J D G Dunn, " 'A Light to the Gentiles,' or 'The End of the Law?' The Significance of the Damascus Road Christophany for Paul," in *Jesus, Paul and the Law,* SPCK, London, 1990, pp 89-107, contra S Kim, *The Origin of Paul's Gospel,* Mohr, Tübingen, 1981.

119 As the title indicates, F Thielman's recent research challenges Sander's view of Paul, *From Plight to Solution: A Jewish Framework for Understanding Paul's View of the Law in Galatians and Romans*, Brill, Leiden, 1989. Cf Thielman's conclusion, 'much scholarship in the last decade has served to isolate Paul - to make him a stranger both to his contemporaries and to the post-enlightenment world' (p121). In contrast to this Thielman argues that Paul 'did not regard Christ and Torah as

mututally exclusive but as complementary' (p119) and that 'Paul's view of the law . . . was based on familiar ideas and echoed a familiar theme: the period of disobedience would end with the arrival of the eschatological age,' (p122).

120 The familiar image of the ingrafting of the olive tree conveys a clear message i.e. the purpose is to reinvigorate an aged tree and to make it more productive, not to replace it with another, cf J Ziesler, *Paul's Letter to the Romans,* TPI Commentaries, SCM, London, 1989 p279.

Chapter 11

A Theme for Romans?

It should be obvious, as a recent writer on the theme of Romans has argued, that since the recipients of the Roman letter were, in most cases, not aristocratic and educated people, but simple folks, slaves, freedmen and small-time craftsmen, whatever the theme of the letter is purported to be, it must be plain to such people - 'if there is one central theme in the letter at all, then it must be evident for the reader on the basis of the text of the letter itself.' (1) Obscure and intricate proposals for a theme for the letter are therefore automatically ruled out because they would not have been obvious when the letter was read aloud in the various house churches of the city. So Romans is, according to Stuhlmacher, about the Pauline gospel - more precisely, 'it is about the Gospel of the divine righteousness in and through Christ'. (2) Whilst not all scholars will accept that the Roman Christians were all of the very low social status described above, (3) nevertheless the fact that at least a substantial part of the church consisted of these means that there is some substance in Stuhlmacher's claim.

But to describe the letter as being about Paul's gospel is not precise enough. That Paul had a gospel about which he was exceedingly proud (4) is not in doubt, but there is disagreement as to what precisely constitutes his gospel. Because of this it is necessary to consider several other important themes in the letter that need to be associated with Paul's gospel if it is to be defined more exactly.

1. *Paul's Gospel and the Righteousness of God*

The first element of Paul's gospel is clearly stated. Paul is not ashamed of the Gospel 'for in it the righteousness of God is revealed', (1:16-17). There is substantial support for the view that the revelation of God's 'dikaiosynē' in the crucifixion and resurrection of Jesus is central to Paul's gospel. 'Dikaiosynē theou' is salvation-creating power (Heilsetzende Macht) - 'God's power reaches for the world, and the world's salvation consists in the fact that it is led back under God's dominion'. So Ernst Käsemann describes righteousness by faith - for him an inalienable constituent of Paul's theology (5).

The central place of righteousness is evident when we consider the content of the thematic verses, Romans 1:16-17. Here we note that four inter-related issues are involved: (1) the Gospel reveals the righteousness of God; (2) the righteousness of God is apprehended by faith; (3) the Gospel is the power of God for salvation to everyone who believes, to the Jew first and also to the Greek; (4) the righteousness of faith in the Gospel is the confirmation and fulfilment of the Old Testament promise of Hab. 2:4 (6).

The appropriateness of righteousness as a, or even the, central theme of Paul's gospel depends on how it is perceived. In (4) above it signifies continuity with the Old Testament. Our starting point must therefore be that whatever the revelation of the divine righteousness signifies, it cannot possibly denote complete or even radical discontinuity. We may express it in this way - there is an overarching unity that includes the apparent discontinuity of the new revelation of God (see Ch.6 on this).

In Chapter 3 we have already argued that 'dikaiosyne theou' is first and foremost a righteousness that demonstrates God's faithfulness to His own righteous nature, as well as being the redemptive action that corresponds to this faithfulness. We stressed there the need to counteract the post-Reformation tendency to stress only the latter of these, thus causing justification to deteriorate into a doctrine concerning the rescue or the new self-understanding of the individual.

We also noted in Chapter 3 and elsewhere that it is wrong to contrast the universality of the Gospel with the particularity of God's revelation to Israel, as if there were an essential polarity between these. The legacy of idealism has left us with the tendency to translate the Gospel into (secular) conceptual form and this has often resulted in an alien logic then being reapplied to the Gospel to produce polarity and opposition where none originally existed in the mind of the apostle. Thus the revelation of righteousness in the Gospel need not necessarily be set in contrast to the particular covenant relationship of God with Israel.

However much we support Käsemann's justifiable attempt to relate righteousness to the whole of creation, we have already argued that to stress the opening up of the covenant to include the whole of creation has been depicted by himself and some of his pupils in such a way that it effectively leaves Israel at the periphery of the divine purpose rather than in the centre stage as in the epistle to the Romans. Doubtless the tendency to contrast universality and particularity is still in evidence here (7).

As has very soon become obvious, one cannot easily discuss the righteousness of God without relating it to the previous activity of God with Israel - as Paul himself does in stating the theme of his letter to the Romans. This brings us to a further element in Paul's gospel which we have already glimpsed in the discussion in the previous chapter, i.e. it could be claimed that Paul's gospel is Israel-centred or Israel-oriented. An alternative description might be to state that Paul's gospel is covenant-oriented. A third possibility is to claim that the divine righteousness revealed in the Gospel is properly described as covenantal righteousness.

J.C. Beker rightly notes that the theocentric focus of 'dikaiosynē theou' points to the hermeneutical field in which it functions. 'The term gathers up in itself the rich connotations of Israel's covenant terminology: 'hesed' (steadfast love), 'emet' (truth) and 'zedekah' (righteousness), especially in its eschatological dimensions as documented, for instance, in Isaiah and the Psalms' (8).

We have argued in the previous chapter that there is substantial evidence in Romans that Paul did, in this letter at least, argue from the Jewish perspective. Despite Sanders and others who sought to explain Paul's differences from Judaism in terms of opposing the Jewish doctrine of election, we would wish with Dunn to maintain that the better understanding of Paul is of one who sees the covenant as being opened up to include Gentiles also. We maintained that it is wrong to think in terms of Paul 'breaking with Judaism' or advocating complete separation from the synagogue.

Our solution is to argue that Paul saw the Christ-event as modifying the Jewish understanding of election, covenant and law. Yet it is a modification, amounting to a transformation, and not simply a termination, dismissal or complete relegation to the old aeon of sin and death (9). Paul's gospel did not include the declaration that Christ is the termination of the law, whatever else he may have meant (10). We noted already that the peculiarity of Paul in Romans is that he is able to emphasize equally two apparently contradictory statements, 'to the Jew first' (1:16, 2:9,10 cf. also 3:1-2) and 'there is no distinction' (3:22, 10:12 cf. also 2:11). When we take together the subject matter of items 3-4 of our introductory paragraph to this chapter, we note the strong emphasis upon the priority of Israel in Paul's gospel. For Paul the gifts and the call of God are irrevocable (Rom. 11:29) and Israel's election still stands even alongside the bringing in of the Gentiles (11).

From 1:16 f. right through to 11:32, the universality of the Gospel is stressed. It is not surprising that so many scholars have regarded this emphasis as that which is truly characteristic of Romans. The gospel is for everyone who has faith whether Jew or Gentile. In sin and in salvation all are alike. And yet the priority of Israel also appears in conjunction with what seems to be a very different emphasis; it is to that other emphasis we must now turn for more detailed consideration.

2. *Paul's Gospel and Divine Impartiality*

In 1:16 f. in the thematic statement for his letter, Paul stresses both the universality of the Gospel and the priority of the Jew. This is followed by the declaration that in the Gospel also is revealed divine wrath or judgement upon sin (v.18 f.). This in turn leads to the declaration in 2:11 that God is impartial in his judgement. Because God is truly impartial in his judgements, there can be no favouritism, 'no distinction' between Jew and Gentile (3:22, 10:12 cf. also 2:11).

How this theme, i.e. divine impartiality in judgement, is developed in Romans has been well set out by Jouette M. Bassler (12). Building on the work of Klostermann, Pohlenz (13) and others, she demonstrates convincingly that divine impartiality is the theme of the first logical unit in Romans, i.e. 1:16 - 2:11. Klostermann had previously noted that the theme of divine retribution, more precisely, fitting or appropriate retribution, is the theme of three periods beginning in 1:22, 1:25 and 1:28 respectively (14). Bassler discovers a fourth subsection in 1:32 -2:3 which parallels the second in that it does not mention a new sin and punishment but expands the message of the one previous giving a pattern lAB/2AB, i.e. 1A 1:22-24, 1B 1:25-27, 2A 1:28-31, 2B 1.32 f.

Thus 2:1 does not start a new argument or stage in the argument, but in diatribe style, draws out a further consequence of the previous argument which reaches its summary conclusion in 2:11. The declaration of divine impartiality in this verse serves both as summary conclusion of what went before and as introductory heading for what comes after it (15). Probably this new section ends with chapter 2, though Meeks argues that Paul's summation in 3:27-31 of his first, fundamental argument shows that in fact the axiom of 2:11 is pivotal of the whole argument, not only of the first half. For the appeal here, also in vivid diatribal style, to the more fundamental axiom, God is one, recalls for the reader again the impartiality of the one God who is obviously therefore not the God of Jews only but also of the Gentiles, who 'will justify circumcision on the basis of faith and uncircumcision through faith'. (16)

The theme of divine impartiality is glimpsed again in ch.11 - for God has consigned all to disobedience, that he might have mercy upon all (11:32); again the following verse warns that God's judgements are inscrutable. Chapter 8 also includes the theme of judgement in that assurance is given that in the final judgement, the elect cannot be separated from the love of God in Christ. The obvious parallel between the judging person of 2:1 and 14:1 has been underlined by Meeks .(17) We will return to this again noting now only that the theme of judgement occurs frequently throughout the letter.

How then may we outline the sequence of Paul's argument in Romans? Immediately upon the announcement of the theme of the letter in 1:16 f., the apostle proceeds to stress the impartiality of God in his judgements. This can be interpreted as functioning as part of an argument concerning the equality of Jew and Gentile in the Gospel (18). It is sometimes understood to be particularly directed against Jewish pride and presumption. Similarly the fact that salvation is by faith and that Abraham can be described as 'the father of us all' may be seen as yet another example of this emphasis upon equality. In effect the whole of Romans 1-8 has often been interpreted as one long argument to demonstrate that the old distinction between Jew and Gentile has been levelled out. From the Gentile perspective this is the good news of the new era in Christ. But from the Jewish perspective it could be seen as a removal of Jewish priority. It is not good news. It is making the Jew equal to the Gentile! (19).

Paul was certainly not unaware of this Jewish reaction. The progress of his argument in Romans from ch.2 to ch.3 indicates this. If we regard the stress on impartiality as concluding at the end of ch.2, then ch.3 still introduces a likely response to it. But if, with Meeks, we regard 2:11 as the pivotal centre of an argument continuing through to ch.4, (20) then the questions concerning the status and the future of the Jews in 3:1 f. stands right in the centre of the argument. However we interpret chs.1-4, we cannot escape the fact that Paul sets statements about impartiality right alongside those concerning Jewish priority.

But what situation in Rome induced Paul to expound his gospel in this unique manner? A traditional approach has been to see the frequent objections in the letter as originating from the apostle's conflicts with Jews or Judaizers. We must now take up the question of what kind of opponents Paul may have in mind or at least what kind of misunderstanding he may wish to counteract.

3. *Judaisers in Romans? Objections to Paul's Gospel*

In 3:8 Paul includes an oblique reference to his being slandered by some people, presumably in Rome, (although it may simply mean that the Romans have had the slander reported to them from elsewhere). The fact that Paul stresses that he is not ashamed of the Gospel could likewise be taken to indicate that there are criticisms of Paul's gospel in circulation at Rome (21).

If 6:1 is a rebuttal of the slander noted in 3:8, this would certainly signify that the slander was being promulgated in Rome and in such a way that Paul finds it necessary to give it a systematic rebuttal. The crucial question, however, is whether in 6:1 f. Paul is simply defending his gospel against misunderstandings of it or whether, as seems more likely, there are Christians in Rome who are in danger of giving adherence to a mistaken gospel, purportedly originating from Paul. This might suggest that the people Paul condemns so sharply and so strikingly in 16:17 are in fact the exponents of this mistaken form of the apostle's message. Who might these people be? If we derive our information from outside Romans, we will probably conclude that these are Jewish Christians who continue to oppose Paul's mission wherever he works (22).

But if we confine ourselves to the information given in Romans itself,(23) then we find no real evidence of Judaizers. We do find the clear statement that the righteousness of God in Christ has been revealed apart from the law, and a sharp contrast between the 'the way of wages' and 'the way of faith' in 4:1 f. But the outcome of this argument, as indicated by the grammar, particularly the emphasis on purpose or intention, is to assert that God's purpose was to save both Jews and Gentiles, i.e. to include both amongst his people (24). This is in fact the goal towards which Paul's argument tends, and it does not readily appear that he is arguing against Judaizers who propose an alternative form of salvation.

It is essential at this point to interpret Rom.3-4 in isolation from Galatians (25). In his attempt to restore justification by faith to its original theological context in Paul's reflection on the relation between Jews and Gentiles (and not within the problem of how man is to be saved), Stendahl warns that to posit 'justification by faith alone' as the centre of Paul's theology 'blocks our access both to the original thought and the original intention of Paul' (26). Further, taking this stance 'obscures the specificity of Paul's arguments' in different letters (27) and makes it possible 'to homogenize Pauline theology since the common denominator could easily be found in generalised theological issues' (28).

In view of this stricture it is essential not to interpret Rom.3-4 as simply another exposition of the doctrine of justification by faith, a repetition of a doctrine already known and formulated elsewhere. Nor is it adequate to maintain that these chapters are Paul's argument for the inclusion of Gentile Christians on equal terms with Jewish believers within the people of God. Surely Paul had already made some progress towards achieving equality. Some kind of recognition or agreement was achieved at the Council of Jerusalem even if it was only with one party in the

Jerusalem community as Lüdemann suggests (29). Since Romans comes late in Paul's writings we would claim that it is somewhat anachronistic to see Paul as having continually to repeat his arguments for the full equality of Gentile Christians as if the on-going success of his Gentile mission had of itself no abiding or at least cumulative theological significance.

In any case, the restatement in another letter of even the same doctrinal argument does not necessarily mean that it must serve the same function in each of two differing contexts. Even if Stendahl is correct in his thesis that Paul's doctrine of justification originated in Paul's mind from his grappling with the problem of how to defend the place of the Gentiles, (30) we need to distinguish origins from later use. Thus the theological statement of a doctrine or an axiom in one specific context does not preclude its re-use in another context to draw out further or different social implications (31). We need to take seriously Kee's warning that there is no inherent function in any genre (and apply the same logic to Paul's apparent repetition of a major theological axiom) (32). Thus content or form of argument in Rom.3-4 does not in and by itself prove or guarantee its inherent function in the letter. This must be determined by the total contents of the letter and other broader considerations.

What we have sought to demonstrate above is that it is completely unwarranted to argue from the apparent similarity between the content of Rom.3-4 and Gal.3-4 that the same opposition, i.e. Judaizers, can be presupposed to exist in both communities. In Galatians, as distinct from Romans, the chief function of Paul's argument is to insist that Gentile Christians do not need to become proselytes to Judaism; whether or not circumcision is obligatory for Christian believers is a crucial issue in the debate, but in Romans circumcision in this sense is not an issue. In Romans Paul does not fight the same battle as he fought already in Galatians, whatever the opposition to him may be in this letter.

Stuhlmacher claims that Paul had heard that there was criticism of his preaching and mission in Rome and that 'in all likelihood, this criticism derived from Jewish-Christian sources and was the result of disputes which Paul had to fight out in Galatia, Philippi and Corinth with the counter-missionaries who had appeared against him there' (33). Elsewhere Stuhlmacher, in a more detailed presentation of his argument, again asserts that these objections against Paul's doctrine and person emanate preeminently from Jewish Christian sources (34). This position is further supported by Hengel's research which suggests an early dating for the letter of James (35). We note, however, in passing that here we are still dealing in the main with evidence which comes from sources other than the Roman letter itself.

Stuhlmacher does take seriously Stendahl's warning against interpreting justification polemically. He rightly stresses the apologetic element in the letter (36) but despite this, it is hard to resist the suspicion that the old tendency to see objections against Paul's gospel as always emanating from a Jewish or Jewish-Christian source has not yet been completely relinquished.

In considering the evidence for a 'Judaizing Christianity' in Rome, Wedderburn takes seriously 'Ambrosiaster's' statement that some of the earliest Roman Christians were Jews and that the Romans accepted faith in Christ 'although according to a Jewish rite' (37). He finds it hard to think whence this picture of the Roman church might have arisen except through historical tradition. Wedderburn points out that not all who professed this Judaizing form of Christianity need have been Jews by birth - they could have been proselytes prior to accepting the Gospel. He also notes Schmithals' conclusion that Paul's intended readers must have been Judaizing Gentile Christians; (38) this is because of the paradoxical fact that the Roman Christians addressed were clearly Gentiles, and yet the argument of Rom 1-11 has to be seen as a discussion with the synagogue.

Wedderburn finds further support for Ambrosiaster's witness in the letter to the Hebrews, a letter 'being sent to Italy', and 'most likely Rome, a writing that makes best sense if directed to Christians in danger of succumbing to the attractions of the Jewish cult, or perhaps returning to it' (39). What is significant for our purposes, however, is that Wedderburn after considering yet further information from the first letter of Clement concludes that the evidence for the nature of the Christian tradition at Rome remains tantalizingly scanty and 'that they were originally of a Judaizing character, must remain a hypothesis, nothing more'. (40).

Our conviction is that the presence of Judaizing Christians in Rome remains not only a hypothesis, but also a very weak one. The absence of any pressure to accept circumcision may indeed mean that the Roman Christians were mainly proselytes; but the absence of this element of the Judaizers' theology and Paul's conciliatory attitude to circumcision tends, we think, towards other more plausible explanations. We do support Wedderburn's thesis that 'the way in which food and drink are superseded in Rom.14:17, rather than circumcision and uncircumcision, perhaps suggests the presence in Rome of a form of Judaizing Christianity which was more moderate in its demands upon non-Jewish Christians than Paul's opponents in Galatia were, ... requiring only that Gentile Christians keep a basic minimum of Jewish ritual requirements that would make fellowship between Jewish and non-Jewish Christians possible without compromising the former's faithfulness to Judaism ' (41). But is it not only complicating our understanding of the situation at Rome if we fail to distinguish clearly between extreme and moderate forms of Judaizing? Räisänen similarly speaks of a soft or Torah-centric form of legalism! (42) But if love for God, or even fear of his judgement are adequate motives for obedience, then surely it is wrong to caricature these as 'earning salvation', or thereby constituting a claim upon God based on merit (43).

It is extremely significant that the discussion of the law in Rom.7:7 f. does not point towards Judaizers in Rome. Paul's purpose here is to exonerate the law and to demonstrate that its weakness is due to human sin that is only overcome in Christ and through the Spirit (ch.8). Only through the Spirit of God working in them can the elect live in confident hope of vindication at the final judgement (8:18 f.). Even the statement, 'I speak to those who know the law ' (7:1) in no-wise indicates Judaizers. In fact it need not necessarily indicate Jews but proselytes or god-worshippers who have lived in close contact with Judaism.

We may conclude this section by attempting briefly to summarize our reasons for rejecting the view that there are any Judaizing Christians in the house churches at Rome.

1) Recent research cautions against using sources other than the primary text to identify opponents.
2) Paul's letters should be interpreted in the first instance individually rather than in conjunction with his other letters . (44)
3) Most of the arguments for Judaizers are based on supposed parallels in other letters. They also tend to be cumulative rather than carrying conviction from their own individual content. (45)
4) There is often a failure in such discussion to distinguish arguments about the validity of Judaism and about the significance of living a Jewish life style from arguments with Judaizers concerning entrance or initiation into Judaism as proselytes.
5) It is our view that the attempt to classify the majority of Paul's opponents as Judaizing counter-missionaries is invalid because it fails adequately to take into account the diversity of early Christianity.
6) Even if we were to draw a parallel between Paul's opponents in Galatians, Corinthians and Romans, there is now support for the view that Paul's opponents in Corinthians were most likely to have been some kind of pneumatics (46).

7) We find it arbitrary to link Rom.3:8 with 16:17 and to presume that these people are necessarily Judaizers. It is just possible from the content of the slander in 3:8 to view this text, with Lüdemann, in its biblical-theological context as originating from the Jewish-Christian, anti-Pauline struggle in the period between the conference visit to Jerusalem and the visit to deliver the collection; but even this author nevertheless admits that the hypothesis is not demonstrable that Paul intended in 3:8 to repulse the attacks of Jewish-Christians in Rome (47).

From this survey we conclude that it is unwarranted to regard the contents of Romans as being largely determined by Jewish objections to Paul's gospel. The objections are in fact questions proposed and promptly repudiated by Paul himself, whatever their actual point of origin.

4. *The Faithfulness of God in Romans*

It is our contention that Paul in Romans argues in favour of the faithfulness of God in face of contradictory interpretations of the significance of the Christ-event. The current missionary situation as outlined in Romans 9:30 f. probably led to these differing view-points. There was no dispute about the actual situation - Gentiles are responding positively to the Gospel - but Israel for the most part rejects it. Paul is deeply grieved by this situation as he reiterates at the beginning of chapters 9, 10 and 11. But he is not pessimistic either about God or about Israel.

With the coming of Jesus Christ, the special relationship of Israel is brought into question. For the early Christians - particularly the Gentiles - there were several possible interpretations of the place of Israel after the Christ-event: (1) The Jews are still in their privileged position within the covenant: (2) They are now in the same position as Gentiles, i.e. they have access to God only by virtue of faith in Christ: or (3) The Jews are in a worse position because they have rejected the Gospel - they are in fact rejected by God and therefore in an inferior position to Gentiles.

Paul and his gospel were inevitably implicated in the disputes concern- ing the place of Israel after the Christ-event (48). He describes himself as 'apostle to the Gentiles' having a commission to bring about the obedience of faith among the Gentiles. Irrespective of whether or not he did preach to Jews in their synagogues, Paul met with little success in winning them to his gospel. Thus it was possible that Gentile Christians might deduce from both of these, i.e. from his own stated calling and from his lack of success with Jews, that God has in fact rejected the Jews.

If, as is possible, the Roman Christians were aware of Paul's correspondence with the Galatians, they would know that he had argued with them that Gentiles who accept circumcision are in fact severing themselves from Christ. Thus in the minds of some Gentile Christians, Judaism itself may have been equated with separation from Christ. It was then only a short step to see the Jews not merely as 'rejecting' (the Gospel) but as 'rejected'.

Moreover, if Paul gave public expression to his view of the Jews as being 'hardened' by God - in an attempt to explain his lack of success with the Gospel message among them, and then devoted most of his energies to working amongst Gentiles, both of these factors could have contributed to the conviction that God had given up Israel (cf. Romans 1:24,26,28).

As we have already noted, if Hellenists like Stephen had influenced Gentile Christians, then this radical theology could easily have led to the view of the old covenant and of Judaism itself as obsolete, now superseded in the new aeon of Christ (49).

Whatever the source, we do find evidence of a theology of Israel's rejection in Romans 11:13-24, 'You will say, 'branches were broken off so that I might be grafted in' ' (v.19). It is to repudiate such formulations that Paul writes Romans 9-11 and possibly the entire letter. The fact that Paul uses the dialogical style of the diatribe is not, as we have already argued, a valid reason for maintaining (1) that the statement reflects no specific situation at all,'(50) or (2) that it addresses only a hypothetical situation that arose only later in the history of the church. In our opinion, Paul addresses a real instance, probably the very first instance, of supersessionist theology in which Jews are displaced by Gentile believers as the new people of God, the new community of salvation (51).

Paul explicitly states that he sets forth his affirmation concerning Israel's election in face of Gentile Christians who were 'wise in their own conceits' (v.25); they had developed 'their own philosophy of history'. (52).Stendahl sees Paul as being forced to upbraid Gentile Christians for their haughty attitude to the Jews 'presumably for the reason that he may have found something unnerving in the missionary zeal of his bragging Gentile converts over against the Jewish people' (53). We agree with Stendahl that the basic components in these Christians' perverted theology are pride and boasting. They have mistakenly seen themselves as the exclusive object of God's redemptive purpose. Paul strongly rejects this inflated self-centredness (cf.12:3) (54) because he realises that this is not only contrary to a proper understanding of faith (cf.12:4 f.) (55) but also that a God who gives up his people cannot be trusted. The real issue for Paul is the reliability of a God who allows one covenant or one set of promises to fail, reject one people in favour of another in what could be construed as an arbitrary fashion.

So for Paul, despite the present resistance of the Jews to his gospel, 'it is not as though the word of God has failed' (9:6). Romans 9-11 and possibly the entire letter seeks in different ways to uphold this statement (56). But even this thesis needs further clarification. Some scholars have been happy to see in Romans Paul's argument for a church of Jews and Gentiles, equal in faith in Christ. Thus for them, when Paul has fully affirmed the safety of the 'elect in Christ' whom nothing can separate from the love of God (8:31-39) there is then really nothing more to be said - all else must be superfluous. Thus F.W. Beare says, 'We have left out of consideration three chapters (9-11) of this letter, chiefly because they do not form an integral part of the main argument. They are a kind of supplement in which Paul struggles with the failure of his own nation. We cannot feel that the apostle is at his best here, and we are inclined to ask if he has not got himself into inextricable (and needless) difficulties by attempting to salvage some remnant of racial privilege for the historic Israel - 'Israel according to the flesh' - in despite of his own fundamental position that all men are in the same position before God.' (57) Dodd likewise accuses Paul of a certain residual patriotism (58).

But although he could have legitimately done so, Paul did not finish his argument at the end of chapter 8. This is because he is not concerned only with the salvation of individual Jewish and Gentile Christians, but with God's covenant people Israel. God's faithfulness to them has to be demonstrated if God's glory and good name as a faithful God is to be vindicated.

Another form of the same Gentile-Christian interpretation of Paul is to maintain that so long as a righteous remnant of Jews is preserved, then God's honour stands intact. At the end of ch.9 Paul maintains that God, in continuity with the pattern already revealed in scripture, now calls a remnant from within Israel to faith in the Gospel (9:27) whilst the majority of Jews stumble over a stumbling stone (9:32 f.) According to 11:5 these are the elect remnant of God's gracious choice - 'leimma kat' eklogēn charitos'. Unlike the rest ('hoi loipoi') of the Jews who have been hardened by God, these elect few, among them Paul himself, are proof that God's word has not failed (59). They are the proof and sign that God is faithful to his covenant promises with Abraham and his offspring.

Some Gentile scholars would once again feel that this is all that needs to be said to demonstrate divine faithfulness. But this is not so for Paul. Paul refuses in Romans to equate the remnant with the seed of Abraham ('sperma 'Abraam') to whom the promise was to come . (60) It is to Israel as a whole that the promises were made and Paul could not be content with the present existence of a 'saved' remnant whilst the rest of the nation is 'broken off'. Instead he argues that the present existence of a believing remnant, although sufficient in itself to demonstrate that God's word in the present is not failing, is evidence of God's purposes for the nation of Israel as a whole. The 'elect' are not saved in and for themselves but they stand as a sign, a first-fruits of God's commitment to save Israel as a whole. So Paul does not conclude his argument at 8:39 or at 11:10, (61) but continues until he concludes with the salvation of 'all Israel' in 11.25 f. Only in this way can God's faithfulness be truly vindicated according to Paul's theology (62).

It is not that God is compelled by anything in Israel, by her virtuous actions or her lack of them, or even by her specific ethnic identity, but only because of his own self-commitment is he obligated to save her. Paul is quite clear that if God has committed himself to Israel, His glory can only be vindicated in the achievement of that to which He gave His word (63). This is why the existence of a believing remnant of Jews, or even the formation of a church out of believing Jews and Gentiles, is still insufficient for the apostle's theology. Our conclusion therefore is this - that the fact that the real climax of Paul's argument is reached only at the end of Romans 11 is proof that a major if not the major theme of Paul in the letter is to vindicate the faithfulness of God both in relation to the Christ-event and in His covenant relationship with Israel.

Our tentative thesis therefore is this - that Paul in Romans sets forth his gospel as the revelation of the righteousness of God in the Christ-event which he depicts as being simultaneously (a) the confirmation of the covenant promises to Israel and (b) the opening up of its blessings to Gentiles also. This righteousness which was until now not fully understood or experienced, has finally appeared in the vindicating resurrection of Jesus Christ. The faithfulness of God to His promises is revealed simultaneously with his impartiality in opening up the covenant to include Gentiles also. The letter can therefore be described as having as its subject matter, a reinterpretation of covenant righteousness in the light of the Christ-event.

In Paul's description of the renewed covenant the emphasis is not upon that which separates or distinguishes Jew and Gentile, but it focuses instead on the theme 'to the Jew first and also to the Gentile'. For the apostle, in contrast to many of his interpreters, there is no absolute incongruity in including within the same letter the twin themes 'to the Jew first' and 'there is no distinction'. It could indeed be argued that the latter of these relates to the topic of divine impartiality while the former denotes divine faithfulness.

It would be perfectly feasible and legitimate to use, as many modern interpreters do, language other than covenant terminology to describe Paul's theological perspective in Romans on the community of faith. Cullmann debated with Bultmann the merits of a 'heilsgeschichtlich' approach. Munck likewise stressed 'Heilsgeschichte' and Paul's special role within it. More traditional approaches have spoken of membership in the church, in the new or eschatological Israel, or simply in the people of God. Recently more open-ended descriptions such as 'the new community of salvation' (64) seem to be preferred in contrast to what some see as the stark exclusiveness of a Christological emphasis upon the justification of the ungodly.

The legitimate scholarly concern not simply to take over Jewish terminology and theology without substantial Christological modification is understandable and not to be lightly dismissed. But the problems created by an over-emphasis on the discontinuity introduced by the Christ-event, to which many post-Holocaust biblical interpreters have become sensitized, provide firm evidence that a more balanced approach is long over-due (65). Despite much scholarly debate on the extent to which Paul renounced the categories and framework of his Jewish faith, we cannot escape the conviction that covenantal theology was still basic to his thinking in Romans, especially chs.9-11.

We do not, of course, view this theological framework simplistically as Judaism plus Jesus the Messiah. Our view is that everything in Paul's life was transformed by his Damascus experience. Nor are we unaware of the problems caused by a naive covenantalism for inter-faith dialogue in our pluralist modern world (66). But as a vehicle for describing the thought and world of the apostle himself, we believe there is more accuracy and less anachronism with this than with more modern models or terminology, particularly in seeking to elucidate his view of Israel in Romans. We are also not convinced by the argument that Paul's infrequent use of explicit covenantal terminology means it was not central to his thought. His own peculiar situation as apostle to the Gentiles and the fact that generally accepted assumptions do not need to be frequently repeated are, we believe, sufficient reason to explain this phenomenon. (67)

We do not deny that for Paul, participation means participation in Christ. But we are also concerned about what this means. Is it participation in Christ as 'the termination of the law' or in Christ as 'goal of the law' and confirmer of the promises to the patriarchs? If Christ is for Paul the inaugurator of a new covenant (1 Cor. 11:25), viewed in the context of the olive-tree analogy, it becomes clear that in Romans this should be understood as denoting a 'renewed' covenant. This emphasis is necessary to continually remind believers of the continuity in God's self-commitment to Israel. In no way is it intended to diminish the significance of the vindicating resurrection of Jesus which for Paul was the first step in the transformation of all things, including of course one's view of covenant.(68)

Perhaps it is better therefore to argue for 'covenant' as a central (Pauline) conviction rather than for covenant simply as concept (69). As an underlying convictional centre this indicates the self-commitment of God to Israel. As a theological term it bears all the varied associations of its long history. It is open to discussion how many of these are present in Paul's writings and in Romans in particular (70). But if Jesus Christ is seen by Paul as the one in whom God came to restore the world unto Himself, then covenant as conviction is the term par excellence which specifically and uniquely describes this divine self-commitment. Thus when Paul maintains that the gifts and the call of God are irrevocable or that God has not rejected His people, he is expressing his covenantal convictions. 'To the Jew first', occurring as it does in the theme verses of 1:16-17 , denotes how early in the letter Paul wishes to indicate his adherence to such convictions. However, our approach to Romans has not been to argue that Paul writes to the Romans his central theological convictions, whether they were covenantal or otherwise, but to regard the apostle as presenting theological arguments designed to correct wrong tendencies in the Roman house-churches (71).

5. *Divine Faithfulness and Divine Impartiality*

We have sought to maintain that it is something in the Roman situation that causes Paul to argue as he does. Can we find any basis in the letter itself why the theme of divine impartiality in judgement should be included and be given prominence in the earlier chapters? We have already argued that the faithfulness of God is a theme that required emphasis because of a mistaken view of the covenant whereby Gentile Christians saw themselves as displacing the 'rejected' Jews. Is there any similar justification for the emphasis on divine impartiality?

We have already noted the stress on divine impartiality in judgement in Rom.1-2 and possibly also in Rom.3-4. If Paul's theme is the reinterpretation of covenantal faith, whence then this emphasis upon judgement? Most likely it stems from the need to oppose false covenantal faith, i.e. presumption of favoured status apart from the responsible obedience implied by this relationship. Gentile Christian presumption is denounced in ch.11 and doubtless it is parallel to the more frequently discussed Jewish presumption in relation to favoured status in 2:17 f.

Jew and Gentile are alike in their capacity for covenant breaking and for making wrong judgements on their neighbour because of an inflated self-estimate (72).

It was all too easy for Jews to misinterpret the covenant as divine favouritism towards Israel, remembering only her privileges and distinctiveness, but forgetting the obligations involved in covenant loyalty. The justice of the God of Israel was an important issue for First-Century Diaspora Jews conscious of being a minority among the nations (73). It was precisely in the context of covenant faith in the Gentile world that debate concerning the justice and impartiality of God would originate.

Even apart from a particular context, it could be argued that Paul for logical reasons alone needed to include a discussion of divine impartiality as a foil in advance against the criticism he was likely to receive for promising Israel's salvation in Rom.11. That Paul, despite his stress on faith, is still optimistic concerning the future of his own nation has not escaped the critical attention of some modern interpreters who see this mainly as an unfortunate residue of patriotism (74). For the purpose of this chapter it is sufficient to argue that if Paul's theme in Romans is, as we have suggested, covenantal faith, then both logically and contextually there is every reason why Paul should include as part of this, a discussion of divine impartiality.

In the Roman context, it would be particularly relevant to raise this issue because here it was not simply a discussion of Israel over against paganism, but a discussion of Jews in relation to believing Gentiles (75). If, as we have shown to be likely, there was also arrogant boasting by Gentiles (over against Jews) of their relation to God, then it was even more imperative for Paul to discuss divine impartiality in judgement. The apostle has to make clear that the Romans will not be judged by their own inflated self-estimate but by the righteous judgement of an impartial God, and not simply by their professed faith but also by their works (originating from that faith).

This calling into question of the Roman Christians' own judgements may also itself be part of the reason for Paul's use of the theme of impartiality. A clear connection can be demonstrated between the condemnation of judging in ch.14:4 and the similar criticism voiced in 2:1. (76). As Wayne Meeks notes, 'commentators, as far as I can see, have paid no attention to the striking parallel (with 14:4) in form, substance and function with the apostrophe that startles every reader in the middle of the first argument in the letter, "Therefore you are without excuse, o man, everyone who judges, for in judging the other you condemn yourself." (2:1). God's judgement relativises our own and therefore those acts of judging one another that divide the people of God run directly contrary to the universal judgement of the one God.

But what is crucial in the Roman situation is that misconceptions of covenantal faith were being combined with powerful racial and cultural divisions to draw distinctions where none ought to have existed. The boasting of one group over another had both a theological and a racial-cultural basis and was therefore all the more serious because of its complexity. [(77)] The way Paul characterises the issue between strong and weak does embrace specifically Jewish categories but it is noteworthy that despite this, he takes pains to state the issue in terms general enough that a former Jew is not necessarily on one side and a former Gentile on the other [(78)]. It is for this reason preferable to view Paul as a addressing men generally in 1:18-2:16 and not simply outlining the divine judgement of Gentiles separate from Jews [(79)]. All are judged for what they have done whether they are Jews or Greeks. Paul's ultimate sanction against partial judging is to remind the Romans that it is God who condemns and God who acquits, not one's fellow believer or even oneself (8:33b-34a).

Thus cultural and racial differences are not ultimate but rather the impartial judgement of God. Like the household slave, the Christian can have only one master (14:4). Yet despite his refusal to acknowledge distinctions, Paul does not insist that the differences between Jews and Gentiles are removed. 'Rather, he argues that both are accepted by God with their distinguishing features' [(80)]

From this brief survey we conclude that the stress on divine impartiality was included by Paul for several reasons: (a) logical - as a foil against the accusation of favouritism; (b) theological - to oppose the boasting of Roman Gentile Christians; and (c) pastoral - to relativise and put a stop to the uncharitable judgements within the Roman house churches [(81)]. Its inclusion in the first section of the letter may indicate a similarity with I Cor.1-4 where Paul gives a general foundational perspective for his responses to particular issues in subsequent chapters . [(82)]

What is important for the purpose of this chapter is that this conclusion is fully in accord with our previous discussion of divine faithfulness. Paul's discussion of covenant faith was introduced by a necessary stress upon impartial divine judgement to prevent misunderstanding of his views on the relationship between Jews and Gentiles after the Christ-event.

6. *Objections in Romans and their Role in relation to the Structure and Theme of the Letter*

Having introduced his letter by stressing impartiality Paul is now able in ch.3 to introduce a number of questions which he intends to treat in the letter. The first issue arises directly from the content of ch.2; (83) if God is truly impartial in his judging of Jews as well as Gentiles, then of what significance, if any, is it to be Jewish? What is the advantage of circumcision? (3:1-2). This is clearly a question about covenant faith - if God has a covenant but judges those within the covenant with impartiality, how then can there be any advantage in being in covenant with Him?

We have already argued in Chapter 3 that Rom.3 is a key to the structure and content of the letter. We paid particular attention to the questions Paul raises in 3:1-8. (84) In this discussion it was difficult to decide on the relation of some of the questions to each other, and the relationship between ch.3 and ch.9, though the main connections were clear enough.

Rather than look at every question Paul asks in the letter, though this itself is instructive and supportive of our argument, we will maintain that the major themes in Romans are introduced by a wrong inference usually repudiated by 'mē genoito' - 'God forbid'. It will be helpful if we set out these ten questions which fall into this category. They are as follows:

3:3 What if some were unfaithful? Does their faithlessness nullify the faithfulness of God?
3:5 But if our wickedness serves to show the justice of God, what shall we say? That God is unjust to inflict wrath on us?
3:3 Do we then overthrow the law by this faith?
6:1 What shall we say then? Are we to continue in sin that grace may abound?
6:15 What then? Are we to sin because we are not under law but under grace?
7:7 What then shall we say? That the law is sin?
7:13 Did that which is good, then, bring death to me?
9:14 What shall we say then? Is there injustice on God's part?
11:1 I ask, then, has God rejected His people?
11:11 So I ask, have they stumbled so as to fall?

By stressing the common introductory formula for objections (ti oun eroumen), (85) and ignoring the absence of the strong repudiation (mē genoito), 3:1, 4:1, 8:31 and 9:30 could also be included in our list. (86) All of these are in the same diatribe style and all, apart possibly from 8:31, (87) cohere around the theme of covenant faith and its implications. However, the ten we have already noted are adequate to establish the case which we wish to argue here.

We are presuming that Paul's questions/objections are carefully and deliberately introduced by him *to set bounds to the argument.* Thus the scope of the questions indicates that Paul intends to conduct a discussion with his audience on a range of (mis) understandings of life within the covenant.

(a) *Objections in Romans 3-4*

It should be noted that the objection in 9:14 virtually reduplicates that in 3:5. This is a major issue questioning, as it does, the right of divine judgement upon those whose failure to believe the Gospel is overruled by God as a means of bringing the good news to the Gentiles. If God has a purpose for the world, how can He judge those by means of whom that purpose is realized, even if he only uses them in a negative way? But Paul wishes categorically to affirm that judgement is as universal as the Gospel. He wishes to emphasize both the kindness and severity of the God of the covenant. Thus neither Jews nor Gentile Christians can presume that they stand outside the sphere of judgement, because they are within the covenant.

The basic question, however, is introduced in 3:1 and fully formulated in 3:3. Does the faithlessness of God's people nullify the covenant (i.e. the faithfulness of God)? It is this question of divine covenant faithfulness and its correlative, obedient human loyalty or faith, (88) that is central to Paul's argument throughout Romans.

The third question in 3:31 aims to show that the new faith in Christ is fully in accordance with God's purpose as revealed in scripture. It is fully in keeping with the faith of Abraham and the original constitution of the people of God. It should be emphasized here that we do not wish to argue against the view that justification by faith can legitimately be seen as a topic in Rom.3-4. Our proposal is that the topics dealt with are not necessarily those raised by Judaizers or even by Jewish-Christian objectors, but topics which have some relevance for the Roman Christians' situation and which Paul therefore desires to discuss with them. We prefer to see the discussion of faith in Rom.3:1 - 4:25 as set in the wider reference of covenant faith and loyalty (89). Thus the appropriate response to divine faithfulness is that exemplified by Abraham who, according to Rom.4, believed in spite of the appearance of all earthly realities and hoped in the God who creates out of nothing.

Thus the original constitution of the people of God and their subsequent continuance is determined by the model of Abraham, the first of the faithful. Who are the true children of Abraham, the true people of God, is an important subject in Rom.4 as well as in Rom.9. Thus Abraham rather than Moses or even David is the figure par excellence to answer this question and for Paul the scriptural story of Abraham plays a vital role in the formulation of his answer [(90)].

The correlative of faith is obedience and the obedience that faith produces is a significant topic in the letter as Paul Minear rightly noted [(91)]. The obedience of Christ and the disobedience of Adam are central to ch.5 and the preparation for ch.6. The awful effects of Adam's sin are contrasted with the glorious outcome of the obedience of Jesus. The opposite of faith is presumption. Faith implies the recognition of one's weakness and insufficiency. But the presumptuous man presumes that he is more than adequate to live by his own power and resources. In terms of covenant faith it is not the proud presumptuousness of the Roman Gentile Christians that is required as an adequate response to God's mercy, but a reverent fear (11:20); boasting in one's own merit or achievements stands in contradiction to the life of faith (3:27 f.; cf. also 11:6,18,20).

Even though the law itself is part of the heritage that God gave to Israel, to boast in the law and use it only as a badge for a favoured people without performing its requirements is also in direct contradiction to the life of faith [(92)]. So all boasting, whether by Jews (cf.2:17-29) or Gentile Christians (11:13 f.) is alike condemned by Paul.

(b) *Objections and the Law in Romans 6-8*

Of the ten questions Paul asks, five of them deal with various aspects of the law. We have already looked at the content of 3:1-4:25 and now we need to look at the remaining four questions. The first two questions i.e. 6:1 and 6:15 deal with the problem of sin within the Christian life. Are Christians to continue to sin so that grace may abound? (6:1). This possibly implies the argument that Paul uses elsewhere in Romans, i.e. that God is able to use even the disobedience of the Jews for His own glory. How can sin be judged if it can be used to promote the divine purpose?

The second question seems to arise either from a Jewish (Christian) source or from a libertine source. We have opposed the former and therefore stress that this question suggests that some Roman Christians saw their emancipation from the law as the gateway to moral freedom, without commitment to a corresponding Christian ethical standard. Paul counters this by a stress upon obedience to Christ entered into upon baptism.

The other two questions about the law in 7:7 and 7:13 represent Paul's attempt to exculpate the law without denying its complicity in sin. This argument by Paul is most illuminating in that it shows the apostle upholding his own gospel whilst at the same time seeking to show that the law itself is holy.

The theme of obedience to Christ implied in baptism is central in 6:1-7:6 especially 6:12-18. It is hard to escape the conclusion that some people in Rome were disputing the role of the law in daily life. The clear paraenesis in 6:12-13 - 'Let not sin reign in your bodies', 'do not yield your members' - makes it difficult to view this section as purely theoretical doctrinal statements about the life of faith. Did some Roman Christians who wished to keep the law in daily life argue against others who did not feel this obligation? Again did some of the latter misinterpret this 'freedom' as licence i.e. were some Roman Christians perceived to be 'at risk' because they were living without the protection of the law (by Jewish Christians)? Or were they actually 'at risk' not because of this, but because they used a theological stance as a reason for licentiousness? We cannot be certain but it seems probable that at least the temptation to licentiousness was a reality for some Roman Christians and a proper understanding of the role of the law post-Christum was essential for their own well-being (and not just as a theoretical response to their Jewish opponents' arguments) (93).

It is also important to note that whilst obedience is shown as the way to righteousness (6:16), there is also a stress upon commitment to a pattern of teaching, 'typos didachē' (94). The obvious meaning here is that to be under grace means to obey Christ - it is not a life without obligation. In this sense it is similar to life under the law (and Paul is careful not to say that the law itself enslaves but rather that it is sin which makes life under the law slavery, i.e. what holds captive (7:6) is not the law but the law's condemnation (95).

Thus the dispute which may have arisen in Rome was not simply about whether one could lead a moral life apart from the law (i.e. between Christians and Jews) but also about whether being a Christian involved any specific obligations for every day life and behaviour. After all, Paul had said in Galatians 'For freedom Christ has set us free' (5:17) and some Roman Gentile Christians may have refused to bind themselves by any rules for living and may have (mistakenly) opposed all others who did not feel absolutely free whether in relation to food or festivals or even payment of taxes (96). 'There is no distinction' may have been a slogan bandied around in Rome. If the law is obsolete, all distinctions that it made are obsolete also, and a Jewish lifestyle for Christians is 'de facto' an anachronism.

Some such situation gave Paul the difficult task of defending both the integrity of the law itself and at the same time 'freedom from the law' in Christ. What has not been sufficiently noted is that Paul achieves this not by saying that the law itself is slavery and sin, but by a theology of death with Christ in baptism so that Christians have died (and not the law) (97). In this way Paul can defend both the rights of his Gentile converts and also give a meaningful function to the law in relation to God's covenantal purpose. The law had a valid role divinely instituted but this role was subsidiary to the covenantal purpose as a whole. The promises are not dependent on the law and their confirmation has been 'apart from the law.' The law is not an end in itself but has its end (goal) in Jesus Christ. Only through the power of the life-giving spirit can the weakness of the law and the perverting power of sin be overcome. We can see that this is the conclusion Paul is leading to when we read Rom.7:25 in conjunction with 8:1-17 and 10:4. (98).

Thus believers are not absolutely free, but freed from sin for obligation to Christ, to be fulfilled by the power of the Spirit. Nor are believers at risk of condemnation because they are not under the protection of the law; the Spirit will intercede for them and therefore God will be for them, so that none can stand against them in the judgement (8:31 f.). (99).

The social obligation of Christians is further spelled out in 13:8 f. 'Owe no one anything except to love one another, for he who loves his neighbour has fulfilled the law'. This last reference to the law in Romans is, surprisingly, also positive and indicates clearly that the fulfilment of the law is a perfectly valid goal for believers in the sense already indicated in 8:3 f. 'For God has done what the law, weakened by the flesh could not do, sending His own Son ... in order that the just requirement (dikaiōma) of the law might be fulfilled in us ...'. In the light of this, it is worth reminding ourselves that very early in the letter, Paul confessed himself as being 'under obligation' both to Greeks and barbarians (100).

It would seem from this overview of the way Paul deals with the law in Romans, that he fights on two fronts at once. He wishes to maintain the rights of Gentiles to live in freedom from the law, but he also refuses either to condemn the law itself or to take sides with those who see their release from the law's demands as release from all constraints whatsoever.

Thus Paul has to give as positive an understanding of the law as he possibly can because there are some Christians in Rome who have misinterpreted the covenant, and probably also the role of the law within the covenant (101). He is not willing to identify himself with those who see the 'old' covenant as obsolete, the law itself as sinful, and Jewish scriptures and culture as being both anachronistic and wrong for all Christians (cf.15:4) (102).

We have now considered all Paul's questions apart from those in chs.9-11. Since these formed our starting point for this view of the letter, we do not need to argue their (obvious) connection with the covenant theme. Only 9:14 remains. Is there injustice on God's part? The justice of God's ways with the world is questioned. Doubtless this includes His treatment of Israel in the context of His providential care for them amongst the nations. Here the introductory emphasis upon divine impartiality in judgement interacts with the major theme of divine faithfulness as Paul comes to the crucial question concerning the future of Israel. Is God just to save only a righteous remnant or is He bound by His covenant to save all Israel? Alternately, is God not too kind to Israel? Is He right to bear with patience and longsuffering 'vessels ripe for destruction'? (103).

7. *Review of Methodology*

In our consideration of the ten questions above, we believe we have demonstrated that it is possible to give a coherent interpretation of their content when they are viewed under the theme of the reinterpretation of the covenant. (104) A summary of our methodology will be helpful at this point in support of our conclusion.

1. In structuring his letter, Paul advances his argument by a series of theses (sometimes elaborated) which trigger questions or objections, producing a recurrent pattern. We believe these questions are deliberately emphasised by Paul to highlight issues of deep concern to the Roman Christians.
2. We have attempted to give particular emphasis to those aspects of Romans that are unique in Paul's letters e.g. the phrase 'to the Jew first' the discussion of Israel in chs.9-11 and Paul's comments on circumcision in chs.2-3.
3. Following the emphasis on 9-11 noted in (1), we have taken these chapters as the apex of Paul's argument in the letter, using the arguments already proposed in chapter 3 of this volume.
4. We have not chosen to make chs.14-15 the main section of the letter because we see them as requiring as their basis the arguments of ch.11, particularly Paul's emphasis upon God's irrevocable election of Israel.
5. We do not wish to make a rigid separation between doctrine and paraenesis in Paul's letters and therefore we are able also to stress the significance of chs.14-15 as embodying the essential implications of the

recognition that it is God's purpose for Jews and Gentiles to share His covenant and live together in harmony.

6. Although Paul makes use of the diatribe style in Romans, we nevertheless view his questions as relating to or reflecting concrete issues in the Christian community there. In this respect, despite the diatribe style, we view Romans as similar to Paul's other letters.

7. But in view of the diatribe style of the letter, we would not wish to maintain that every topic which Paul discusses must, without exception, have direct relevance to Rome. Rather we maintain that Paul's total argument is a corrective to a misunderstanding of the covenant at Rome and that some subsidiary or supplementary issues may be raised as part of his own response and their inclusion warranted as supplementary parts of a major argument which is 'in toto' directed to the situation at Rome. Thus some parts of the letter may in fact originate derivatively from Paul's chosen theme and have only an indirect bearing on the situation in Rome.

8. We do not presume that Paul's theological statements addressed to the Romans are identical with his own theology 'per se' i.e. we believe that here, as in other letters, Paul formulates theological statements in response to, and to meet the needs of, particular local problems. Therefore in asserting that the reinterpretation of the covenant in the light of the Christ-event is the theme of the letter, we are not asserting that Paul always and everywhere centres his theology around this theme (though it may be feasible to argue thus). What we are maintaining is that Paul chose this theme as a focus for his responses to the Romans because it was the most effective way to repudiate their particular misconceptions.

9. We have sought to repudiate the view that Paul's gospel was every where opposed by Judaizers. We see Paul's statements in Romans as directed almost exclusively to the Romans themselves, though it may be that there was some danger from certain errors from outside the Christian community. But, from our perspective, Paul's main concern is to remind the Romans of the claims of the Gospel to which both he and they were committed, - 'by way of reminder' (15:32).

10. We have emphasized Paul's concern for the Roman Christians, rather than his own personal interests i.e. his forthcoming visit to Jerusalem with the collection and his planned mission to Spain. But we see his arguments in the letter as having a bearing on both of these. The emphasis on the covenant links the Romans with the poor saints in Jerusalem and with all Jews as well as reminding them of their obligation to help Paul in his work of bringing Gentiles also within its (the covenant's) sphere.

11. *A Theme for Romans?*

11. We have taken the view that the 'greater' includes the 'lesser', that the themes of individual chapters or sections of Romans cannot be determined 'piecemeal' as if they had some meaning of their own apart from the whole. We have presumed therefore that Paul was operating on the basis of a coherent (covenant) theme in writing even this long letter and that therefore all sections of it must be interpreted in the light of its overall purpose. This is particularly relevant in the case of Paul's statements about the law.

12. We have also given particular weight to Paul's concluding remarks in ch.15. The important exhortation to 'welcome one another' in 15:7 is founded upon the Christological statement 'For ..... Christ became a servant to the circumcised to show God's truthfulness and in order that the Gentiles might glorify God for His mercy'. The implication is that if Jesus and Paul have sought the salvation of both Jews and Gentiles, the Roman Christians should follow their example. So too Paul's reference to the collection; 'For Macedonia and Achaia have been pleased to make some contribution to the poor among the saints at Jerusalem'; they were pleased to do it, and indeed they are in debt to them, for if the Gentiles have come to share in their spiritual blessings, they ought also to be of service to them in material blessings (15:26-27). These both imply the sharing together of Jews and Gentiles, and the indebtedness of Gentiles to Israel. Similarly an earlier reference likewise asserts that the (Jewish) scriptures were 'written for our instruction' (15:4). Paul's call for the Romans to strive together with him in prayer for his safety and for the acceptance of the collection in Jerusalem again denotes the mutual obligations of Jewish and Gentile Christians and their indebtedness to Israel.

8. *Proselytes in Rome?*

As we come to the conclusion of this chapter, we cannot avoid discussing an hypothesis that has become increasingly attractive during the period of research. The hypothesis is that there may have been a considerable number of proselytes among the Christians at Rome. As Schmithals has observed, there are some ambiguities in the way Paul addresses the community there. We have noted already his significant statement 'circumcision indeed is of value' (2:25; 3:1-2). Also since we have not been persuaded by the argument that Paul was opposed by Judaizers in Rome, we are obligated to offer some alternative explanation to account for his choice of material in the letter, particularly his treatment of the law.

A Christian perspective on the role of the law 'post-Christum' would have had some relevance for all Christians. But for whom would it have had most significance? It seems to us that it must have been of vital importance for proselytes, who, having taken on the role of the law, then may have had to relinquish their acquired practices (or at least substantially to revise them) on being won over to the new messianic faith.

As a result of this, some of these may then have begun to view their adherence to Judaism as simply part of their sinful past, part of the old aeon now rendered obsolete by the Christ-event. It is also probable that there was a division of opinion and that some Christian proselytes disagreed with this radical perspective, remaining fully convinced that they ought to retain their acquired Jewishness alongside faith in Christ.

If, in addition, some of these proselytes now felt a deep insecurity, because of this on-going debate concerning the significance of Jewish practices within the new messianic faith, they would require reassurance in respect of the purpose of God for Judaism, past and present, and its relation to the new messianic movement of which they were now a part. If Paul had acquiesced in the mistaken views of some Roman Christians that Israel had been rejected by God, then the Jewish life style of both Jewish and proselyte Christians would most certainly be rendered anachronistic. If Judaism is truly judged to have been superseded, then Jewish Christians cannot ever possibly be regarded as equal with Gentile Christians, so long as the former continue to follow a life style which is, by definition, a legacy from a sinful past.

In such a situation, Paul's pastoral concern would take precedence above all else and must inevitably focus on the spiritual welfare of such insecure people, however 'weak' or 'strong' their faith may actually be. Though Paul associates himself with the strong, contrary to Watson, he does not take the part of either group - but affirms the right of each to live according to their own convictions, and then calls upon them to give recognition to the freedom of others to differ from them in their everyday life. They are to accept each other freely as Christ accepted them and live together in harmony, despite their abiding differences.

The outcome of all this would have meant that some proselytes continued to adhere to their chosen home within the circle of Jewish Christians probably still living in association with the synagogue. Others however would discard their acquired Jewish life style and make links with the Gentile house-churches. Paul's concern is not to destroy or hinder 'the one for whom Christ also died', (14:15).

We are aware, of course, that the same dilemma concerning the practice of their Jewish way of life must have also arisen in an acute form for Christians of Jewish birth. We still feel, however, that the dilemma would have been most acute for those who had already converted to Judaism and then been tempted to relinquish their acquired faith. Paul's deepest concern is with those Christians, from whatever background, who find themselves caught in the middle, in the conflict between other more confident Christians. He counsels the stronger to care for these, and the vulnerable are advised not to go against their own deep convictions despite pressure to be guided by other people's consciences. Whatever life-style Christian proselytes decide to follow, they are clearly advised by Paul that they cannot entirely separate themselves from the Jewish roots of their faith - the analogy of the olive tree makes it plain that branches of themselves do not constitute a tree.

We recognise that the presence of proselytes in any numbers must remain an hypothesis. [105] It is certainly not possible to decide with any degree of confidence whether there was a considerable number of proselytes in the Christian community at Rome. There is a real likelihood that there were *some*, and also that they may have been very much involved in a dispute concerning the relevance of 'Jewishness' 'post-Christum'.

All that we can do here is simply to assert that it would seem particularly appropriate if a letter dealing with a theme such as the reinterpretation of the covenant were sent to a community which included a not inconsiderable number of proselytes.

NOTES

1 Cf. P Stuhlmacher, "The Theme of Romans," Australian Biblical Review, 36 (1988) 31-44 (33) cf. also L. Morris, "The Theme of Romans", in *Apostolic History and the Gospel: Festschrift for F.F. Bruce,* ed W Gasque et al, Paternoster, Exeter, 1970, 249-63.

2 Op. cit.32.

3 On the diversity of the Roman house-churches, see R. Jewett, "Between Spite and Condemnation : Roman House-Churches in the Light of Rom. 14-16", a paper presented at the "Paul and Community" seminar, SNTS Meeting, Dublin, July 1989. Jewett builds on the recent study of Peter Lampe, *Die stadtrömische Christen in den ersten beiden Jahrhunderten: zur Socialgeschichte* (WUNT 2,18: Mohr/Siebeck, 1987 2 Aufl 1989).

4 cf. Halvor Moxnes, "Honour, Shame, and the Outside World in Paul's Letter to the Romans", in *The Social World of Formative Christianity and Judaism: Essays in Tribute to Howard Clark Kee,* ed J Neusner, P Borgen, E Frerichs and R Horsley, Fortress Philadelphia, 1988, 207-218. Cf also by the same author "Honour and Righteousness in Romans", Journal for the Study of the New Testament, 32 (1988) 61-77. See also Stuhlmacher op.cit 34-36.

5 "The Righteousness of God in Paul", in *New Testament Questions of Today* ET by W J Montague, SCM London 1969, 169-82 (182).

6 Cf. J C Beker, "The Faithfulness of God and the Priority of Israel in Paul's Letter to the Romans", originally in the Harvard Theological Review, 79 (1986), now in *Christians among Jews and Greeks: Festschrift for Krister Stendahl,* ed G W E Nicklesburg and G W MacRae, Philadelphia, Fortress, 1986, 10-16 (13).

7 Cf. Chapter 4 of this volume esp.57 n.34.

8 Op.cit p.15.

9 Contra E Käsemann who maintains that 'the apostle's adversary is the devout Jew, not only as the mirror-image of his own past-though that too - but as the reality of the religious man'. "Paul and Israel", *New Testament Questions of Today,* 182-87 (184). Cf. also Käsemann's *Commentary on Romans,* E.T. by G W Bromiley, SCM, London 1980, 282-3.

10 See chapter 5 of this volume, "Christ the End of the Law: Romans 10:4." We now take the view that it is best to translate 'telos' as goal, following in part C E B Cranfield, *Romans ICC* , Clark, Edinburgh, 1975, 1979, Vol.2 519; even Käsemann admits that 'systematic theology of every stripe argues that goal or meaning, fulfilment can be meant' and that 'lexically all these meanings are possible', (*Commentary on Romans* 282), though he himself categorically rejects them. Cf. also R. Jewett,"The Law and the Co-Existence of Jews and Gentiles in Romans", Interpretation 39 (1985) 341-56 (351f), and S. Westerholm, *Israel's Law and the Church's Faith : Paul and his Recent Interpreters*, Eerdmans, Grand Rapids, 1988 esp.130f. and 169f.

11 Cf. Beker of.cit. 13f.

12 *Divine Impartiality: Paul and a Theological Axiom,* Scholars Press, Chico, 1982.

13 M Pohlenz, "Paulus und die Stoa", ZNW,XLII (1949) 69-104.

14 "Die adäquate Vergeltung in Röm.1:22-31, ZNW XXXIII (1933) 1-6."

15 Bassler considers 2:11 - 'there is no partiality with God', to be the pivot of the argument in 1:16-2:29, op.cit. 153; see also 123-37.

16 Cf. "Judgement and the Brother: Romans 14:1-15:13", in *Tradition and Interpretation in the New Testament : Essays in Honour of E. Earle Ellis* ed. by G F Hawthorne with Otto Betz, Eerdmans, Grand Rapids, 1987, 290-300 (296).

17 Ibid. Meeks notes that 'the root `krin-' becomes a leitmotif of our text', (291). Cf. `ho krinōn', 2:1, 14:4; `krinō' occurs in 2:1,3,12,16,27; 3:4,6,7; 14:3,4,5,10,13,22; `krima' in 2:2,3; 3:8; 5:16; 11:33; 13:2; cf. also `diakrinomenos' and `katakekritai' in 14:23.

18 K Stendahl claims that 'Paul's argument about justification by faith' neither grows out of his dissatisfaction with Judaism, nor is intended as a frontal attack on legalism but instead 'was hammered out by Paul for the very specific and limited purpose of defending the rights of Gentile coverts to be full and genuine heirs of the promises of God to Israel'. *Paul Among*

Jews and Gentiles, Fortress, Philadelphia, 1976, 130-32. For Stendahl justification 'justified' the status of Gentile Christians as honorary Jews, op.cit. 5 and 130. Cf also E P Sanders, *Paul, the Law and the Jewish People,* Fortress 1983, 32-36 and 154-62.

19 Cf. K Haacker, "Der Römerbrief als Friedensmemorandum", New Testament Studies, Vol.36 (1990) 25-41 (36f).

20 Op cit 296.

21 But see C K Barrett's view on this, 'I am not ashamed of the Gospel', *Foi et salut selon S. Paul,* Analecta biblica 42 Rome, 1970, 19-50.

22 Stuhlmacher refers to criticism of Paul's gospel arising out of Paul's previous disputes with 'counter-missionaries' in Galatia, Philippi and Corinth, op.cit.30f.

23 Cf. J Ziesler, *Paul's Letter to the Romans,* TPI New Testament Commentaries, Trinity Press International, Philadelphia, SCM London 1989, 40f.

24 Note the teleological and inclusive emphasis of 4:16, 'dia touto ek pisteōs, hina kata charin, eis to einai bebaian epangelian panti to spermati' followed by 'ou monon alla kai', cf Bassler op.cit.159. Cf. also Beker's comment, 'Romans 4 maintains the distinctiveness of Jew and Gentile as Abraham's seed', op.cit 16.

25 Cf. Paul Sampley, "Romans and Galatians: Comparison and Contrast", in *Understanding the Word: Essays in Honour of Bernard W. Anderson,* ed. J T Butler, E W Conrad and E C Ollenburger, JSOT. Sup. 37, Sheffield 1985, 315-39. See also A G M Wedderburn, *The Reasons for Romans,* Clark, Edinburgh 1989, 35-37. U Wilcken's view is that Romans is a repetition of Galatians in the light of subsequent experience and a new situation, "Über Abfassungszweck und Aufbau des Römerbriefes", in *Rechtfertigung als Freiheit: Paulusstudien,* Neukirchen 1974, 110-70 (143). In keeping with his stress on the contingency and coherence of Paul's statements in his letters, J.C. Beker, after a detailed comparison between Gals. 3 and Rom. 4, concludes that the disparity between them on the issue of continuity and discontinuity is to be accounted for by the different contexts and differing audiences addressed. *Paul the Apostle,* Fortress, Philadelphia, 1980, 98-100.

26 Op cit 26.

27 Op cit 3.

28 Op cit 5.

29 *Opposition to Paul in Jewish Christianity* ET by E J Boring, Fortress, Minneapolis 1989 (35f).

30 Op cit 27.

31 Cf. M Barth, "Jews and Gentiles: The Social Character of Justification in Paul", Journal of Ecumenical Studies, 5 (1968) 78f.

32 *Knowing the Truth: A Sociological Approach to New Testament Interpretation,* Fortress, Philadelphia, 1989, 24.

33 Op cit 31. Stuhlmacher is broadly in agreement with the approach of his former student, M. Kettunen *Der Abfassungszweck des Römerbriefes,* Helsinki 1979.

34 "Der Abfassungszweck des Römerbriefs", ZNW, 79(1986) 180-93 (191f).

35 Cf. M Hengel, "Der Jakobsbrief als antipaulinische Polemik", in *Tradition and Interpretation in the New Testament* (n.16 above) 248-78, cf. also Stuhlmacher's recent commentary, *Der Brief an die Römer*, NTD 6, Vandenhoeck und Ruprecht, Göttingen 1989 esp13f, 49, 222f.

36 "The Theme of Romans", 35.

37 Op cit 51f.

38 Op cit 52f.

39 Ibid.

40 Op cit 54.

41 Op cit 61

42 "Legalism and Salvation by the Law", in *Die paulinischen Literatur und Theologie* ed S. Pedersen, Aros, Aarhus, 1980, 62-83 (64). Cf. also Westerholm op.cit.132.

43 See the excellent discussion of this issue in Westerholm (op.cit. 133f). In fairness to Wedderburn, he is most careful to define 'Judaizing Christianity' as 'as a form of Christianity which treats Christianity as simply part of Judaism, and more important, requires of all its adherents, whether they are Jews or not, that they observe the Jewish Law as the Jewish law either in whole or in part '(op.cit.50). He also (rightly) opposes Kettunen's support for the presence in Rome of Judaizing opponents in the form of a counter-mission such as one finds in Galatia (op.cit.99).

44 See J L Sumney, *Identifying Paul's Opponents: The Question of Method in 2 Corinthians,* Sheffield Academic Press, Sheffield (1990) 186f.

45 Ibid. Note Sumney's critique of Lüdemann for not consistently keeping to the principle of interpreting letters individually, and for allowing his reconstructions to dominate his exegesis and thus determine the identification of Paul's opponents, op.cit. 34-40.

46 Cf. R P Martin, "The Opponents of Paul in 2 Corinthians",*Tradition and Interpretation in the New Testament* (see n.16 above) 279-89. Cf. also Sumney op.cit. 189-90. J.J. Gunther lists eight different identities for Paul's opponents, *St.Paul's Opponents and their Background : A Study of Apocalyptic and Jewish Sectarian Teachings,* Nov. Test. Sup. 35, Brill, Leiden, 1973.

47 Op cit 110-11.

48 W Marxsen states that the Gospel requires both Jew and Gentile to distinguish between his self-awareness before he became a Christian, and his self-awareness after he became a Christian, *Introduction to the New Testament,* Oxford 1968, 105.

49 See Chapter 8 esp. 105; cf also D Fraikin's suggestion, 'Israel is more than all individual Jews. Somehow, at some point, the rejection of the Gospel by individual Jews or synagogues had led to the theological conclusion that

Israel has rejected the Gospel. It remained only to explain 'the fact'. The fact, of course, is the result of an interpretation.' "The Rhetorical Function of the Jews in Romans," *Anti-Judaism in Early Christianity,* Vol 1, ed P Richardson with D Granskou, Wilfred Laurier University, Waterloo, 1986, 101f. Cf also G Eichholz's comment, 'the addressee is the young church at Rome which sees Israel's election as invalid.' *Die Theologie des Paulus im Umriss,* Neukirchen-Vluyn, 1977, 291.

50 As we have previously argued, the objections in Romans are not simply theoretical, cf. S Stowers, *The Diatribe and Paul's Letter to the Romans,* Chico, Scholars Press 1981. Stowers claims that there is some evidence of 'real objections from the audience' in the writings of Epictetus and Dio of Prusa (128). He is quite clear that this is true of Paul's letters also - 'objections do not simply grow out of the internal logic of the argumentation, but also reflect the teachers' experience of objections and false thinking or behaviour which is typical of his audience'. (177)

51 We do not propose to *argue* that Paul opposed every kind of supersessionist theology, rather we *presume* this to be the case; what we have already written in earlier essays should have made this evident and even a casual reading of Rom II should be sufficient to establish Paul's opposition to all such views. Translations such as the RSV of Rom II:17b 'and you, a wild olive shoot, were grafted *in their place*', do not help to discourage 'Gentile Christian imperialism'. Some of the Roman Christians may not have wanted Paul to go to Jerusalem or to associate themselves with the collection, cf Wedderburn, op cit 74; cf also Dunn, *Romans,* Vol 2, 880f.

52 Cf. T W Manson, *Romans* in *Peake's Commentary on the Bible*, ed. M. Black and H H Rowley London, 1962, 940-53 (949) Cf. also O. Glombitza's description of the Roman Christians as 'geschichtlos', because they had erected their own view of the Gospel and of history into a sort of 'Heilsegoismus'. "Welche Sorge treibt den Apostel Paulus zu den Sätzen Rom II:25f?" Novum Testamentum VII (1964) 312f. Cf 12:16, 'Live in harmony with one another; do not be haughty but associate with the humble.'

53 "In No Other Name", *Christian Witness and the Jewish People*, ed. A. Sovik, Lutheran World Federation, Geneva, 1976, 48-53(53).

54 Käsemann regards the whole of Rom 12 as directed against 'enthusiasm' 'the chapter may be explained in detail from that perspective', *Commentary*, 332 f.Cf. also 359, 364. According to the grafting analogy, the ingrafting serves the function of invigorating the tree, cf Ziesler, *Romans,* op cit, 279.

55 Cf. R Jewett, *Christian Tolerance: Paul's Message to the Modern Church,* Westminster, Philadelphia, 1982 esp.59-63. Cf. also C.E.B. Cranfield, *Romans ICC* , Clark Edinburgh, 1975, 1979, Vol.2, 613f.

56 We take this to mean that God is faithful to His covenant promises, and see this affirmation in 9:6 as a reply to the objection in 3:3 that the faithfulness of some of the Jews nullifies the faithfulness of God. Cf. G Bornkamm, *Paul,* Harper and Row, New York, 1971, 150; N A Dahl, "The Future of

Israel", in *Studies in Paul*, Augsburg, Minneapolis, 1977, 143; H. Hübner, *Gottes Ich und Israel: Zum Schriftgebrauch des Paulus in Römer 9-11*, FRLANT 136, Vandenhoeck und Ruprecht, Göttingen, 1984, 60; also M A Getty, "Paul and the Salvation of Israel: A Perspective on Romans 9-11", Catholic Biblical Quarterly 50 (1988) 456f, 464f (though we do not agree in seeing a reference to Gentiles in 9:6 - this does not occur until 9:22f). For a modification of this view of 9:6, cf. O Hofius, "All Israel will be Saved: Divine Salvation and Israel's Deliverance in Romans 9-11", in The Princeton Seminary Bulletin, Sup. Issue 1, *The Church and Israel: Romans 9-11* (The 1989 Frederick Neumann Symposium on the Theological Interpretation of Scripture) Princeton 1989, 19-39(29). Hofius sees Paul as addressing two questions (1) Has God's word failed? (9:6a-11:10) and (2) Has God rejected His people 11:(1),11f (29-31) Cf. also Scott Hafemann, "The Salvation of Israel in Romans 11:25-32", Ex Auditu Vol.IV (1988) 38-58 (43f) Hafemann rightly notes that before Paul can affirm the salvation of 'all Israel' in 11:25f, he must first demonstrate why the *current* rejection of the Gospel by the majority of Israel has not *already* overthrown God's word (44). See also the literature cited in Chapter 10, n102.

57 In *Paul and His Letters* , Black, London, 1962, 103-4.

58 *Paul's Letter to the Romans,* Hodder & Stoughton, London, 1932, 63; cf. also 43-45, 179, 182f. J C Beker lists a number of scholars among them W Sanday and A C Headlam, Rudolf Bultmann and C H Dodd, all of whom regard Rom. 9-11 as an awkward and unnecessary appendix to Paul's systematic-theological core of Romans, "The Faithfulness of God and the Priority of Israel", (11).

59 The Qumran community regarded themselves as the servant of God whose salvation takes the place of God's promises to ethnic Israel cf. O Hofius, "Das Evangelium und Israel: Erwägungen zu Römer 9-11", Zeitschrift für Theologie und Kirche 83, (1986) 297-324 (305f).

60 Cf. O Hofius, "All Israel will be Saved" (as in n.59) 31,.

61. Cf. Hofius comment 'The extraordinary thing about Paul's exposition in Romans 9-11, however, is that the apostle does not close with this point (ie the remnant) and end the discussion at Rom.11:10' (op cit 31).

62 D Johnson rightly notes that for Paul in Rom.11:1-5, the salvation of a righteous remnant is a sign of hope for the salvation of 'all Israel', and not a substitution for the rest of Israel. "The Structure and Meaning of Romans II", Catholic Biblical Quarterly 46, (1984) 91-103; for Johnson the overriding theme of Rom. II is the salvation of all Israel (92).

63 Cf. J C Beker, *Paul the Apostle,* 332f.

64 In discussing Rom. 9:6, Hofius distinguishes between 'the people of Israel' and the 'Israel which is the community of salvation, op.cit.31. I have just received the recent book by R D Kaylor, *Paul's Covenant Community* (John Knox Press, Atlanta 1988) in which the author's preface states 'my thesis is that the fundamental conviction underlying all of Paul's theological

expression is that in Christ God is acting to bring all humankind, Gentile and Jew, into one community of the new covenant' (iii).

65 In note 9 above, we have noted the opinion of a most revered New Testament scholar about 'the devout Jew', which so offended Markus Barth that he unsuccessfully sought a retraction, "St. Paul - a good Jew", Horizons in Biblical Theology: An International Dialogue, Vol.1 (1979) 7.

66 Cf. K Stendahl, "Christ's Lordship and Religious Pluralism", *Meanings: The Bible as Document and Guide,* Fortress, Philadelphia, 1984, 233-44 (241f).

67 Contemporary Jewish misinterpretation in an exclusive sense may have caused Paul to refer to 'the promises' etc. rather than use explicit covenant terminology. We agree, however, that 'Paul's linguistic inheritance from Judaism and Early Christianity is such that covenantal concepts underlie his theological expressions even when explicit covenantal language is not present' (Kaylor op.cit.43). Kaylor convincingly demonstrates the covenantal dimension of Paul's convictions in such things as (1) the association of general sinfulness with idolatry (2) the divine punishment of idolatry - 'God gave them up' (3) the grounding of his analysis of the human predicament in a theology of creation (4) the connecting of right human-human relations to right divine-human relations (Rom.1) and, (5) most significantly, the language by which he understands the death and resurrection of Jesus is derived from covenant traditions so that righteousness itself is revealed as covenantal ie. relational, rather than primarily ethical or juridical op.cit. 38-40, 45, 51, 60-62.

68 'Paul's innovation is the way in which he interprets the covenant tradition inclusively', Kaylor op.cit. 44; because of the ever-present risk of anti-Judaism in Christian life and theology we do not agree with Käsemann's arguments for 'new' covenant rather than 'renewed'. We fully agree with him that 'right and righteousness can only be ours in so far as God gives them to us anew every day i.e. in faith' but not with his view on the previous page that 'the apostle's real adversary is the devout Jew' - hence our emphasis on 'renewed', Cf. 'Paul and Israel' (n.9 above) 184-5. Cf also M Hooker, "Paul and Coventantal Nomism," in *Paul and Paulinism; Essays in Honour of CK Barrett,* SPCK, London 1982, 47-56. Cf also M A Getty, "Paul on the Covenants and the Future of Israel", Biblical Theology Bulletin, 17 (3) 1987, 92-99

69 We presuppose in this discussion our review of the debate between Dunn and Sanders, in Chapter 10, 146f. Cf. Kaylor's useful distinction between concept and conviction, 'covenant functions at two levels in Paul's theology: at the levels of *idea* and of *conviction*. I do not claim that Paul always consciously had this conviction in mind, or that it is an intellectual concept central to his thought,....the validity of my claim does not rest on the frequency with which 'covenant' or distinctively covenant terminology appears in Paul's letters. My main claim is that the covenant as a conviction rather than an idea functions as a persistent presence and a dominant reality in Paul's life, work and thought'. Op cit iii, cf. also 10-13

and 36f. The merit of this view of Paul is that Paul's conviction that God renews the covenant through Jesus Christ 'does not obliterate his complex intellectual heritage, but provides a unity to all he says'. (13) On Paul's convictions see also D Patte, *Paul's Faith and the Power of the Gospel,* Fortress, Philadelphia, 1983, 10f and G Theissen, *Psychological Aspects of Pauline Theology,* ET, J P Galvin, Fortress, Philadelphia, 1987.

70 On the biblical understanding of covenant see the article on 'diathēkē', in *The Theological Dictionary of the New Testament* E.T., G W Bromiley, Eerdmans Grand Rapids 1964 Vol.2 106-34 and A Jaubert, *La notion d'alliance dans le Judaîsme,* Éditions du Seuil, 1963. Cf. also 'covenant' in *Encyclopaedia Judaica,* Keter, Jerusalem 1971, 1012-22; also D R Hillers, *Covenant: The History of a Biblical Idea,* John Hopkins University, Maryland 1969 and D J McCarthy, *Treaty and Covenant,* Analecta Biblica 21 Rome 1963. R E Clements rightly notes that in the case of 'themes' such as that of the remnant, the concept itself is in many respects more important for understanding the development of thought than the particular occurrence of the term, "A Remnant Chosen by Grace, (Rom.11:5)", *Pauline Studies: Essays presented to F.F. Bruce,* ed. D A Hagner, Paternoster 1980 (107f). With the increase of sociological approaches in biblical interpretation the covenant as a central theme is now re-emerging cf. H.C. Kee's chapter on 'Covenant and Social Identity: An Approach to New Testament Theology' in *Knowing the Truth* 70-102 : cf. also P D Hanson, *The People Called*, Harper and Row, San Francisco 1986 and Alan Segal, *Rebecca's Children: Judaism and Christianity in the Modern World,* Harvard University Press, Cambridge 1986.

71 Paul's statements in his letters arise out of his inner theological convictions but are addressed to the contingent situation. 'What must be denied is the choice between either contingency or coherence, because it is the interaction between these components that characterizes the letter, *Paul the Apostle* (92). Cf. also Beker's recent article, "Paul's Theology : Consistent or Inconsistent", New Testament Studies, Vol.34 (1988) 364-77.

72 Cf. Kaylor op.cit. 32f, 45f.

73. Yet this often was concerned mainly with the explanation for Israel's sufferings at the hand of the nations, rather than in developing the awareness that impartiality should imply equal status for all nations before God. Though Philo is closest to Paul in some aspects, Bassler concludes that 'Philo's' Jewishness did not cause him to define one group as higher, and closer to things divine, but it did provide him with the label for his group (ie. the Jews), op.cit. 65, 118-9.

74 See notes 57-58 above.

75 We do not mean to minimize the significance of the fact noted by Bassler that in Rom. 1:16-2:29, the context seems to demand 'a discussion in terms of Jews and Gentiles *per se.* To argue that God's impartiality embraces both Jews and Gentiles when they become Christians adds a dimension to the argument Paul postpones until 3:21' (op.cit.144). This postponement helps to account for the fact that 'there is less use of explicit Christian

terminology in Romans than in Paul's other letters'. Instead Paul 'emphasized God throughout the letter, but especially in chs. 1-4 and 9-11", H Moxnes, *Theology in Conflict: Studies in Paul's Understanding of God in Romans,* Nov. Test. Sup. 53, Brill, Leiden, 1980(13).

76 Op cit 292f. Paul Minear did make the connection between judging in 2:1 and 14:4, *The Obedience of Faith: The Purposes of Paul in the Epistle to the Romans,* SCM London (1971) 46, 48, 52.

77 This is another reason why Paul began in Romans by discussing Jew and Gentile rather than Jewish Christian and Gentile Christian; he may thereby be indicating the cultural and racial roots of some of the Roman Christians divisive tendencies. Ch 12:1-2 is the heading for what follows in the next three chapters; note the use of 'phronein' and related terms in 12:3, 16, 17; 14:6; 15:5; note also 'dokimazien' in 12:2 and 14:22, (cf also 1:28, 2:18). The Romans are not to please themselves (15:1), but to discern what is pleasing to God (12:1) and thus please their neighbour (15:2) as Christ did (15:3). Cf Wedderburn, op cit 76f. See also p170 and notes 51-55 above.

78 Cf. Meeks op.cit.292f. We agree that the issue in ch.14 'is a question concerning food being deemed 'profane', 'koinos", and that it is somewhat broader than 1 Cor.8-10, involving not only meat from pagan markets, 'but 'kashrut' or at least some modified food taboos, like those in Acts 15:20,29; 21:15.' Ziesler argues that 'the non-eaters were not only Jewish Christians with kosher scruples, but also Gentile Christians who, as in Corinth, feared to eat food that had been, or might have been, sacrificed to idols, op cit 17, (cf.also 322-6).

79 Paul's use of generic reference to 'anthrōpoi' and frequent applications of 'pas' denote the fact that God's judgement recognises no ethnic distinctions, Cf. Bassler op.cit 139. Cf. also G. Bornkamm, 'Paul in the first part (1:18f) frees the natural understanding of God and the world from its Greek presuppositions through specific Jewish terms and thoughts, and again in the second part bursts the boundaries of the Jewish understanding of law and judgement through the references to the law the Gentiles know'. "The Revelation of God's Wrath in Rom. 1-3". *Early Christian Experience*. E.T. Paul Hammer SCM, London 1969, 46-70(61).

80 Cf. Bassler op.cit, 163 cf. also Jewett , *Christian Tolerance*, 62f,

81 Cf. Dunn, *Romans,* Vol.1, lvif.

82 Cf. N A Dahl, "The Church in Corinth", in *Studies in Paul,* Augsburg 1977, 40-61.

83 The significance of this must not be overlooked; when Paul connects chs. 2 and 3 in this direct way, it means that he self-consciously sets out to highlight the apparent tension between divine impartiality and divine faithfulness. We therefore use the term 'questions' rather than 'objections' to emphasise that however and wherever they may have originated, the questions/objections in Romans come to us from *Paul himself*. By stressing questions rather than objections, we are drawing attention to the fact that Paul is *constructing* an argument by use of questions rather than *reconstructing* an earlier incident that may have

occurred in his missionary activity. The questions are therefore not unexpected but deliberately planned and introduced by Paul - he is not so naive as to introduce 'straw men' or hypothetical arguments which he cannot satisfactorily demolish, so that 'he becomes embarrassed and, in the end, dismisses the subject awkwardly'. Contra Dodd op.cit.70-71.

84 In order to avoid needless repetition, we will presume the findings and bibliography of our more precise consideration of questions/objections in chapter 3, "Romans 3 as a Key to the Structure and Thought of the Letter". Cf also C Cosgrove, "What if some have not believed? The Occasion and Thrust of Romans 3:1-8" ZNW, 78 (1987), 90-105.

85 M Black notes the formal characteristics of this question/answer as :(1) an objection is raised by the formula 'ti (oun) eroumen' (what shall we say?) (3:5, 4:1, 6:1, 7:7, 8:31, 9:14,30) or 'ti oun' ('What then') (3:1, 9, 6:15, 11:7). The objection is rejected by the formula 'mē genoito' ('by no means', 'Heaven forbid') (3:4, 6, 31; 6:2, 15, 7:7, 13; 9:14, 11:1, 11). *Romans New Century Bible,* Oliphants, London, 1973(30). In his study of Romans 5-8, N A Dahl noted how Paul's argument advances by means of a series of theses that are then elaborated or give rise to questions, which are in fact triggered by Paul's initial statement eg. 6:1-14 is triggered by 5:20-21, 6:15-7:6 by 6:14, 7:7-12 by 7:5-6 and 7:13-25 by 7:12. "Missionary Theology in the Epistle to the Romans", *Studies in Paul*, op cit, 70-94. Paul's way of structuring his argument is clearest in chs.6-7. Paul effectively uses rhetorical exaggeration to emphasise his point, cf Ziesler op cit 94; Dunn notes (in chs 9-11) the use of larger conclusions than the preceding section warrants, to provide a transition to the next stage of the argument, op cit 519. When I began my doctoral research on Romans, I studied these chapters to demonstrate Paul's use of questions and objections; my thesis, "The Purpose of Paul in the Letter to the Romans", (University of Edinburgh 1972), developed out of this study.

86 Eg. Scott Hafemann in his recent perceptive study of Romans II devotes some attention to Paul's construction of chs. 9-11. 'Paul knows that this answer (ie. 9:6f) to the problem of Israel's rejection of the Messiah will spawn a host of objections. Thus, in typical diatribe style, he now proceeds to take up these questions by anticipating where his arguments will lead his reader and then posing the next logical question *himself* to answer it' (op.cit.45-6) Hafemann structures 9:14 - 11:32 as follows: (1) Paul's support for the integrity of God's word, which leads to the question of 9:14a : 'Is God unjust?' (2) The justice of God in 9:14-29, which leads to the question of 9:31 : 'Why did the Gentiles attain righteousness while Israel did not?' (3) The failure of the Jew in 9:30-10:21, which leads to the question of 11:1: 'Has God rejected His people?'. (4) The role of the remnant as a sign of the faithfulness of God in 11:10, which leads to the question of 11:11: 'Has Israel stumbled so that they have fallen?'. (Ibid) We note that this author sees four major questions in 9-11 and uses 9:30 along with the other three which are fomally repudiated.

87 This verse can also be seen as closely linked to the covenant theme if, with N A Dahl, we see Rom. 2:15-16 as a reaction to the Jewish claim to possess special advocates for the final judgement. Not the Torah but Christ and/or the Spirit will be the advocate for Christians ie. He will be the advocate in the renewed covenant to parallel Torah and Miswot. "Paulus som foresprakare", STK, 18,(1942)174 (I am indebted to J. Bassler for this reference, cf. op.cit.148, 260f n91-2).

88 Cf *Faith and Obedience in Romans : A Study in Romans 1-4* by Glenn N Davies (Sheffield Academic Press, Sheffield 1990)

89 Ziesler refers to the unpublished thesis of Wendy Dabourne, *The Faithfulness of God and the Doctrine of Justification in Romans 1:16-4:25* (Cambridge 1988) in which the author mounts a powerful argument for seeing God's faithfulness as the 'governing strand', and the doctrine of justification as a secondary one. Op cit 41 note (a).

90 Cf. also Lloyd Gaston's interesting study, "Abraham and the Righteousness of God", in *Paul and the Torah,* University of British Columbia Press, Vancouver 1987, 45-63. Cf also Chapter 3, 32.

91 Op cit Appendix 2, "Gratitude and Mission in the Epistle to the Romans", op.cit.102-10.

92 Cf. Dunn, *Romans,* Vol.2 596f.

93 Cf. Wedderburn op.cit.137f. Cf also Westerholme, op cit ,198f.

94 Cf. Stuhlmacher, "Der Abfassungszweck des Römerbriefes", 189.

95 Cf. C E B. Cranfield, *Romans : A Shorter Commentary,* Clark Edinburgh, 1985, 152.

96 In the light of 'opheilas', 'opheilete' in 13:7-8, we are inclined to include the duty to pay taxes as part of Paul's stress upon Christian obligation, (probably following Jesus' words on the same theme). If Romans was written in late 57 or early 58, then this was a period when there was such unrest about payment of taxes in Rome that Nero had to mitigate the most grievous burdens of the taxation (Tacitus - ann 13.50.1, Suetonius, Nero 10.1). The previous discplinary measures of Claudius against the Jews would also have been familiar to Paul since Aquila and Priscilla had been forced to leave Rome because of them. (Acts 18:2). Serious unrest involving the Christian community in Rome would undermine Paul's plans to visit them en route to further work in Spain cf. J Friedrich, W Pohlmann, P Stuhlmacher, "Zur historischen Situation und Intention von Römer 13:1-7", Zeitschrift für Theologie und Kirche 73 (1976) 131-66; cf. also Wedderburn op.cit 62f; Moxnes rightly discusses Paul's attitude to the Roman authorities in his essay on Honour and Shame (n.4 above) and suggests that 'Paul's main goal in this passage was to warn Christian enthusiasts who wanted their Christian freedom to spill over into civic life' (212); cf. also Käsemann, *Romans*, 357.

97 Cf. Dunn op.cit.597.

98. Käsemann makes a positive connection between 7:1-25 and 8:1-39 in combining both of these under the title "The End of the Law in the Power of the Spirit, *Romans.* 186.99. See note 87 above.

99 See n87 above.

100 Cf. Otto Michel's comment, 'Paul is placed under obligation to all people and all levels of culture. 'Opheiletēs einai' is an image for the laws concerning debts and expresses the fact that Paul himself was declared debtor; the turn of phrase is very strong and says that Paul knew that he was indebted in his whole existence to the Gentiles'. *Der Brief an die Römer* 14 Aufl, Vandenhoeck und Ruprecht, Göttingen, 1978, 84.

101 The situational aspects of Paul's view of the law in Romans have not sufficiently been taken into account in many of the numerous recent publications on the theme and Paul's image often suffers as a result. We do not intend to discuss recent views of the law here - in our view they would not drastically alter what we have written above; but see esp. Westerholm's excellent overview of the discussion (n.10 above) esp. chs. 10-11 (198-222); J D G Dunn, *Jesus, Paul and the Law,* SPCK, London, 1990, esp. the author's additional notes appended to earlier published essays (105f, 174f, 206f and 237f); F. Thielman, *From Plight to Solution : A Jewish Framework for Understanding Paul's View of the Law in Galatians and Romans,* Nov. Test. Sup. LXI, Brill, Leiden 1990 esp. 87-116; B L Martin, *Christ and the Law in Paul*, Nov. Test. Sup. LXII, Brill, Leiden, 1989, esp. 131f where the author states, 'Lexically it is possible that 'telos' means 'goal' but normally in Romans it means 'end"; H Räisänen, *Paul and the Law* WUNT 29 Mohr, Tübingen, 1983; C E B Cranfield, "Give a Dog a Bad Name: A Note on H. Räisänen's *Paul and the Law*" Journal for the Study of the New Testament, 38 (90) 77-85; R Badenas, *Christ the End of the Law Romans 10:4 in Pauline Perspective* JSNT Sup.10, Sheffield Academic Press, Sheffield 1985 and H Hübner, *Law in Paul's Thought* E.T. C G Greig, Clark, Edinburgh 1984.

102 Markus Barth maintains that in speaking of the temporary validity of the Torah, we actually relegate Israel to the position of fossil; for the Jew repeal or abolition of the Torah means 'cutting the vital nerve of Jewish people'. op.cit.13-14.

103 The final response to these questions, however, is in 11:32 'For God has consigned (sunekleisen) all men to disobedience that he may have mercy upon all'. The ultimate freedom of God was certainly recognised by Paul and Philo alike - however there was still much debate about the interpretation of Israel's history, past, present and future, eg. Rom. 2:4, 9:22, and esp. 11:22.

104 Although we have identifed these questions as part of Paul's rhetorical strategy in the letter, space does not permit us to consider further the significant topic of Paul's rhetoric in Romans.

105 W Schmithals maintains that the earliest converts in Rome were former God-fearers, adherents to the synagogue who nevertheless can be addressed as Gentiles, *Der Römerbrief als historisches Problem*, Gütersloher Verlaghaus Gütersloh, 1975, 73f, 83f. Despite much debate in recent years there is still good reason to believe that proselytes provided the most fruitful source of converts cf. J. Gager op cit. 67-88; A. Overman",

The God-Fearers: Some Neglected Features", JSNT 32 (1988) 17-26; T. Finn, "The God-Fearers Reconsidered", CBQ 47 (1985), 75-84; F. Siegert, "Die Gottesfürchtige und Sympathisanten", JSJ, 4 (1973) 109-64; Emil Schürer, *The History of the Jewish People in the Age of Jesus Christ*, rev. and ed G Vermes, F Millar, M Goodman, Clark, Edinburgh, 1985, Vol III, 166-72; E M Smallwood, "The Alleged Jewish Tendencies of Poppaea Sabina", JTS, 10 (1959) 329 -55 and *The Jews under Roman Rule*, Brill, Leiden 1976 esp. 202f (Smallwood notes Dio Cassius' report that the Jews were converting many to their way of life); cf. also R. Stark's thesis that Christianity's rapid growth after 150 can only be explained if Jews continued to be a major source of Christian converts until as late as the fourth century. This would support the view that even in its earlier development Christianity was still somewhat dependent on Judaism, and not as successful in winning converts from paganism as is often accepted, "Jewish Conversion and the Rise of Christianity: Rethinking the Received Wisdom", SBL Seminar Papers, 1986, 314-329.

Chapter 12

General Conclusion

Whilst the frequency with which certain words or themes appear in Romans may not, as we have argued, prove decisive in determining the theme of the letter, due significance must nevertheless be accorded to a dominant theme indicated by 'dikaiosynē', 'dikaioō', 'dikaios' and related terms. (1) We are in agreement with the view that sees righteousness as a central issue in the letter. We wish to qualify this opinion by seeking clarification concerning the precise understanding of the theme in relation to the *total* argument of the letter.

Thus we wish to insist that righteousness is the righteousness of the covenant i.e. that righteousness whereby we describe the divine initiative in offering, maintaining and fulfilling the covenant. (2) As such it concerns not just the individual but the people of God - it is corporate rather that individualistic. (3) From this perspective we can identify a continuous emphasis throughout Rom 1-11 upon the faithfulness and integrity of God.

We must stress that this is not an emphasis glimpsed only occasionally or subtly derived from various nuances, but rather a carefully constructed argument in which Paul explicitly defends the integrity and faithfulness of God. We could have termed this simply a defence of divine righteousness, but we have preferred to stress faithfulness and consistency or integrity., recognising the fact that in Romans the righteousness, faithfulness and truthfulness of God are virtual equivalents. (4)

Despite the fact that Paul employs the diatribe style, by focussing on the major questions/objections which he himself introduces, we were able to identify an ongoing discourse with divine integrity 'post-Christum' as its theme. The advantage of this rhetorical style is that it enables Paul to maintain a certain distance in his paraenesis in keeping with the fact that he has not yet visited the Roman Christians. (5) But the rhetorical device should not be allowed to hide the fact that Paul is informed to some extent about the situation in Rome and actually addresses the Christians there. One should not differentiate too sharply the pedagogical and paraenetic elements or emphases in the letter. (6) There are many links across different sections of Romans that indicate that, however apparently theoretical Paul's argument, it was nevertheless written with some awareness of a specific 'Sitz im Leben.' (7)

Thus we cannot accept the view that Paul's discussion of God's righteous acts and judgements originated in response to the objection that his gospel led to 'unrighteousness' - in the sense of offering 'cheap grace'. We have not found any real evidence of Judaizers in Romans and this particular hypothesis lacks conviction.

As Morris and Moxnes have indicated in differing ways, the theme in Romans has to do with God, if word-frequency is any indication at all. (8) Thus it would appear most likely that the tumult caused by the Christ-event and the subsequent general lack of positive response from Jews to the preaching of the Gospel had led to a crisis concerning divine credibility. (9) The character or righteousness of God required vindication.

Since Paul was instrumental in creating some of the confusion by his founding Gentile Christian churches, so too he was necessarily involved in seeking an explanation of divine faithfulness, particularly in relation to the covenant with Israel. Paul attempts an overview of divine grace and judgement that will offer a solution of the problem of continuity and discontinuity between the faith of Israel and the new messianic faith. He has to provide explanations and solutions that will relate the interpretation of God's act in Christ to His ongoing relationship with Israel and his newly revealed relationship with Gentiles also. (10)

Whatever the law's precise failings, the role of the law had to be reviewed so as to explain why Gentiles need not keep it and what is its relationship, if any, to Christ. In Romans Paul is not interested simply in showing the failings inherent in the practice of the law. He is more concerned to show that the law did have a positive role - as a witness to the Gospel in pointing to Christ who is its goal (10:4) because faith in him 'establishes the law' (3:31). (11)

Whether it was the result of his own outspoken comments in Galatians falling upon Roman ears all too willing to adopt a critical view of Judaism, or whether it was simply the Roman situation itself that compelled him, Paul, possibly for the first time in his apostolic career, finds himself cast in a role of the defender of Israel against Gentiles. Since he is forced to present the Gospel in continuity with God's revelation to Israel, then he must be as positive as possible in respect of the law, the faithful remnant, election and the covenant. Doubtless his criticisms of Israel's misunderstandings of these topics were already well known to his converts, but what is now required is a statement of the positive content Paul could still attach to these. In Romans Paul offers this reassessment by means of a reinterpretation of the covenant.

We noted already that there exists in Romans a certain tension between divine righteousness and divine impartiality. This tension became most apparent in our discussion of God's relationship with Israel, though it also had specific connection with the doing of what the law requires (ch.2). Its resolution is implicit in the demonstration of God's righteousness in the Christ-event; but it will be fully resolved only in the consummation of history when Israel's restoration will serve as the prelude to the full redemption of the world, (12) (and if we use words carefully, as we should, it is only of the latter event, that the word 'fulfilment' properly applies). This reminds us that for Paul in Romans the future dimension of righteousness (or ultimate vindication) is also significant and especially in relation to Israel.

But Paul previews not only God's purpose for Israel in the future but also in Israel's past history, in order to reassess the meaning of Christian life in the present. He was forced to do this to counteract a misunderstanding of God's action in Christ (13) that tended to contrast God's past and present dealing with humans in such a way that Judaism (and Jewishness) was simplistically perceived as necessarily standing in opposition to faith in Christ. So Paul argues for God's integrity of purpose in such a way as not to deprive the past of all salvation significance, and so as not to endow the present with too great finality ie. believers live in hope of adoption according to Rom. 8:14f (14)

Paul was fully aware that the evaluation of one's past - whether as Gentiles, proselytes or Jews - was crucial for a right understanding of the present. Only by identifying a positive role for the law within the covenant relation with Israel, and by claiming a positive future for the now 'unbelieving' Israel, could Paul hope to provide grounds for a Gentile Christian majority at Rome to regain respect - and therefore tolerance, for those Christians with Jewish scruples who still wished to follow their own convictions.

We note in passing that we have depicted Paul here as standing in opposition to a stark contrast between a Christian present and a Jewish past. In this we are consciously depicting Paul as a theologian of transformation rather than of sharp discontinuity. (15) Through the transforming influence of the Spirit as in the case of the scriptures also, the past can be taken up into the present in a transformed existence. (16)

However if there were proselytes in Rome who were confused as to whether they ought to continue to follow a Jewish life-style, Paul had a duty to clarify whether they were obligated 'to continue in the state in which they were called' (1 Cor 7:20); obviously they could only do so with confidence if 'Jewishness' as such could be given some positive significance alongside faith in Christ. The same, we have already noted, would apply to a Jewish-Christian minority oppressed by a Gentile-Christian majority.

Both such 'weak in faith' would require renewal of hope such as might spring not only from supporting theological argument but also from greater social acceptance. (17) So one aim of Paul's argument concerning divine faithfulness in Romans may be to strengthen the hope of the weak whose confidence in God's purpose for Jews in particular, had been undermined by recent experiences in Rome. (18) For such the irrevocability of God's promises to Israel would be exceedingly important.

We noted initially however, that the reason why Paul took up the covenant theme was because Gentile Christians had misinterpreted its meaning. Thus the primary purpose of arguing in favour of divine faithfulness is to repudiate the arrogant Gentiles' presumption that they had displaced Israel.

Accompanied by this arrogance was a related presumption that salvation by faith meant 'cheap grace' - in the sense that sin and its judgement were no longer seen as serious issues for the new 'elect' in Christ! We take the view that in Rom. 6, Paul does not oppose Jewish misinterpretations of his Gentile gospel, but rather the misconceptions of righteousness in everyday life already prevalent among the Roman Gentile Christians. It seems that a form of Gentile Christian 'enthusiasm', if we may coin a phrase, had begun to emerge in Rome in the conflict concerning Christian identity among the Roman Christians. (19) In response to this Paul stresses the obedience of faith - that in fact righteousness must be lived by those united with Christ in baptism. He stresses also the symbolic separation of those in Christ from their former sinful existence (6:1-7:6), and points to the life- giving Spirit as the way to the future adoption as sons of God (8:23). He also stresses the fact of the coming judgement of all (8:31f) by the judge who is truly impartial .

We conclude therefore that Paul in Romans is concerned to show that 'God himself is righteous' in keeping covenant, and that He justifies him who has faith in Jesus ie. the one who lives in the obedient righteousness of faith now made possible by the transforming power of the Spirit. (20) But most important of all we see that Paul is arguing concerning the identity of the new believing community. Whatever its identity, it cannot simply be a sectarian re-definition of itself over against Judaism. Paul's forte, we have already noted, was that he interpreted the covenant inclusively, not exclusively. It was Paul's reinterpretation of Abraham as the model for all believers that makes Abraham truly 'the father of the faithful'.

It is at this point that we begin to discover those elements in Romans that have caused it to be interpreted as a foundation charter for Christianity. In it, because of a related group of circumstances, Paul was to expound the identity of the new movement (21) in such a way that positive links with its Jewish roots was retained, that a positive hope for Israel is shown to be still viable, and that the church is truly seen to be a unity of Jews and Gentiles linked together in a faith that promises both the restoration of Israel and of the whole creation.

Our reconstruction of the sequence of events that produced the letter to the Romans may be summarised as follows. The subsequent interaction and reaction between Jews and Christians following upon the advent of the Christian message in Rome eventually led to a conflict concerning Jewish identity in which Jewish Christians and proselytes were inevitably deeply involved. This conflict was further intensified by Gentile Christians seeking to distance themselves from their Jewish roots and to create a separate identity for their Gentile Christianity. (22)

In Romans Paul opposes this separatism and uses the occasion to forge a clear identity for the new messianic movement that roots it inextricably in God's historic revelation to Israel. In taking as his theme, the reinterpretation of the covenant in the light of the Christ-event, Paul found the means to depict the continuity and discontinuity in God's purposes for the world that was essential for the proper self-understanding of the Roman Christian community. But in so doing he has provided a letter which has incidentally served as the normative definition of Christian faith down the centuries. Partly due to this particular history, one of the problems surrounding the interpretation of the letter today is that the debate concerning its contents is still for many scholars a debate concerning the identity of Christian faith itself. Fortunately for his students Paul's own expression of Christian faith in Romans is one that allows for both cultural and theological diversity in Christ.

NOTES

1 The impressive and persistent use of this set of terms is well documented by Wedderburn, demonstrating how much more Paul concentrates on these in Romans than in Galatians (op cit 108-12). We disagree with Wedderburn's suggestion that 'the accusation had been levelled against Paul's gospel and ministry that they were unrighteous, and that Paul had then to defend himself against the charge by showing that they were in fact righteous' (112).

2 H C Kee notes that 'in all four of the Gospels, Jesus is represented as engaged in redefining the covenant'. He deplores the fact that approaches to New Testament theology over the past three decades have begun with Jesus, but then proceeded to treat the emergence of the new community as a subsequent development not envisaged by Jesus (op cit. 84-86). Following P D Hanson's, *The People Called* and Alan Segal's, *Rebecca's Children,*

Kee sees the basic issue between early Christianity and Judaism as revolving around what constituted the covenant community.

3 New paradigms for New Testament interpretation such as a hermeneutic of solidarity with Judaism have moved beyond the individualism of the existentialist approach. Sociological approaches have reinforced this; cf Kee's comment, 'knowledge throughout the range of human inquiry is social in nature and oriented within a community sharing convictions and assumptions', (op cit. 6). Cf. also W Meek's, "Understanding Early Christian Ethics", JBL 105 (1986), 3-11. It is significant that J C Beker (rightly) asserts that Paul's apocalyptic interpretation of the Christ-event is not individualistic but a pragmatic, ecclesial consensus-building which takes place in and for the Body of Christ, "Paul's Theology: Consistent or Inconsistent?", New Testament Studies, Vol 34 (1988), 364-77 (370f).

4 We support here the claim of S K Williams that in Romans, 'the righteousness of God, the faithfulness of God and the truthfulness of God are intended as virtual equivalents' by Paul, "The Righteousness of God in Romans", JBL 99 (1980) 241-90 (268).

5 Following Kee's emphasis upon the social reason for the choice of the stylistic form adopted by the writer, (op cit. 105), and bearing in mind that the diatribe 'may more usefully, if not precisely, be described as a mode rather than a genre', cf. A Malherbe, *Moral Exhortation: A Greco-Roman Sourcebook,* Westminster, Philadelphia, 1986, (129).

6 In this we are attempting to avoid the fallacy of allowing genre *per se* to determine the meaning - it is the author's specific use of genre in this instance that is crucial. Meeks and Stowers seem to prefer to stress the protreptic aspect of the diatribe, cf. Meeks, "Judgement and the Brother" op cit. 295, Stowers op cit. 117f, 152f, 174f;

7. We have already linked the judging person in 2:1 and 14:4, but see also `paristēmi' in 6:13, 19; 12:1, and 14:10 (16:2).

8. Cf. L Morris, op cit. 249f and Moxnes, *Theology in Conflict: Studies in Paul's Understanding of God in Romans,* op cit. 14f, 32f. Morris also gives useful statistics on the frequency with which Paul uses various terms, the most surprising being that 'theos' occurs no less than 153 times; 'nomos' occurs 72 times, 'Christos' 65, 'harmartia' 48, 'kurios' 43 and 'pistis' 40. Morris concludes that 'Romans is indeed a book about God, but it is about God in action' (252). On this see also Chapter 11, 179f and notes 17, 77, 96-100 above.

9 Cf. Scroggs, 'In the face of Israel's rejection of God's righteousness, both the value of the actual Israel and the trustworthiness of God are at stake', "Paul as Rhetorician: Two Homilies in Romans 1-11", *Jews, Greeks and Christians: Essays in Honour of W.D. Davies,* ed E Hamerton-Kelly and R Scroggs, Brill, Leiden, 1976 282f.

10 Cf. H Boers, "The Problem of Jews and Gentiles in the Macro-Structure of Romans",SEA 47 (1982), 184-96.

11. The question of the meaning of 3:31 and 10:4 is still very much debated. It is our view that Pauls intends to give positive meaning to the law in both cf.

T Rhine, *Faith Establishes the Law* SBL Diss Series, 55, Chico 1981, and "Nomos Dikaiosynes and the Meaning of Romans 10:4", CBQ 47 (1985) 486-99; cf. also R Hays, *Echoes of Scripture in the Letters of Paul*, Yale University Press, New Haven and London, 1989, 53f and 75f. Note esp. Hays' comment 'when he (Paul) says that his message confirmed the law, he refers not to the specific commandments of the Pentateuch, but to the witness of scripture, read as a *narrative* about God's gracious election of a people.' Cf also Chapter 4 where we noted that the discussion of faith and works has its proper context in the theme of election (50-52).

12 'In sum, the intersections of apocalyptic and wisdom traditions in Romans 9-11 afford Paul the means of maintaining a theological tension between God's faithfulness and God's impartiality, a tension he never resolves because it is constitutive of the character of God', E E Johnson, *The Function of Apocalyptic and Wisdom: Traditions in Romans 9-11* SBL Diss Series 109, Atlanta 1989, (175). Bassler rightly notes that absolute impartiality was not posited by anyone, op cit 186. Käsemann also warns against 'regarding God's righteousness as simply a property of the divine nature (as distinct from faithfulness in the context of the community) because it postulates what cannot be convincingly intellectualised', "The Righteousness of God in Paul," *New Testament Questions of Today*, SCM, (1969), 166-82 (186).

13 Such an attitude is typical of the enthusiasm of those won over to new ideologies or faiths and could perhaps therefore be most typical of Hellenistic Christianity Cf. W Lütgert, Der Römerbrief als historisches Problem, BFChTH, 17, 1913, 69-79. Cf. also Käsemann on Paul's polemic against 'enthusiasts', *Commentary* 228-33, 242, 332f, 350, 359, 364.

14 Cf. Käsemann's title for 8:18-30 "Being in the Spirit as Standing in Hope", op cit.229f.

15 Cf. Chapter 5, "Christ The End of the Law". This view derives from our understanding of 'telos' in 10:4. Cf also Chapter 7, 105 n37 and R Badenas, op cit 144f.

16 Cf. Hays' discussion of the meaning of 'telos' in 2 Cor. 3:13, op.cit 131-53 esp. 152; 'where God's Spirit is at work, the community is being transformed into the image of Christ and liberated to see, when they read Scripture, that the old covenant prefigured precisely this transformation'.

17 As Watson rightly emphasises op cit. 145-6. Note the phrase 'God of hope' (15:13); according to Morris, Romans has more than 24 per cent of the New Testament references to hope, op cit. 254.

18 We bear in mind here the long-term effects of the banishment of Jews from Rome by Claudius, cf W Wiefel, "The Jewish Community in Ancient Rome and the Origins of Roman Christianity" in *The Romans Debate* op cit. 100-119. Moxnes is one of the few scholars to note that the crisis over the identity of the Jewish community caused by the Christian movement would be felt most acutely by Christian Jews caught in a conflict over loyalties in different directions, op cit. p34.

19 See Chapter 11 n113. above. It is difficult to determine to what extent these radical Christians regard themselves as Pauline. In any case we see here a form of Hellenistic Christianity which Paul feels obliged to correct by inculcating a deeper appreciation of God's relation to Israel. Cf Chapter 8, esp 105f.

20 As Minear's and Davies' studies (Chapter 12, n88 above) emphasize, obedience is a significant theme throughout Romans; it is used in relation to Paul and the Gentiles, to Jesus Christ and specifically to the Roman Christians (1:5, 5:19, 15:18). There is also a parallel emphasis upon obligation and indebtedness (1:14, 8:12, 13:8) and Christians as obedient slaves in 6:16f. Cf also Michel as in n.100 above. Cf also Chapter 11,195 n96.

21 Cf. Kee's stress on the relation between covenant and social identity: op.cit 70-102.

22 Dunn notes 'the growing self-confidence of the Gentile Christians in their sense of increasing independence from the synagogue and over against the returning Jewish Christians'. Paul envisages 'a community well into the process of developing its own distinct identity over against the Jewish community from which it had emerged,' *Romans,* Vol 1, liii.

Index of Modern Authors